Praise for *Pulling Together*

"The culture in sport to 'win at any cost' was something many of us experienced to our detriment, but few of us talk about. All athletes, coaches, and parents should read *Pulling Together*, as Jason Dorland bravely speaks out against our broken system while offering an alternative: a culture in sport based on love and support."

STEPHANIE DIXON,
seven-time Paralympic champion,
Canada Sports Hall of Fame

"Having spent more than twenty-five years in high-performance sport, it's clear to me we are consistently ignoring the *why*—why a young person competes and what motivates them to be their best. Jason Dorland has again told a moving and compelling story about the joy found in challenging oneself. For me, this is mandatory reading for both coach and athlete."

DUFF GIBSON,
Olympic and world champion;
founder of Dark Horse Athletic

"*Pulling Together* takes the reader through a memorable journey of the rites of passage, not only of the coach, as he focuses on personal growth, but of his student-athletes as they grow through the discipline and dedication of sport within academia. While I am a believer in the Canadian High Performance sport system, I also appreciate that the voices of challenge, including Jason's, are heard as we continue to grow, improve, and build future generations of athletes."

LORRAINE LAFRENIÈRE,
CEO, Coaching Association of Canada

"A well-told story that brings to life the journey of a coach and a group of athletes and how, through navigating adversity and striving for success, all are found standing a head taller. Jason shares a compelling illustration of the enduring power of sport to unlock human potential."

TERRY DILLON,
two-time Olympic rower;
CEO, Rowing Canada

"It has been said that sport doesn't build character so much as it reveals character—and Jason Dorland's *Pulling Together* is the embodiment of that thought. He was himself an elite athlete, an Olympic rower, and from years of coaching he developed a sports philosophy profoundly different from the old-school 'stick-and-carrot' methods. He found his way in producing not just elite athletes, but elite human beings: winners before the finish line, winners well beyond any line."

ROY MACGREGOR,
author; columnist, *The Globe and Mail*

"*Pulling Together* is an honest look into what courage, grit, and a powerful mindset can really accomplish. A must read for all coaches who want to understand the real meaning of developing young women and men of the next generation through sport."

DR. BETH MCCHARLES,
performance coach

"At a time when business and sporting cultures are (rightly) coming under greater scrutiny than ever, *Pulling Together* shows a better, thoughtful way forward to optimize every moment of the ups and downs of competition and teamwork."

CATH BISHOP,
Olympic medallist and World Champion rower

"I see sport as a paradox. On one side, the winner takes all. Winning is delightful, yet often difficult. After overcoming the challenges, being the best is undeniably fun. That said, if you win or lose, the end moment of high-performance sport is remarkably short. As I age, mature, and reflect, I have to agree with many of Dorland's points. It's who you become on the journey that matters most. What kind of character traits are we nurturing in young adults through sport? How are we using sport to make the next generation better than we could ever be? This book will help you wade through the philosophy of coaching to find an answer that is right for you."

ADAM KREEK,
Olympic champion; management
consultant, KreekSpeak Business Solutions

"In this inspirational and engaging book, Jason Dorland shares life-changing lessons on achieving one's true and full potential. This book will help make you a better leader, athlete, and person."

DR. JIM AFREMOW,
author, *The Champion's Mind*

"*Pulling Together* is a inspiring and genuine testament to what can be achieved through positive, athlete-centered coaching and a focus on process. Dorland's athletes gain so much more from his mentorship than just wins and medals."

GREG HUGHES,
head coach, Heavyweight Men,
Princeton University

"Many coaches are so focused on the techniques and tactics of a sport that they forget the number one rule: you coach a person, not a sport. *Pulling Together* shares a lifetime of lessons from an Olympic athlete and elite coach so that you can create an environment that will help your athletes reach their potential in sport and life."

JOHN O'SULLIVAN,
founder, Changing the Game

"Jason's story is about much more than rowing. It's about struggling and learning and realizing that all too often the most formidable competition is *you*. No matter what you're trying to improve—times, scores, standards, or sales—a destructive attitude about competition is self-defeating. *Pulling Together* is a better way."

JAMES MCKEOUGH,
VP, Copylab

"Dorland's deeply personal convictions of what ignites high performance and what invites human potential are timely. In a world where athletes, coaches, organizational leaders, and politicians are reaching for anything that will create a win, Jason reminds us of those themes that will sustain and shape our finest selves into the future."

IAN CHISHOLM,
partner, Roy Group

PULLING TOGETHER

A COACH'S JOURNEY *to* UNCOVER
the MINDSET *of* TRUE POTENTIAL

JASON DORLAND

foreword *by* David Meggyesy

H
HERITAGE

Victoria | Vancouver | Calgary

Heritage House Publishing Company Ltd.
heritagehouse.ca

CATALOGUING INFORMATION AVAILABLE
FROM LIBRARY AND ARCHIVES CANADA

978-1-77203-173-7 (pbk)
978-1-77203-174-4 (epub)
978-1-77203-175-1 (epdf)

Edited by Melva Maclean
Proofread by Sarah Weber
Cover and interior design by Setareh Ashrafologhalai
Cover photo by Jason Dorland

The interior of this book was produced on 100% post-consumer
recycled paper, processed chlorine free, and printed with vegeta-
ble-based inks.

We acknowledge the financial support of the Government of Canada
through the Canada Book Fund (CBF) and the Canada Council for
the Arts, and the Province of British Columbia through the British
Columbia Arts Council and the Book Publishing Tax Credit.

21 20 19 18 17   1 2 3 4 5

Printed in Canada

—— ⊣ ⊢ ——

CARL DORLAND
*I couldn't have hoped for a more loving
and supportive dad and mentor.
I'm grateful for my time with you.
And proud of everything you stood for.*

PETER YATES
I miss you, my friend.

JOHN WALKER
A man who lived with "fire in the belly."

JACK NICHOLSON
A man who loved rowing more than anything else.

JOSEF TKACZICK
*A loving father and husband who wanted
what we all want for our children:
To live life fearlessly, with their wings
spread to their fullest.*

—— ⊣ ⊢ ——

ACKNOWLEDGEMENTS

TO MY NINETY-ONE-YEAR-OLD mom, and first draft editor, Eleanor: Thanks for joining me on this writing journey. I'll cherish our conversations.

To Robyn and Mataya: I would need another book to express my gratitude. I trust you know how I feel. Thank you.

To my sister, Wendy: You're an exceptional coach. Thanks for your love and support.

To my brothers, Scott and Paul: Thanks for your support throughout my Ridley coaching journey.

To Fraser MacKay: Thanks for being the quintessential "wingman." What we accomplished at Ridley wouldn't have happened without you.

To Paul DeVillis: Your knowledge, commitment, and support played an enormous role in our success. Thank you.

To Conrad Cowherd: "Best hands in the business!" Thanks, for keeping all of us *in line*.

To Jonathan Leigh: Glad you called! Thank you.

To Roy MacGregor: Appreciate the push! Thanks.

To Jim Kingstone: Your kid gloved and wise counsel kept this venture moving forward. Thank you.

To Peter McCoppin: Your passionate belief in me gave me resolve. Thank you.

To Anu Bhalla: On so many levels, thank you.

To all of my first draft readers: Thank you for your time and comments. It all helped.

To the parents who understood what I was trying to do: Thank you for your trust, patience, and support.

To every Ridley rower who truly understood the meaning of donning an orange and black singlet: Thanks for your commitment.

To every athlete I had the privilege of knowing and working with during my time at Ridley: Thanks for all of it.

To Winston Cook: You were the perfect partner in crime. Glad you reached out.

To Melva MacLean, the editor of this book: Thank you for your insights, understanding, and support. As before, it was a pleasure working with you.

To the team at Heritage House: Thank you for bringing this story to the masses. I appreciate your belief in this project.

To all of those early readers who provided a liner of endorsement: Thanks for taking the time. I truly appreciate your support.

To David Meggyesy: Thanks for stepping up. Your words are perfect: thoughtful, wise, and inspiring.

To David Walker: Thanks for believing in me and this crazy little venture. It means the world!

And, of course, to the boys: I will never forget this ride. Thank you, for trusting in me.

FOREWORD

——┤ ┠——

OLYMPIAN ROWER, JASON Dorland, has written an engaging story showcasing his 2014 Ridley College rowing crew. It is a treasure trove of wisdom and coaching perspective for athletes, parents, coaches, and executives alike. Jason's message, in the form of a question, is this: *What is the best way for coaches to support their athletes in reaching their potential, and experience the essence, power, and beauty of their athletic endeavour?* Witnessing how this question is answered over the course of a rowing season is a deeply moving experience. And, for those with a measuring stick, Jason's approach produced exceptional results—his team won multiple national championships.

I met Jason in 2014 at the Joy of Sculling Conference in Saratoga, New York. I attended Jason's presentation and was struck by our shared view of how sport can be a profound positive learning and growth experience for both coaches and athletes.

We each shared the view that traditional coaching, or what I call shame-based coaching, focused on winning, was absolutely limited in its ability to encourage athletic excellence and personal growth. He and I agreed that the mainstream approach to coaching emphasized the dysfunctional and archaic notion that sport is warfare and opponents the enemy. That's because the punch line of this view is that if you lose *the game*, you are less of a person.

What Jason presented at the conference and expands upon in *Pulling Together* is how positive-relational coaching produces optimal results. Why? Because athletes feel fully supported and safe in their quest to achieve excellence. Jason's holistic approach does not skimp on either the physical or mental hard work. It is truly an athlete-centred, integral approach to coaching.

An essential aspect of Jason's coaching philosophy is whether or not coaches focus on the extrinsic results, winning and losing, in contrast to the intrinsic joy of getting better—achieving excellence. "Where is the fun in good enough?" asks Dorland of his athletes. Mastery in sport, certainly in many aspects of living, is a process of awareness and growth. Achieving excellence is a verb, a continual progression. How we look at competition is also key, either as a dreaded fear-driven event to be avoided or as an invitation to excel.

Jason's coaching philosophy surrounding high performance reinforces that a holistic approach produces better results—because it's a competitive strategy! Reaching one's potential is not a straight-line procedure. Often it involves two steps forward, one step back, and curve balls do occur, as seen often with Jason's crew. However, the point and message to his athletes was that by committing to and focusing on process, or the "controllables" as he calls them, the "winning" will take care of itself.

Pulling Together is an extraordinary book. It should be mandatory reading for all coaches. As a former high school, college, and professional athlete I'll say this: What athlete wouldn't want to have a coach who embraces the messages expressed in Jason's book?

DAVID MEGGYESY
National Football League, retired; author, *Out of Their League*;
co-founder, Sports Energy and Consciousness Group
sportsenergygroup.com

PROLOGUE

—⊢ ⊣—

"**T**HE MOST DEVASTATING moment of my life" is how I used to describe my Olympic failure in rowing at the 1988 Seoul Summer Games. Back then, I was a poster child for an aggressive and combative type of athlete. I saw every competitor as an enemy. And I defined myself by the results: a winner when I won or a loser when I lost. In the end, the definition of "Olympic loser" would prove too much for me. I would struggle for years to find a new personal identity and a new purpose in life after competitive rowing.

It was a Canadian National Team, two-time Olympic, middle distance runner named Robyn Meagher who changed my life. Saved my life might be more accurate. Her process-centred approach to competition and her notion that we are here to travel, not arrive, unsettled me. My whole life had been about pursuing stuff: accomplishments, titles, compliments, and all things outside of me. Every moment of my existence had been about arriving at a destination and then, shortly after, looking for another. Never once had I considered that the messed-up life I had arrived at was the result of the messed-up way I was living it. Never once had I realized that winning was a limited goal—that it is, and should be, a by-product of striving for personal and team excellence; that compassion, empathy, love for yourself, your endeavours, your team and your competitors, is the foundation for a successful competitive strategy.

I chronicled all this and more in my memoir *Chariots and Horses*. I shared my tumultuous journey in the hopes of cultivating a healthier outlook, not only for athletes, but for anyone striving for greater purpose in their own lives. When the book hit the stores, I wasn't prepared for the response, not just from the general public, but from other Olympians. When the letters and emails came in, thanking me for telling my story, which many referred to as *their* story, I wasn't ready to hear it. I wasn't flattered. I was angry. Angry that so many athletes—too many athletes—had had similar experiences with their Olympic journeys. All along, I'd thought I was an anomaly.

After a disastrous first attempt at coaching, I decided to incorporate what I'd learned from Robyn, now my wife, on my second attempt at it. The result was nothing short of extraordinary. When you create an emotionally safe environment for athletes, they feel free to fail but also, ultimately, achieve success on levels they'd never dreamt of before. I began to see that winning results and taking care of athletes were synonymous. Others didn't.

Over the two years prior to the 2010 Vancouver/Whistler Olympics, I tried to get on the presenters' list at the Coaching Association of Canada (CAC) national conference in Ottawa. A year after those Games, in 2011, I was finally approved to present. I was told confidentially that my message didn't jive with the folks at Own the Podium (OTP), a sports funding organization. Furthermore, I was told that having me present in the lead-up to the Vancouver Games might be "awkward." No surprise, I had been quite outspoken regarding the impact of the OTP initiative on the athletes.

OTP's mandate was to facilitate funds that provided athletes with better coaches, better facilities, and a lifestyle that would afford them the opportunity to train full-time. I was all in support of that. However, I felt the name they had chosen with which to brand themselves was far too brash and did nothing to support athletes' all-important mental and emotional components that would allow them to perform and reach their true potential. To me, OTP was to an athlete's motivation what jet fuel was to a bonfire.

I was less than impressed. Olympians generally don't need added outside pressure to perform. They already put enough pressure on themselves. Why change any athlete's emotional playing field from *I want to win* to *I have to win*? These are two incredibly different paradigms from which to perform. They draw on different sources of motivation: one excitement; the other fear. Not surprisingly, it's the first one that creates a more desirable environment in terms of efficacy, sustainability, and outcome.

Even worse, the message made it clear to the athletes that if they didn't win or "own the podium," they shouldn't expect a celebration. The new message to all Canadians, athletes and spectators alike, was that Canada was only interested in celebrating winners. Ironically, that message ran counter to the very spirit the Games claim to be about as indicated in its own creed: "The most important thing in the Olympic Games is not to win but to take part." Instead, OTP's message in Vancouver conveyed, "Thanks for coming. Now let's get these Games started so we can kick your ass and prove how good we are."

Even the foreign press saw the name as un-Canadian. Like we were trying to be something or someone we weren't. It was painful to watch, and even more painful for the athletes who had to try to live up to the expectations. Is it any wonder that so many of our Canadian athletes went to Vancouver, only to blow up during the first week of competition?

As Stephen Brunt, a reporter with the *Globe and Mail*, one of Canada's leading national papers, shared so perfectly in his video essay following the Games, "We didn't really need to own anything." Brunt suggested that perhaps the confidence and swagger that OTP was trying to inspire in our athletes was actually there all along. And that if OTP had left well enough alone, they may have had a better start to the Games. And, perhaps even more pertinent, that during intense competition "it feels good to let your heart show."

Three-quarters of the way through my talk at the CAC conference, two high-level national team coaches got up and left. I wasn't offended. I was used to it. It had happened before. I reminded myself of Robyn's response every time it did: "We do the best we can with what we know," and that's what they know.

In the question and answer period, however, I could sense a change in focus in those who stayed. Just by the questions and the stories they shared, I knew that the old-school coaches who had been raised in the same stick-and-carrot culture that I had been were slowly making way for a new generation of younger, more progressive individuals who wanted not only to produce winning teams, but also to support the personal development of their young athletes. It was encouraging to see a more holistic approach to inspiring high performance on the verge of becoming the new normal.

Then, an all too common occurrence unfolded. When the line-up of coaches who had individual questions was gone, with the room empty, a lone coach approached me. This was something that I had sadly grown accustomed to. It happened at almost every coaching conference where I had ever presented.

It would start with them introducing themselves to me and then explaining they were an Olympian from a previous Games, and now they were trying their hand at coaching. We would talk about their experience at their Olympics and then right on queue, they would tear up and start to cry. Those tears would begin just as they shared how things had gone for them *after* their Olympics were over. I would stand there and do what I had done countless times before—listen.

On the odd occasion it ended with a hug. I would give them my card and encourage them to call any time they wanted to talk. I was tired of it. The system was broken and continuing to fail our Canadian athletes. Something had to change.

On the train ride home, despite the predictable behaviour of some of our nation's top sporting coaches and decision makers, I felt it had been time well spent. It was now getting close to a decade of giving these talks, and I was encouraged by the shift in the type of coaches who were now attending.

Over the years, I'd received countless requests from these coaches about writing a book on coaching. I was hesitant. I wasn't interested in writing a "how-to" book, but I wanted to share Robyn's, and now my, philosophy. The result is this book: an opportunity to showcase this coaching philosophy and, at the same time, tell a remarkable story about a group of young athletes I had the privilege of coaching. Enjoy!

JASON DORLAND
Victoria, BC, 2017

INTRODUCTION

—┤ ├——

T HE WEATHER WAS cold for late spring in Port Dalhousie, Ontario, showers on and off since the racing had begun. It was Sunday, May 29, 1983. I was eighteen years old, and it was the finals of the Canadian Schoolboy Rowing Championships, as it was known back then. It would be my last regatta before entering university.

Earlier in the day, the younger half of our crew had won the senior coxed four event, while the remaining seniors—myself included—had won the straight four. Combined, we were a fast eight, the fastest crew I'd ever rowed in. Two weeks earlier we'd beaten the best crews in the United States at their national championships. We were expected to do the same at home today.

Ridley College had a reputation for having fast rowing crews. Ours was another one in a long line of successful teams. Our coach, Neil Campbell, was revered for his ability to take awkward teenage boys and make remarkably fast crews of them. Like all of his crews before us, we were well prepared and ready for this championship eight race—the last race of the day.

The water was perfectly flat—ideal for racing. The air was cool and still. The mist almost too thick to breathe. As we sat in our boat waiting for the starter to call us to attention, the rain returned. A little at first, then a lot. The sound of it pelting the surface of the water around us grew louder and louder. Over that distracting noise, our coxie called out intermittent commands for us to stay focused and keep our boat aligned.

Finally, the starter began to poll the crews. We sat poised and ready to begin when a familiar sound came creeping from the finish line. Barely audible at first. Then it grew. And grew and grew:

"Row Blacks, row Blacks, row Blacks, row!"

It was Ridley's rowing cheer, a chant that stirred deep passions within our rowers but drove our competitors crazy. They looked over at us. We were all big guys, and I remember thinking, *Wow, I wouldn't want to be in your boat right now!*

Rob Silk, who was sitting two seats in front of me, turned around with a confident smile and said, "They're screwed. Let's get this race started. Now!"

As if on cue, the starter sounded his horn to release the crews from their motionless states.

Rowing is a painful sport. It's hard to escape that, but I've had a handful of races in my time where the pain seemed elusive. This race was one of them. I could feel the pain, just not the intense burn that I associated with training. Instead, a strange sensation came over me. Time seemed to slow. The strokes were purposeful, strong, and in unison. The boat felt light and fast.

Within moments we could see all of our competitors behind us. When we crossed the finish line four and a half minutes later, the chanting, which had disappeared temporarily, returned. This time it was even louder.

Standing on the podium with my best friends beside me, I was quietly thrilled with our accomplishment. Winning that trophy was a big deal for all of us. It was a proud moment feeling the exuberant energy coming from our supporters, but I was also sad. Being a rower at Ridley had been my persona for four years. And, regardless of how tough our coach had been on each of us, he had also been a source of comfort. Rowing back to the boathouse soaking wet, I was even more aware of what was now coming to an end, and oblivious to what was about to begin.

RIDLEY HAD BEEN my home since day one. I was born on the campus in 1964, the son of a schoolmaster. The late Dr. Hamilton, Ridley's third headmaster, had hired my dad, Carl Dorland, three years earlier. The life I, my brothers, Scott and Paul, and my sister, Wendy, knew growing up there was pure magic. The campus was all manicured fields and wooded areas and the buildings classic Ivy League–style architecture. It was a childhood most kids could only dream of. We were fortunate to have lived it.

During the day, from September to June, we attended Edith Cavell, a local public school, but after school, in the evenings and on the weekends, we played on the School's sixty-odd acres. Come July, when all of the boarding students left for the summer break, we owned every square inch of the place.

With the other "staff brats," I would race out the door after breakfast each summer morning and meet my friends in the front courtyard to plan the day: baseball, soccer, and football on the fields, tennis on the courts, ball hockey in the outdoor arena and, sometimes, on rainy days, hide and seek in the spooky old gym. The day's activities were capped off with a swim before dinner. We splashed and played tirelessly, washing away the sweat and grime of the day until one of our parents announced that it was time to come home. When evenings came, we biked around the perimeter of the grounds, played tag in the woods and, when we were old enough to stay out past dark, flashlight tag on the main fields.

That was our life. In the same way you feel comfort and safety in the arms of a parent carrying you from a cold car to your warm bed, Ridley's campus held and protected us. Yes, perhaps an idealistic cocoon that sheltered us far too much. But we didn't know any differently, and so we loved it.

When we grew old enough to attend Ridley, most of us did; as sons and daughters of teachers, our schooling was provided at a cost our parents could afford, one normally reserved for the financial elite. Of course, that meant we had to give our moms and dads over to twenty-four-hour-a-day access by the students who paid full tuition. For the most part, we saw it as a fair exchange: sharing our parents with a few hundred teenagers for the chance to go to one of Canada's most distinguished private independent schools.

During the early 1970s, Ridley went through perhaps the most significant single change in its history: it started admitting girls. Not necessarily a popular decision at the time, but Richard Bradley, the headmaster, saw it as essential not only to Ridley's survival, but to a more progressive, relevant, and all-encompassing education for Ridley students. Eventually, Mr. Bradley would be vindicated. Ridley became the trendsetter; the majority of independent schools in Canada would eventually follow suit.

School events were a big part of life at Ridley, and most of them focused on the arts and athletics. As a pre-teen, I looked forward to attending school plays and musicals. They were excellent. In the winter, the "Assault at Arms" was a one-night spectacle of athletic precision in gymnastics and other team events. Colonel Iggulden, or "The Colonel" as we affectionately referred to him, would run students through their paces followed by the Cadet Band marching into the gymnasium playing "Ridley Go." It was the stuff of movies. The traditions were a little corny at times, but this was a nostalgic period that filled us with a sense of belonging, a feeling that resonated throughout the School. It was the essence of the place.

If Ridley was known for anything in those days, it was the unquestioning commitment to sports. The powers that be saw sports as an integral part of our education; if you liked sports, and the majority of us did, there was a good chance you would enjoy your time at Ridley. Students spent a minimum of two hours each day dedicated to their athletic passions.

On a crisp autumn day, there was no better time spent than watching a football game against one of the rival independent schools like Upper Canada, St. Andrews, or Appleby. We'd cheer along with our traditional male cheerleaders, who were unapologetically leading a mass of seemingly crazed students through songs and cheers that dated back to the School's beginning. Our voices echoed across the campus in a school spirit one would be hard-pressed to find anywhere else. The pride that I, and others, took from those moments was palpable. Our belief in the "Spirit of Ridley" was our touchstone. It brought us closer together and forever made us a family.

For all of the attention that Ridley's sports teams attracted, the rowing crews garnered particular notoriety and prominence. Beginning in the late 1960s, Ridley won multiple national and international races. In 1968, Neil Campbell, himself a Ridlean and a multiple Olympian, took the reins of the fledgling program and ran full bore with it. He recruited an impressive assembly of supporting coaches and built an armada of crews that soon dominated rowing waters in Canada, the United States, and overseas in Great Britain.

My dad, following in his own father's footsteps, had rowed for the St. Catharines Rowing Club and, in 1971, he began managing Ridley's rowing program, seeing it through to his retirement in the late 1980s. There weren't too many evenings when Dad wasn't on the phone with other coaches or hosting them at boat club meetings in our living room, where they discussed the upcoming regattas, fundraising, and all things administrative. It was an exciting time for the Ridley rowing program.

In grade ten, it became my turn to row. I had some shoes to fill. My two older brothers, Scott and Paul, each had rowed in previous winning heavy eight crews. They had won every major high school race there was, including gold at the Henley Royal Regatta in England, the most prestigious rowing regatta in the world.

For many young rowers in those early heavy eight crews, Neil Campbell assumed not just the role of coach, but of surrogate father to most. His rebellious character was larger than life, and this proved irresistible to the young men who religiously followed his training regimen and hung on every word he said. As impressionable teens without our parents around, we relied on him to provide leadership, values, and life skills. He taught us the meaning of commitment and sacrifice. And, for many, myself included, he helped redefine what we perceived as our physical and mental limitations. The results of that tutelage were some astoundingly fast crews.

By the time I graduated from Ridley, I had been a part of a few myself. It was an unforgettable time. I lived to row. Each day, during class, I would watch the clock, counting the hours and minutes until it was time to leave for practice. Whether it was indoor winter training or spring training on the water, the butterflies in my stomach intensified with each passing moment as I anticipated the workout session for the day. Like so many athletes who use sport as an escape, rowing was a safe haven for me, a place where I belonged and was understood.

It is a strange attraction to be sure—a sport that you don't play but rather endure. There are no goals scored. No time outs for a drink of water and advice from your coach with thirty seconds on the clock. It's simply full-on aggression from the word go. Each day you show up, you know you'll be lifting your barbell or pulling your first stroke until you feel ill. It hurts like hell in the moment. The pain is inescapable, but the rush of surviving it, beating it, conquering it and then, on some inexplicable level, wanting more, is an experience I've not replicated with any other endeavour.

I felt I belonged to something larger than myself. I was in a group of odd misfits who had found one another through a discipline that few understood or were willing to embrace. On top of that, there was a pride of membership in the craziness—knowing you were part of a very small group that could reach physical exhaustion and keep going. Egotistic in nature indeed, maybe even self-mutilating. But, hell, we were teenage boys. We believed our role in the world was defined through our physical accomplishments. Yes, the races we won were gratifying on some level, but it was mostly knowing that, with focus, determination, and a work ethic, there wasn't much, if anything, you couldn't do.

In *Chariots and Horses*, I examined how, as a young athlete I had embraced the combative model of attaining high performance I'd been taught, a model in which making our competitor the enemy, and therefore someone to defeat, was the foundational source of our motivation. Over the years, I had discovered that that paradigm was limited.

In 2010, when Jonathan Leigh, Ridley's headmaster at the time, offered me the job of director of rowing, I saw it as my opportunity to pay forward what I had learned rowing for Neil, but I also wanted to tweak Neil's gift—put my own spin on it. I wanted to show the current Ridley athletes that experiencing their competitors as people to work with synergistically would create opportunities for high performance beyond their imagination. Instead of creating teams that aspired to win at all costs, I wanted to build a culture of high-performance teams that aspired to reach a higher purpose.

CHAPTER ONE

————┤ ├————

THE LATE SUMMER dew felt cool on my feet as it reached past the edge of my Birkenstocks. It was the first staff meeting of the year. As I walked through the schoolhouse doors, the Westminster chimes signalled eight and two quarters. When I was young, and that close to the clock tower, I would feel a stirring in my chest. Now, the days of my youth, and the soulful analog vibrations, were long gone, replaced by a more efficient and cost-effective imposter: a digital timekeeper as the ultimate metaphor for change.

Nevertheless, I was reminded that, as much as I was on time, I was also late—a few decades late, give or take. This would be my fourth and, as Robyn and I had decided earlier that summer, my final year at Ridley. We would be going home to the West Coast at the end of the school year and its subsequent racing season. I had made Robyn a promise: to return home at the first sign of trouble. The trouble I sensed was that the excitement for the rowing program I'd felt with Jonathan Leigh had wavered since his recent departure. I had signed on to build a high-performance rowing program and, in my mind, the opportunity to fulfill my pledge to do so was fading.

By the time Jonathan Leigh was hired as headmaster in 2004, Ridley had, over the years, lost its reputation for sporting excellence. One of his goals was to see sports regain some competitive focus. Although he was more of an artist, Jonathan had first heard of

Ridley while he was attending boarding school during the late 1960s in England. His roommate, a competitive rower, had been knocked out of the Princess Elizabeth Challenge Cup at Henley by a boatload of Canadians from a then unknown school named Ridley College. When Jonathan arrived at Ridley decades later as its newly appointed head, he was shocked to learn that the rowing program was no longer the dominant player it had once been.

IT WAS THE spring of 2007 that I received my first phone call from him. Robyn and I, and our young daughter, Mataya, were living in Victoria, on Vancouver Island in British Columbia. I was teaching in the visual arts program at a school in town, Glenlyon Norfolk, and enjoying a break from coaching. My previous job at Shawnigan Lake School, about forty-five minutes' drive north of Victoria, had involved coaching rowing as well as teaching full-time. As much as I had enjoyed the coaching and treasured my time with the young men I had the opportunity to work with, the work was exhausting. I would teach a full load of classes, work duty nights in one of the residences and, on top of that, coach sometimes twenty-five hours a week, not including regattas. Now, with a young child, I wanted some family time.

Jonathan's ask was to the point: come back to Ridley and, as he put it, "reignite the rowing program." Although flattered, I was enjoying my time solely in the classroom and away from the sport. Rowing had owned me for the better part of my youth and now, approaching fifty, I wasn't missing the countless hours of sacrifice that I believed were required to achieve what Jonathan wanted. I said no. After a subsequent call the next year, and another in 2009, I became genuinely intrigued. And, after four years of not sitting in a coach boat, I entertained the notion. Jonathan's insistence that I was the right candidate for the job was based on some success I had garnered at Shawnigan Lake School. At the time, the culture at Shawnigan placed a respectable amount of importance on the sports teams it produced, in rugby and, to a lesser extent, in rowing. The boys I coached had won numerous national championships, including the Calder Cleland Memorial Cup two years in a row—the prize for winning the senior heavy eight race.

From what I had heard about the student body at Ridley, unlike at Shawnigan, the pickings would be slim. My question was how could I build a rowing program without athletes? And when I thought about moving our family back to St. Catharines and leaving Vancouver Island and our house, I had misgivings. We loved our life on the coast and had never imagined leaving, even if only temporarily, but the offer, as unlikely as it first seemed, continued to occupy space in my mind, and with each passing day that space grew.

Over that time, Jonathan was persuasive, not in a pushy salesman way, but with an obvious excitement to get the job done. He was charming to the core and a masterful storyteller. He would report on the state of the school, and how much he and other alumni wanted the rowing program rebuilt. He made it clear that his dream was to return to the English Henley with a heavy eight from Ridley. *Just like the old days!*

It was his damn British accent that was the killer. Those Brits can work magic with the English language, and Jonathan was as good as any. I felt as though I was speaking with Mr. Bradley, my British headmaster when I was a young student at Ridley. Every phone call that I had with Jonathan took me back to my childhood and the excitement I had felt when my dad was running the program. I was just beginning to realize how important that time in my life had been. Nostalgia lit a yearning in me to return to Ridley and recreate the magic of those impressionable years.

Underlying everything, there was the pure challenge of the task. With all of the success that I had experienced coaching at Shawnigan, there were some people who felt the only reason we had done so well was because of the abundance of athletes, the ideal location, and the financial support of the school. If I could go to Ridley and rebuild its program to the same level, and then some, it would prove that my philosophy of high performance, the backbone of what we had built at Shawnigan, was the bulletproof strategy I believed it was.

I started to look at it logically. Our home? We could rent it. All of our stuff? We could store it. My gardens? We could hire someone to take care of them. School for Mataya? They had schools in St. Catharines—hell, she could go to Ridley! Each time I set up a roadblock, I could also easily remove it. *Jase, buddy, you could do this*, I said to myself.

In the end, what made sense of this seemingly irrational venture was the chance to be with family. Both Robyn and I had aging parents in the east: mine in St. Catharines and hers in Mulgrave, Nova Scotia. If we moved to Ontario, we could support our parents, and Mataya would have a chance to get know her aunts, uncles, and cousins, the ones who lived there and on the East Coast.

When I got on the phone with some Ridley "Old Boys," and we talked about the rowing days we knew and loved, the job transformed from one that I *should* do to one that I *had* to do. It was worth the shot. I knew I could turn things around if given the chance. And, if I didn't, who would? It was time to have a deciding conversation with Robyn.

We sat quietly on the large rock outcropping in front of our house. "So, what do you think?" I asked to begin the conversation.

After a long moment of silence, Robyn responded. "I'm trying to imagine myself living in Ontario. Away from all of this." She gestured to the massive trees on our property. "Beginning my counselling practice again from scratch. Living in a strange city." She paused for a bit. "This move wouldn't be my first choice," she continued. "The West Coast is my home, Jason. I feel a part it and it a part of me. There is a sense of ease for me in just being here."

I had never seen Robyn so serious. Perhaps, in my excitement to make the venture happen, I hadn't considered the full impact of what I was asking of her.

There was another long pause, and then she thoughtfully continued. "I couldn't care less about the job. You coaching at Ridley. It's not a part of my past. What makes this possible for me is knowing that Mataya will be across town from your parents and will be able to spend vacations with my parents. I'm aware of this all happening at a key moment in their lives. That's what I find appealing about this. Nothing more."

"I understand that," I said.

"Sometimes I'm not so sure you do. You're chasing again, Jason. Just like you've done before. You're going after another dream that you've built up in your mind to be more than it is. It's just a coaching job."

I thought quietly for a moment before responding. "I don't see this as chasing. Do I want to take on this challenge? Yes, I do. Would I love to prove that what I achieved as a coach at Shawnigan wasn't a fluke? You bet! But I also see the perks that come with this move. I want Mataya to experience a piece of what I knew growing up: life on the Ridley campus. And, as you mentioned, seeing my folks and yours more often is a bonus."

More extended silence before she said: "The only thing that will allow me to go forward with this is knowing that we can return to our home, this house. I don't want to move away forever. If we can rent this house, I'll go. But at the first sign of something going wrong in St. Catharines, we're leaving. Okay?"

"Done! I wouldn't have it any other way," I agreed.

One of the arrangements with the School was that we would live in staff housing so we didn't have to buy another home. Furthermore, living on campus was the experience that I so desperately wanted for Mataya: the other staff children, the freedom and protection of the campus, the incredible facilities, and the sense of community.

I wanted all of it for her. When I received word that we would be living in the bungalow on the corner of Ridley Road and Victoria Street, I was gob-smacked.

"*No way... can't be!*" I said.

That had been one of my childhood homes. Now Robyn, Mataya, our dog, Katie, and I were moving back to it. I felt as giddy as any kid on Christmas morning.

Robyn, Mataya, and Katie went first. They stayed with my mom and dad in their home on Lake Ontario while I remained in Victoria to ready our house for our tenants. I joined them a few days later—completely exhausted. The next day we drove over to the School to see the campus and our new home. The state of the front yard and gardens was surprising. It had looked more cared for when we'd looked at it on Google Maps. Now, the house looked rough.

Robyn and Mataya noticed.

We knocked on an open front door and went in. Soon after entering the hall and calling "anyone home?" a young woman came up from the basement. We introduced ourselves and asked if she was okay with us having a look around.

"It stinks in here!" said an unimpressed six-year-old, as we walked down the main hall.

"Shhhhhh. Mataya. Easy does it," I said quietly.

She was right though—it did smell. Every part of the house looked neglected. Nothing like how I remembered it. The walls were cracked. The paint was faded and the floors worn. This was *not* my childhood home.

Venturing downstairs we found the source of the smell. There had clearly been some water damage, and parts of the ceiling tiles were covered in black mould. Robyn and I looked at one another, each thinking the same thing: *This was not what we signed on for.*

Returning to the main floor, Robyn and Mataya veered toward the living room while I went down the hall to find my old bedroom. It looked tiny. Of course it would. I was more than twice the size I had been thirty-five years earlier. The view out my bedroom window was different too. Back then I would have had to stand on my desk to gain this vantage point. I smiled, remembering "the Colonel," our neighbour back then, bent over pulling pesky weeds from his backyard vegetable garden. The campus looked different too: the trees were taller, and there was now a large cast iron fence around the perimeter of the grounds that looked out of place.

Regardless of the impressions, the memories were still alive in every inch of that room. The cats we had back then. The furniture. All of it vividly as I had remembered it.

"Is this going to be my room?"

I looked up. Mataya was standing at the door.

"It is. This was my room when I was your age, Mataya. What do you think?"

"It's kinda dirty. And the closet door isn't even attached."

She was right. Just like the rowing program that I was stepping into, this place needed a lot of work.

As the three of us made our way out the front door, returning to the familiar but long forgotten humidity of a southern Ontario summer, the excitement that I had arrived with was fading. Negotiating the cracking and uneven cement steps, I began to feel the dream of sharing my childhood home with my family slipping away.

"Well, with a little paint and some flowers, we can get this house looking like a home," I said in an attempt to keep things positive.

When I turned to face Mataya, I noticed she was crying.

Robyn motioned for me to come closer. "Is it too late to go home?"

The first couple of months back were rough, but with a bit of work, the black mould was removed, the walls painted, the floors replaced, and the closet doors hung. That was the easy part. The hard part was accepting that the Ridley of my youth had changed: it was now an educational institution more focused on business. In fact, some grads referred to it as "Ridley, Inc." It wasn't a criticism. The business of running a boarding school was more competitive than ever.

Without bums in beds, schools like Ridley closed their doors forever. A sad commentary, to be sure, but one I came to accept.

My job, as it turned out, was far more challenging than I could have ever imagined. Perhaps, not surprisingly, there were more than a few coaches who were quite happy that Ridley was no longer being a contender. Rebuilding the program presented additional competition they'd sooner not have to contend with. Add to the mix that it was an ex-Ridley boy coming home to coach, and you had a perfect storm for some resentment. Then there were my own expectations and the relentless self-inflicted pressure that resulted. On top of that was the expectation of the School, alumni, and parents to succeed. Failure was simply not an option. I was determined to turn this program around, no matter what it took.

The result was a twenty-four-hour clock that rarely shut off. Always processing. Always thinking, *What more could I do to make this program successful?* This new venture had become all consuming. On top of that was the fact that our parents were at stages in their lives that, although perhaps inevitable, provided added stress. Robyn's dad had experienced a sudden stroke during our second year back and had passed away a few months later. What made that particularly challenging was that he had been the caregiver for Robyn's mom, who had a very aggressive form of Alzheimer's. She would die within the year.

My parents, too, had had their challenges. At eighty-five, my mom was the caregiver for my eighty-five-year-old dad, whose dementia was proving more and more challenging. One night during our first year back, my mom went into septic shock. After almost losing her, we made the heart-wrenching decision to find a care home for my dad. It would be tough to leave him, but it was time for us to go home.

RIDLEY'S ATHLETIC DIRECTOR, Jay Tredway, as well as Ed Kidd, Ridley's tenth, and newest, headmaster, were waiting for me. Ed began the meeting. "First of all, Jason, thanks for making time to come in early today."

"Of course. No problem," I replied.

"We all know this is a busy time of year," he continued. "So, I'll get right to the point of this meeting. We've decided to terminate the position of director of rowing going forward. But you'll continue in that full capacity for the remaining year. If you wish to stay on at Ridley after that, you will have to go back into the classroom and teach. You would be permitted to continue coaching rowing, and I would obviously encourage that, but teaching would be your main focus within the School."

I paused a moment. "Well, I had a sense that Ridley was moving in that direction. Robyn and I have already decided that this would be our last year, regardless of any decision by the School. Truthfully, we were ready to leave in July but agreed that it was important for me to stay on and graduate the current athletes I'm coaching. I owe it to them."

"As much as I'm sorry to hear that," Ed replied, "I'm not overly surprised. If you decide to change your mind, I'd be happy to have that conversation at a later date."

"Fair enough, but I can't see us changing our minds, Ed. We're ready to go home."

Jay was quiet as Ed and I continued.

"How do you see your last year playing out? What would you like to do?"

"Well, I think it would be fitting to return to England and race at Henley," I answered.

"That's a terrific idea," he said. "And what an ideal swan song for you."

"Well, it's not me I'm worried about. It's the boys. Some of them have been rowing at Ridley for four years, and finishing at the Henley Royal Regatta would be a perfect way to end their high school rowing careers."

I waited a moment while Ed thought about my plan.

"What about you coming over to watch the crew race?" I added.

"Hmmm, what are the dates?"

"Late June, early July," I answered, hoping that he was seriously considering the trip.

"Ah, I can't. We're hosting a conference here at the School then. There's just no way I could make it. I'm sorry, Jason, it would be so great to watch those boys race."

"Oh well. If there's a way to make it work, perhaps we can revisit it in June," I offered.

With a clear direction for my final year, we called an end to our brief meeting. As concerned as I was about the notion of Ridley's rowing program possibly dwindling once again, it wasn't my battle. I had already chosen to let it go anyway. It was time for me and my family to go back home.

I was, however, quietly disappointed that Ed wouldn't be able to join us overseas. I thought that if he could just experience Henley, he might better understand the significance of Ridley rowing on the international stage and perhaps have a change of heart regarding the future of rowing at the School. I was saddened, but regardless, it was time for me to do what I'd been doing for the past three years: focus on the athletes.

My next stop was a local coffee shop where I'd be meeting with Fraser MacKay, a Ridley Old Boy from 1973 who had rowed with my oldest brother, Scott, in a few of Neil's legendary heavy eights and won everything there was to win nationally and abroad—including Henley. Fraser was now a doctor in the Niagara region with a genuine passion for the Ridley rowing program, providing him an incredible knack for fundraising. To date, we had raised several hundred thousand dollars.

I informed Fraser of the School's decision to terminate my position. Like me, he wasn't surprised. We had both sensed a shift in the School's administration over the last number of months. During my first two years while most of the onerous heavy lifting was underway, Fraser and I would meet here weekly at our "office" as we called it, to review the progress we were making and brainstorm further initiatives. Aside from his sage advice in dealing with the School, alumni, parents, and the local rowing community, he had proven a constant source of emotional sustenance. I enjoyed our meetings. We would share stories from the past and get excited about where we thought Ridley rowing could go in the future. Now, both knowing that future was in jeopardy, we discussed my exit plan and, more importantly, how to get the boys to England.

CHAPTER TWO

—————⊢ ⊢—————

T HE SPRING 2013 racing season had been a bust for almost every rowing school in Canada, and in some parts of the US. As a coach and an athlete, I had never experienced anything like it before. Extreme weather conditions resulted in every major regatta being cancelled or its scheduled events compromised. Even the Canadian Secondary Schools Rowing Association (Schoolboys) Championship was cancelled for the first time in its history because of high winds that refused to let up.

Weeks earlier, at the Stotesbury Cup Regatta, hosted each year in Philadelphia, a record rainfall flooded the Schuylkill River. The largest high school regatta in the world was almost cancelled for fear that trees floating downstream would compromise the safety of the racing shells and the athletes in them. Eventually, after a long wait, crews were able to race on a compacted schedule. Not an ideal outcome, but when you sign on for a sport that takes place out of doors on exposed waterways, sometimes you have to concede to Mother Nature.

The weekend after, the US Schoolboy Championships hosted that year in Camden, New Jersey, just barely managed to get racing in over the two-day event. The wind was relentless and the conditions were less than ideal. In early May, the smaller local St. Catharines regattas, which act as warm-ups to the major national championships later in the month, were cancelled as well. It was truly an unbelievable season of racing, or non-racing, depending how you looked at it. Not surprisingly, the returning crew members were eager to experience a full season of regattas, and the sooner we got started the better.

Most of our current crop of rowers had been with the rowing program since grade nine or ten. They had witnessed the success of the 2012 crew first-hand and now had dreams of following in those large footsteps. It was my goal to see that through, and now, with racing in England officially an option, I was ready to end my time at Ridley the way I'd started it, with a process-centred rowing program.

The boys' heavy eight had long been the flagship of Ridley's rowing program, and this year's crew, like so many before it, were big, strong, and keen. As was so often the case with crews that I had coached, I didn't have many athletes to select from. This year, there would be no selection given we only had eight rowers to begin with.

Our small pool of athletes was the reason I viewed the Henley Royal Regatta in England as just an option. I didn't believe in sending crews to Henley if they hadn't earned it or weren't capable of getting to the finals. Most of the events involved five days of match racing—elimination style—where the competition got stiffer as you progressed. It took a significant chunk of change to send a crew overseas. Since most of it would come from the parents, I wasn't about to waste money that wasn't mine. I knew the parents had already thrown enough of their hard-earned cash at the School without having to pony up for an overseas trip. If we were going to make this commitment, we'd need to be fast enough and then some.

I had believed that our 2012 Henley crew would make it to the finals, and with good reason. The guys had won the eight final at the Canadian Schoolboy, setting a course record. They'd finished a close second to the fastest US crew at Stotesbury. Still, we were knocked out by an average British crew on the second day of racing.

That was a wake-up call for me. Our loss told me that the British crews had their programs in order and were producing outstanding rowers. From the 1970s through the early 2000s, Canadian and American schools had often prevailed on the Thames. The times were changing. If you were fast enough to be a national champion in Canada or the US, it didn't necessarily mean you were fast enough to win the English Henley. We would have to dig much deeper with our new crew.

So much of the success I experienced in my coaching career had been the result of the culture I had fostered. When I came back to Ridley to begin this undertaking, the question I heard most often from alumni was, "What do you see as your biggest challenge, technique or fitness?"

As much as those are obvious influences with regard to boat speed, they are limited by one essential ingredient—a team's culture. I believe culture is the foundation upon which the technique and fitness transpire. If the culture isn't optimal, not surprisingly every component of an athlete's training will invariably be compromised.

As a rowing coach, I understand there are limited areas of influence when it comes to coaching. Yes, I know enough about the sport to make boats go fast. But what has differentiated my crews from their competitors is the *why*—the why in how our athletes chose to show up every day. And given that the shells are similar in structure—sometimes identical—you have to find the areas where you can have the greatest impact on your crews. Some coaches choose fitness, while others choose technique. For me, I've always chosen culture. I see it as integral to the success of any team. Not surprisingly, it's the most challenging to shift and, therefore, one has to be patient—not always a common trademark of most coaches.

Throughout my coaching career, there have been many moments of self-doubt, times when I've stood on the bank of a river or lake and watched competitors' crews rowing by only to think, *How the hell are we going to compete with that boat? Those boys are huge and there's no question their coach knows more about rowing than I do!* In most instances, we prevailed—we found a way to win.

When I first began coaching years ago, I'd train my crews with a personal intensity that I was no longer comfortable with. The goal was always to make sure that they were fitter and tougher and meaner than any other boat on the water. My method then was simple. Entice them into winning because I had convinced them there was no greater feeling than knowing you were better than your competitors. Or, more often than not, shame them to avoid losing because there was no lesser feeling than having your ass handed to you on a platter.

In the same way my coaches had taught me what they themselves had been taught, I continued that widely held tradition. Why not? It worked. And like the saying goes, "If it ain't broke, don't fix it." This combative mindset that I instilled in my athletes quite often did work, but now I saw it as outdated and ultimately limited. As I grew older and began to reflect on the lifelong impact of this combative approach to high performance on the athletes I had coached, I realized it was time to change. Synchronicity being what it is, it was a woman who set me straight.

How many men have had their outlook on life turned upside down by a woman only to then achieve success on a level never before seen? Yes—a rhetorical question. And don't bother trying to answer it. The number is embarrassing. My point being, if I had never had my approach to competition challenged, I would have never had reason to think there was another, let alone a more effective and successful, way to achieve it.

When I met Robyn, she taught me that it was the journey and not the destination that was important. At first I mocked her. To suggest that life was about being awake to every single moment, not just the point of arrival, was so far from my coaching and life philosophy and strategy that I couldn't even begin to grasp how anyone, let alone an internationally ranked runner, would consider it a viable road map to success. I thought Robyn's ideas were ludicrous, until I watched her storybook race at the 1994 Commonwealth Games, held in Victoria, British Columbia.

Robyn and I had met on a blind date a week earlier. After a couple of hours walking on the beach in Cadboro Bay, talking about mundane first date stuff, I figured it was time to get onto some topics that had a little more weight. I knew she had the final of the women's 3000 metres coming up, and being a guy who was a little obsessed with outcomes—as in winning—I figured there was only one question worth asking. "Are you going to win?"

Her answer was shocking. Instead of telling me that she was going to win, she told me she was hoping to do her best. Her best? Her explanation included some lame story about being so sick throughout the winter and spring that she really wasn't properly prepared for the event. My cynical inner voice was having a heyday: *If you're not prepared, don't bother racing!* The way she saw it, the race was an opportunity to "give it her best shot and see what happens." At this point, I had heard enough and awkwardly ended the date. In fact I remember feeling embarrassed for her when she "really wasn't expecting much." Not surprisingly, I felt Robyn lacked the confidence and bravado that I would have expected from an elite middle distance runner of her calibre. Needless to say, I predicted Robyn's race would be a gong show. She was going to get killed and she knew it. And sure enough, one lap into the race, Robyn was tied for last.

What happened over the next few minutes was just short of a Hollywood movie. Close to the halfway mark, slowly but surely Robyn began to reel in her competitors one at a time. Soon she was sitting fourth with three laps to go and her teammate Angela Chalmers leading the field.

The crowd knew that if Robyn could find her way to third, that would mean both a gold and bronze medal for Canada. Shortly thereafter, Robyn produced another gear and moved into third and then into second. The stadium went crazy when Angela and Robyn crossed the finish line one-two, producing one of the most memorable races from the Games.

As I watched Robyn climb the podium and gracefully accept her silver medal, I was dumbfounded. How was it possible? Not prepared? Not anticipating a great race? Not going in with the intent of winning? And she'd turned in a performance as good as anyone could—fit or otherwise. In one race, she had challenged my entire belief system around what was required to win.

That one race was the beginning of the end for me as a competitor and coach who focused on chasing wins. When we purposefully step back far enough to notice how pathetic our contribution to humankind has been and what our unimpressive legacy will ultimately look like, it's a humbling moment that screams for not just our attention, but also our action.

Now at the age of thirty-one, I realized that I had it backwards. We are here to serve others, plain and simple. When we embrace that ideology, we serve ourselves like no other way possible. Once my childish attempts at protecting and serving my tenuous ego gave in to Robyn's mindset, who she was and how well she did what she did became an example of how life could be if one simply stopped chasing. Robyn had figured it out decades before me: focus on the concerns of others. Until that moment of realization, even my coaching—the service of my athletes, so I thought—had truly been about me.

I, like so many coaches, obtained my sense of self-worth from my athletes' accomplishments. If my crews were worthy of winning, then I too was worthy. Disturbing to think that I pushed young teens to limits beyond most people's perception of normal physical pain so that I could stand out as the accomplished and winning coach. But it's what I did. Granted, there was no gun to their heads and they could have quit. And, true enough, they won some big races and learned a few things about life. But the risk of emotional damage had been too great.

When I finally decided to change my ways and consequently my reasons for coaching, not surprisingly perhaps, I did so without compromise. It wasn't easy, either. When life is about how and why you get out of bed each day, it's a challenge to suddenly remember to choose to step out on the other side. What this change looked like and how this influenced my coaching, and ultimately my athletes, was this: love is the foundation of our pursuit of high performance, not just mindless hard work. Love for self. Love for the endeavour, in this case rowing. Love for team. And, finally, love for the competitor. My new number one job as I saw it was to create opportunities for the young athletes that I was working with to arrive at this understanding on their own and in their own time. But arrive they must.

What followed were years of coaching focused on the athletes' needs, not just mine. Sure, winning was fun. But how we were arriving there was so much more deserving of the races these young men were winning. The race results were simply now the by-product of the work, commitment, sacrifice, and "love" they had embraced. The understanding that win or lose they were still the same people and weren't defined by those results allowed them the freedom to fail. That freedom to fail unleashed a new level of performance.

Having Robyn as a shining example for my rowers from the get-go made it an easier sell for the athletes who were skeptical of the "love bullshit." They learned that when she'd begun running at a young age, her goals were not to go to multiple Olympic Games or win a Commonwealth and World Cup Silver Medal. She never told anyone that she wanted to be consistently ranked top ten in the world. She never set out to reach the highest level of physical and mental preparedness of her career in her final years, after seventeen years on the national team. Holy shit, who does that anyway? Finishes seventeen years of elite international competition at the top of their game? Not many.

Robyn's accomplishments screamed for the young athletes' attention, and got it. They came to understand and acknowledge that all of these remarkable achievements were the result of her approach to running, her *love* of running. Their success would, therefore, be determined by their *love* of rowing.

After the 2012 Canadian Schoolboy final, where our Ridley heavy eight crew won, it wasn't until the next day that I felt most proud of what they had accomplished. I was reading the local paper's article on the regatta and noticed that they had interviewed our coxie. One of the questions from the reporter was, "What makes you guys so fast?" The answer was beautiful and telling. "There's a lot of love in this boat." My job was done. They had arrived. They had figured out the source of their greatest strength—love. Yes, I was proud they had won, but I was more proud of the fact that I had helped teenage boys learn how to love one another.

In mid-August I sent our current boys an email explaining our plans and coinciding expectations for the next ten months. They understood clearly that showing up on September 1 ready to train was in all of our best interests. Yes, there'd be some time to acclimatize, but they knew we'd have to be up to our prescribed mileage in short order.

Our weekly schedule would have the boys sculling in small boats as much as possible. Even though the eight would be the priority boat for the year, sculling would ultimately serve the finesse part of the stroke that we aspired to. True, my reputation as a coach was that of producing crews that pulled hard and raced aggressively, but rowing fast involved proper technique as well. And ours would have to be better.

The beautiful thing about sculling in a single is that the boat speed a rower is able to achieve is indicative of so many components—fitness, technique, and grit—all of it has to be there. If we could get each of the rowers to become efficient scullers, then their combined effort would probably produce a faster eight.

Location plays a huge part in training a crew. Coaching on Vancouver Island means you can be on the water twelve months of the year, with the exception of the odd snowstorm. In St. Catharines, you're off the water from November until April. Four months is a long time. How could we be competitive with the schools on the West Coast and the majority of US schools also training outdoors?

When I first arrived at Ridley, I presented Jay with a list of all of the things that would support a high-performance rowing program. One of them was an indoor tank. After much research, I made a trip to New Haven to meet with a manufacturer and have a trial row. The tanks, made by the Durham Boat Company, were the closest thing to rowing outdoors I had ever experienced. Along with the natural feeling the design provided, there were many other perks. Foremost for me was that the tanks were not built into the ground. Instead, they were made of a hard resin that sat on top of the floor. That translated into a better line of sight for the coach, more physical hands-on coaching, and easier accessibility to the tanks if there were ever leaks or damage. Given that the price was right, the decision was easy.

The installation took less than a week, including a few hours to fill each tank with a hose. These enormously large tubs would essentially represent the corresponding port and starboard sides of the boat. Almost half of our 2012/13 crew had been novice. Therefore, using the tank to "catch up" technically to the more experienced crews made it an invaluable asset.

Now, with our 2013/14 group, we aspired to what I now referred to as "tank technique." This essentially meant that, in a tank with as close to ideal conditions as one could ever hope for, an athlete could strive for as close to a perfect stroke as possible. That was my thinking, anyhow. Once a week, we ran through drills and exercises in our tank in the pursuit of that perfect stroke. Furthermore, given the tank came with a rigging system that allowed rowers to scull, we could ensure that part of their development as well.

It was ideal. Sure, we weren't on the water every day, but at least when our athletes sat in the tank they were going to learn how to row as perfectly as possible, whereas teams at schools that rowed year-round often developed poor rowing technique that was re-emphasized each time they took a stroke.

There is an expression in rowing made popular by Mike Spraklen, one of Canada's most successful national team rowing coaches: "Miles make champions." I didn't doubt it. If those miles are shit awful, however, there's no championship waiting at the end of the season. Instead, I believed in the adage "Perfect practice makes perfect." Every mile we put in would have one purpose—make us faster. If we could do that, come race day, we'd be ready.

I had taught an entrepreneurship course for a number of years at my previous school, Glenlyon Norfolk in Victoria, and I had made Jim Collins's book, *Good to Great* required reading. Although the 2008 economic crash calls into question some of his findings, his thoughts on culture and its impact on performance was what resonated most for me. Essentially, Collins lays out important concepts required to take any organization and transform it from good to great. This transformation, not surprisingly, requires some key cultural shifts, along with the implementation of some essential strategies.

One of those strategies is what he refers to as "getting the right people on the bus, and getting the wrong people off." The theory is that your "bus" will go in the direction the people driving it want it to go.

After my first year back at Ridley, I combined simple observation of the program in action with some soft changes. From this observation, it was clear to me who had to go and who had to stay. For me the challenge was in trying to move the program forward with coaches who could buy into a process-centred culture, one in which winning wasn't the goal of the program, but a by-product of the cultural and strategic choices our program made. A subtle distinction, perhaps, but an essential one if we were going to achieve the success I had in mind. Did I want a winning program? Of course. But I saw focusing on what a winning program looked like, as opposed to focusing on winning, as the most effective way to get there.

I had first tried this competitive strategy over a decade ago at Shawnigan Lake School. The young men I worked with the first year there rose to levels I couldn't have imagined and went on to become multiple national champions. Their success validated a coaching strategy that I continued to hone over the years. Now, at Ridley, in order to build the high-performance program that I'd promised, it was essential that everyone embrace the paradigm of solid process combined with the required healthy culture as the foundation. If someone thought that buy-in was impossible, then they had no place on our bus.

Collins also recommends surrounding yourself with people who know as much, or more, as you do about what you want to accomplish. For some team leaders, this strategy can be an enormous challenge. If a leader experiences his or her position from a place of authority first, this strategy—inviting others to join the team—can seem threatening. Filling the bus with people who know more than you do has the potential to challenge one's ego. When you see the strategy through the lens of what's best for the team, the decision becomes clearer and easier. In my case, I simply identified all of the components that were required for us to achieve the high performance we were seeking and began finding experts in each of those areas.

In 2011, when *Chariots and Horses* was published, Winston Cook contacted me on Facebook. He was coaching in Toronto at Upper Canada College, a long-time rival of Ridley's. He shared some notes and reflections of his own journey as an athlete and coach. His thoughts were honest, insightful, and telling of an individual who had battled his own competitive demons and transformed himself as a result.

Indeed, when I had first met Winston at a Junior National Team rowing camp at Shawnigan Lake years earlier, he resembled the coach I had once been. Now, as he put it, he had mellowed. Clearly, there was a shift in his coaching perspective and his approach to high performance. Yes, he still loved winning, but he wasn't about to compromise his values along the way. He was also quick to point out what almost everyone who read the book told me: "You should go hug your wife and say 'Thank you for saving me from myself.'"

We finally met in person and discussed all things rowing, coaching, and life in general. We talked about rowing against each other in our high school days back in the early 1980s when he was competing for St. Catharines Collegiate. He recalled our Ridley crew in 1983. "We were tied with you guys in that final, right up until the race started." Winston also possessed a quick wit.

Given the direction of the conversation and the similarities in our coaching philosophies, I saw Winston as someone I wanted on the bus. I asked him about coming to Ridley to coach. Initially, I wanted him to head up the lightweight program, which had, in Ridley's heyday, been incredibly successful under some memorable coaches from that era. Winston was open to taking those reins but needed some time to sort out a few things in his personal life. Not wanting to push, I gave him some time, and in the fall of 2012 he started working with me and the senior boys.

Winston was, and had been, a volunteer coach for his entire career, which spanned over thirty years. When he wasn't coaching, he owned and ran a successful financial investment company— Henley Financial. As a coach, he had an impressive track record with high school, university, and national junior crews. Not only was he a competitive individual, who inspired his crews to reach impressive goals, he was an exceptional rigger. I knew he had a good eye for rowing technique, but knowing that he was knowledgeable in the field of rigging was a bonus. I had always played it safe with my rigging, using standard rigging measurements for my crews. Although that approach had managed to work so far, having Winston aboard would force me to entertain more aggressive and potentially faster options.

We quickly established a nice working rapport. Not only was Winston highly astute as a coach, he had a playful and relaxed manner with the athletes. He was simply fun to be around. For someone like me, who could be intense, having an entertaining and spirited presence helped to get me to joke around more than I otherwise might have. Now all we had to do was get the right crew on the bus, and we'd be ready to start training.

With more than half of the crew residing in other countries, some of them as far away as Germany, Russia, and Hong Kong, we agreed to schedule optional rows for our first week of training.

The athletes would be arriving at Ridley on different days and, therefore, it made sense to provide some flexibility. It was the last week of August and still seven days before classes began. And, truth be told, the School was more agreeable to optional rows over mandated ones.

After four years of playing the "coaching game" at the School, my strategies had become more refined when it came to getting what we needed. Winston and I knew that if the boys were in town, they'd be at the course ready to row, optional or not. They were as eager as we were to get this year started.

Autumn was my favourite time of year for coaching in St. Catharines. It wasn't too hot, with the humidity pretty much done for the year. Martindale Pond, where we rowed, was quiet now that summer rowing was over. And, of course, there were the trees. There was nothing like the fall colours of the massive deciduous trees that lined the water's edge and protected us on all sides. That beautiful spectacle was just a few weeks away, and with this being my final year, I anticipated it with even more appreciation.

Over the first few days, the boys rowed only in singles. We were determined to take the time early on in the season to strip down the technique of each athlete and then build it up again from the bottom. They bought into the strategy of acquiring free boat speed by simply striving for better technique. That made our plan easier to implement. Having hard-working athletes is one thing. Having mature, big-picture thinking athletes is another. Improved technique, combined with the fitness level that they would achieve this year would ultimately make a crew that would be hard to beat, and they knew it. Their complete buy-in to this approach was paramount.

The best thing about this group was that they understood our philosophy on achieving high performance. As junior rowers in grades nine and ten, they had heard what the 2012 crew was all about. Selling the idea that love could win them a national championship was easy, or at least easier. In 2013, having one athlete continue from the previous year's crew had given us a huge advantage.

That athlete was Igal Flegmann, a cocky Mexican who had started showing up for our indoor ergometer sessions as far back as 2011. He saw the ergometer as a way to improve his fitness for hockey—that's right, hockey! Quite honestly, he rubbed a lot of the guys the wrong way. He was never rude or inappropriate. Instead, just a bit loud and animated—two words I wouldn't have chosen to describe any of the others. There were no false pretenses; he was genuinely full of energy and obviously not afraid of the challenge the senior heavyweight crew had taken on.

With each workout, not surprisingly he began to improve. On one particular day, with ten-minute pieces on the menu, his scores started to challenge those of some of our top guys. In fact, his efficiency scores put him well ahead of many of them. He wasn't pretty to watch on the erg, but he could pull.

Being a sucker for weight efficiency, I began paying more attention to our Mexican Wayne Gretzky. When I was a rower on the national team, I was tall but lighter than most of my competitors. Consequently, there was nothing I enjoyed more than beating my teammates, especially on the erg. Igal may have been a lightweight, but his aggression and tenacity were getting him noticed by the members of the heavyweight crew. Was he ruffling some feathers? You bet he was, and I loved it.

The criterion for making any boat that I've ever coached was clear: the fastest guys will sit on the starting line come race day. Period. It was pretty simple. Show up every day. Train hard. Stay out of trouble.

And let the chips fall where they may. Igal took that simple checklist as an invitation to see if he could crack the heavy eight as a 5-foot-10-inch, 155-pound lightweight. Five months later, he was still a little rough to watch, but man did he ever mess up the water when he pulled.

Now, in 2013, back as a defending national champion and the male captain of rowing, he was our sole leader in the boat. With a group of young mostly novice rowers, he did his best to pass on what he had learned in a few short months the previous year. Despite incredibly challenging circumstances, he did a remarkable job. In fact, if his response after their heat at Canadian Schoolboy Championships that year was any indication of the impact he had made, we'd have an impressive group returning this year.

As I mentioned earlier, the conditions for the 2013 Canadian Schoolboy Championships weekend were horrendous. Shoving the crew off for their first race of the regatta in the eight, Winston and I both knew there was no way they were going to beat the heavily favoured Brentwood crew from the West Coast. We did figure that if they could get into the final, they could possibly medal.

With the races shortened to 1000 metres due to the terrible conditions, all of the crews would have barely three minutes to sort out who was advancing to the final the next day. Every crew's racing strategy that morning would be to get out fast and clean, and hang in until the finish line.

As Winston and I watched the race, we could tell right from the get-go that something was wrong.

"Someone on the starboard side isn't rowing," I said quietly to Winston.

"Yep."

Surprisingly, as the race progressed, our Ridley crew still remained in contention. They weren't leading the field, but they weren't last either.

We learned at the dock that one of our novice boys, TJ, had come off his slide at the start. Not seeing that his seat had disappeared behind him, he had simply pulled his oar across and tried as much as he could not to disrupt the boat. He didn't know the protocol in that situation was to "get your ass out of the boat, pronto, and cheer as your crew rowed by."

Finishing fourth meant our boys wouldn't advance to the final. With only seven rowers and 190 pounds of dead weight sitting in the middle of the boat, they managed to beat two crews. Ridley had a history of stuff like this happening to its crews. Curse? Bad luck? Whatever it was, it was the worst way to end a season. Losing to a crew that was faster than you meant you still got to race. You still got to see how good you were. When you suffered broken equipment or a mishap like this one, it meant that you had no clear ranking coming out of that regatta season. We would be in the dark in terms of assessing ourselves against the other schools for 2013/14.

When I reached our crew at the dock, my first concern was for Igal. All of the other members would be able to return to Ridley the next year and have another try. This was Igal's last race wearing orange and black.

As I put my arms around him, both of us tearing up, I said, "I'm so sorry, Igal."

"Why? Don't be sorry," he replied, fighting back his tears. "That was an amazing race. I'm so proud of these guys. Not one person quit. Nobody gave up. Everyone pulled as hard as they could all of the way down. I'm so proud."

If there was a better response to a situation like that, I couldn't think of it. That's what any coach would want to hear. Clearly, by Igal's account, these boys had learned everything that we had hoped they might. Now our plan moving forward was as it always was, to show up at every regatta and have our best race we possibly could on the day.

Mathew Szymanowski was our newest addition to the group. He was the son of a national team rower from Poland. His dad, Mirek, had rowed for his homeland during the 1980s and been part of some exceptional Polish quads during that decade. When he moved to Canada and put down roots in Kitchener, Ontario, years later, there were no schools nearby with established rowing programs. He had no choice but to coach Mathew on his own.

Later, when Mathew began rowing with a local club, he flourished, managing to earn a bronze medal in the junior single event at the 2012 Canadian Schoolboy Championships. There was lots of potential in Mathew. He was a big boy just like his dad.

The next year, 2013, at the same regatta, Mirek and I started talking about our rowing careers and realized that we had been at the same World Championships together during the 1980s—small world!

We also talked about Mathew coming to Ridley for his grade twelve year. Recognizing the opportunity it would be for Mathew, Mirek made it happen. At first Mathew was understandably quiet and reserved. He had not only transferred schools for his graduating year, but was also aware of the tremendous sacrifices his parents were making to support his rowing dreams. There was a lot riding on his shoulders.

Watching him on the water those first few days, Winston and I both knew that we could help him go faster. His technique was fine, but with some small adjustments there was more bang for his buck waiting—and there was lots of buck!

At the Ontario Erg Championships in 2013 he placed third with a 6:24 time. The will to pull was rare and sometimes hard to teach, but Mathew clearly had it. With his size, strength, and work ethic, he would fit in perfectly and be a terrific addition to our group.

Steve Smyth was also a recent transfer to Ridley. A local boy, he had rowed for the Ridley Graduate Boat Club during the summer and wanted to see how he would fare with our high school program. His first love, however, was hockey, and he made that very clear. He wasn't the tallest rower I'd ever met, but he was physically strong and rowed quite well.

His plan was to play hockey on a high-level team in Niagara Falls and row with us when his schedule permitted. It wasn't my place to say what he could or couldn't do, but my experience told me this arrangement wasn't going to work. I am all for developing young children as multi-sport athletes, but as boys and girls become young men and women, and their sporting dreams begin to narrow, combining two time-consuming sports during the same season was a train wreck in the making. Nevertheless, we were willing to give it a try.

The final addition to our team came in the form of a new coach. Jay and I both knew that if rowing was going to grow and establish some legitimacy within the School, the women's head coach needed to be a full-time paid position. Although Nancy Storrs, a US National Team rower from the 1970s and 1980s had been doing a good job at the helm, we felt the program needed new blood and someone who was hired within the school, not a volunteer position as it stood when I arrived. As qualified as Nancy was, she had been doing double duty all these years: coaching the Ridley Graduate Boat Club throughout the entire year as well as the Ridley College program throughout the school year. A tall order for anyone.

Siobhan was an Old Ridlean from 1996, the same year as Jay. She had grown up on campus and had had a successful career rowing for Ridley and on the Junior National Team before heading off to Western University, where she rowed as a varsity athlete for four years. After completing her master's degree, she began her coaching career in Saskatchewan at the provincial level. From there she moved on to the head coaching position with the Ottawa Rowing Club before working at a National Satellite Development Centre in Welland, Ontario. Jay and I agreed that she was the perfect candidate.

CHAPTER THREE

———| |———

THERE AREN'T TOO many head-style races that have the prestige of Boston's Head-of-the-Charles Regatta (HOTC). If there was ever a race where you wanted to meet the best of the best, this was it. Knowing that, we chose it for our first major regatta of the 2013 fall season. We were slated to race our eight in the youth division. That would enable us to go up against the top high school and club crews in North America and even the United Kingdom. With the race scheduled for the third weekend in October, there wasn't much time to get ready. Given what international travel was like post 9/11 and the makeup of our crew, we had some US border hoops to navigate. In my summer email, I had informed the athletes that we would need everyone to ensure that their ducks were aligned perfectly with regard to passports and visas. There would be a fair amount of travel that year to the regattas we had in mind, and a good number of them were outside Canada.

Ridley's current student body had so many young girls and boys from abroad that the School had someone whose job involved making sure things like this were taken care of. It was imperative that the lines of communication between parents and the School start early so as to prevent any last-minute challenges come departure time. With everything set in motion, there was nothing left to do but prepare for the race.

As it stood, we had five returning athletes from the previous year's heavy eight. With our two new rowers and one athlete moving up from our junior program, we had enough for a crew—barely. Sandy Morrison, having coxed the previous year's heavy eight boat, would occupy that seat once again. Although first impressions might have you thinking he was quiet for a coxie, once in the boat, he was transformed. What I appreciated most about Sandy, aside from his ability to get a boat down a course in a straight line, was that he didn't fill the airwaves with useless drivel. When he spoke in the boat, it was because he had something worthwhile to say. That inherent nuance made him very effective at what he did. We were fortunate in that his dad, as a teenager himself, was a very successful coxie. Bill had helped many St. Catharines crews win Henley Gold during his youth. Now, his son Sandy was carrying on that family tradition.

With the craziness that was the HOTC Regatta, we would need some of that Morrison DNA to help our crew navigate not only the winding Charles River course, but also the many crews we planned on passing. As a lottery entry crew, we would be starting closer to the back of field in the sixty-fourth position. With ten second intervals and eighty-five entries, we were bound to catch up to someone.

The routine that Winston and I had laid out in August had grown into a nice rhythm by the second week of school. Technically, we were making progress. The changes that we were implementing in the tank every Monday were sticking throughout the remaining week on the water. The boys could see the changes each week during our video analysis and, more importantly, they could feel the change in the boat. It was a good start to the year, and both Winston and I were optimistic that we just might pull off this ambitious little venture.

When I had rowed at Ridley, we wouldn't find out what the workout was for the day until Neil pulled up in his coach boat and announced it to us. Although, we usually had a good idea given the pattern that developed, it didn't much matter—all of it was going to hurt.

Now, however, I believed in keeping the athletes informed of our decision making. Granted, I wasn't about to hand over the reins in terms of what work was on the schedule each day but, at the very least, I wanted them to know what was coming down the pipe. This strategy allowed our rowers to prepare for each session in terms of pre-workout meals, supplementing snacks, and the appropriate attire. It encouraged them to take ownership of their choices on and off the water.

We had ten training sessions a week: five on the water, two in the weight room, one on the spin bikes, one in the tank combined with an erg session, and one in the gymnasium, which was usually a basketball game. We knew it was going to be a long year, and keeping things fresh was imperative to not only their physical health, but their mental and emotional states as well.

The tank was the foundation of our technical work. Each week we chose one focus, and we kept on it throughout each subsequent on-water session, building on each focus as we progressed throughout the month. The resulting shift in boat speed was significant.

I was also a big believer in the merits of time well spent in the weight room. While at Ridley under Neil's leadership, weight workouts were the backbone of our winter training. The weights we lifted were mainly focused on building our aerobic base through repetitive circuit training. Yes, strength was important, too. But for Neil it was all about improving our conditioning and mental tenacity through competition.

With the advent of rowing ergometers, I believed we no longer needed those aerobic based circuits. Instead, I chose to have our athletes focus on building strength and power. Fortunately for us, we had the School's physical trainer to rely on when it came to designing our weight-training regimen.

Paul DeVillis was a perfect example of the "right person" on the bus. I met Paul my first week back at the School in 2010. During our initial conversation, I realized he was going to be easy to work with. Not only did we share similar ideas about fitness and strength development, but his calm demeanour and playful sense of humour made for an immediate connection. We chatted extensively about what I was looking for in a weight program for the rowers. Each year, as our athletes developed, we would reassess our direction and make the appropriate changes. In addition, I always knew Paul was up on the latest research on lifting techniques and loading principles. As a coach, I was incredibly fortunate to have such a committed and knowledgeable resource at my fingertips. His passion for learning allowed me trust him completely with the team's needs.

Our early morning weight-training sessions proved tremendous for developing these young athletes. Not only could Winston and I see the physical difference in the boys, but their new-found strength was reflected in their ever-improving erg scores.

The added bonus with Paul was that, as a math teacher at the school, he was my eye-in-the-sky in terms of keeping me informed on the boys' academic progress. All of them were capable students, but Paul made sure they kept their proverbial noses clean when it came to their individual class assignments. They already respected and admired him for what he brought to our team; knowing they had an advocate among the teachers was a huge help for all of us.

As the crews' technique continued to improve, we made sure that their on-water mileage was increasing at a constant and appropriate rate as well. In my opinion, Mike Spraklen described the training effect we were looking for perfectly. His analogy of an oar handle and the blister it produced was simple and clear. Our bodies, in this case the hand and resulting blister, had no choice but to get stronger each time we stressed it. As our hands grew calluses to manage the constant friction from the oar handle, so too did the body grow stronger as we stressed it with more physical work, but as a coach one had to be smart about the duration over which one increased that stress or training load.

In our case, the work that we were able to manage at this stage of the year was the result of the work these young boys had done the year before. Too many coaches would just hurl an inordinate amount of volume at their athletes in the hopes of "toughening them up." It sounds good, but it rarely worked. The mileage we were putting in was significant, but it was appropriate given the context of their stage of development and readiness.

The point of rowing is to race. It's very simple. Crews line up either side by side or in a line one after the next and, when told to begin, they go as hard and as fast as they possibly can from one point to another. The crew that does it in shortest amount of time wins. Easy.

What I've always found curious about watching other coaches work with their athletes, particularly on the ergometer, is the lengths to which some coaches would try to disguise or hide the racing part. Watching coaches tape over the display board on an erg so that the athlete won't be distracted by the feedback, or not posting scores publicly in front of the entire team for fear that the ones who "lost" would somehow feel inferior—that never made sense to me.

I believe the reason that some athletes have so much anxiety about the erg, and in particular the numbers that it spews out, is because of what some coaches and athletes make those numbers mean. It's just a number—feedback and nothing more. It informs you either that your process is working or it's not. When athletes struggle with "the number," it's always because it has been made to mean more than it should.

My strategy at Ridley was, all day, every day, to be transparent about any sort of assessment. And I made it clear that every day was an opportunity to assess. During erg workouts, I would read the scores out to the athletes after each piece—for feedback. It means that today, this is what you scored. And these are everyone else's scores. If athletes think it means that they're losers, or inferior, or shouldn't even bother trying, then it's the job of the coach to explain otherwise to them. By demystifying the meaning of assessment, athletes simply use it as a tool to improve.

My belief was that those numbers were there to inspire—not diminish. By using language that was consistent with that belief, our rowers soon learned that if they showed up every day, believed in the process, and trained to their utmost ability, they would improve. What more could we, or any athlete ask for? Nothing more.

The Five Bridges head race was a local regatta held every year in Welland, a smaller neighbouring city located about thirty minutes south of St. Catharines. The racecourse wound through the heart of the city on the Welland River. With a few weeks until Boston, this was an ideal opportunity to assess our training while comparing our boat speed with that of some of the local high schools and clubs. The distance was a little over five kilometres, a good test for any crew at this stage of the season.

Cosmo Steier had been the stroke of our 2013 crew. He was a local boy from Niagara Falls who had been at Ridley since grade five. He was a top-ranking student and an exceptional athlete. As a member of Ridley's soccer team, a fall term sport, the plan was to have him train with us every morning and as many weekday afternoons as possible.

In his first week back with the soccer team, however, he suffered a severe concussion during a practice. Given the hyper-vigilant climate around concussions and the concerns about continuing to play unchecked, the consensus was that he should sit out for a few weeks. After the second week Cosmo decided there was too much on the line in this his graduating year and decided not to return to the soccer pitch. Instead, he would be joining us full-time when he was given the all clear.

I was honestly disappointed for him. The soccer team was promising. They'd reached their league's gold medal game the previous year. It would've been a terrific experience for Cosmo to continue to play. I won't lie though: given the ambitious goals we had laid out for the year, knowing he'd be with us every day going forward was pretty good news. Toward the end of September, he returned to the crew and resumed his training. At first he struggled but, never one to complain, he simply pushed through the fatigue and was back managing the rest of the team's volume in short order.

One of the challenges of working with a crew comprising mainly grade twelve students, especially in the fall, was the allure of the US colleges and universities. Ridley's heavy eight from 2012 had, indeed, put the School back on the rowing map. Now coaches from some of the top rowing programs in the United States were actively recruiting our current crop of athletes.

Winston and I didn't get upset with the boys when they had recruiting trips—we both knew the game. Hell, I had been recruited to Syracuse University to row for the Orangemen back in 1983, so who was I to complain? Nonetheless, it was still a delicate balance of allowing our top athletes to pursue their post-Ridley rowing and academic goals while maintaining a consistent training regimen for the entire group.

The problem was that Cosmo had inadvertently agreed to a recruiting trip with the University of Pennsylvania (UPenn) for the same weekend as our race in Welland, which meant we wouldn't have our stroke seat for the eight. Knowing UPenn was at the top of Cosmo's list of universities, we weren't about to have him change his plans. It wasn't ideal, but it wasn't going to ruin the entire year either.

Given the number of kilometres that we had logged in small boats up until this point, we would use the regatta as an opportunity to see if all of that time was transferring into real boat speed. Therefore, we made sure that everyone had at least one sculling race. We entered two quads, a coxed four, and number of doubles.

With each crew's subsequent launch, Winston and I took off on our bikes to watch them at various stages of the day's races. When it was all over, we had some good feedback. The changes we had made were working. The boats were responding accordingly, especially our top quad. They posted a substantially faster time than the second place finisher. But the quad wasn't the goal. Ultimately, it was the eight we were after, and although not ideal Boston was going to have to be our first test.

Daniel Tkaczick was from Dusseldorf, Germany. He had come to Ridley two years earlier for grade ten. It wasn't hard to imagine why he—at six feet seven inches—was such an exceptional boat mover. In fact, Daniel rowed like most typical Germans, meaning, he rowed well: clean at the catch and finish, while maintaining good posture throughout the drive and recovery. Germany had a long history of producing extraordinarily fast crews. I would know. It was the undefeated German eight that beat us in the Olympic final in Seoul.

Having Daniel back for his last year at Ridley had been a question mark throughout the summer. His father, an eighty-year-old still incredibly vibrant and brimming with life, had experienced some health setbacks, and Daniel was having second thoughts about spending another year away from him. Understandably, Daniel wanted some time to think about his decision over the summer break. It wasn't until the end of August that I received a text from him informing me that his dad wanted him to return to Ridley and finish what he had started.

I was relieved to hear the news that he was returning, but I was also genuinely happy for Daniel. I knew how much rowing meant to him and, in particular, how fond he was of his teammates. Having him in our training group was a big part of why we had so much potential. Both Winston and I were depending on him to be one of the key members from which we built this crew.

Dmitry Veremeenko was from eastern Russia. He was a young boy who had joined our group the previous year as a grade ten student who was too old to row in our junior program. What Dmitry, or Dima as the boys called to him, lacked in size he more than made up for with his sheer determination. As a novice rower the year before, he had made some enormous strides not only in terms of his technique, but also with his fitness and strength. So much so that Dima ended up stroking our coxed four at both the Canadian and US Schoolboy Championships. He'd had a growth spurt over the summer, and we were happy to have him back as part of our team.

The challenge we now faced with one week to go until we left for Boston was that neither Daniel's nor Dmitry's visas had arrived at the School. The boys were allowed to travel between Canada and their home countries but needed special papers to travel into the United States. If the documents didn't show up on time, we would be forced to find replacements for their seats.

I made daily visits to the office at Ridley where their travel documents were meant to show up. I was still hopeful the frantic phone calls and emails that were now in full swing would result in a green light for both of them. By mid-week, there was still no indication this predicament was going to have a happy ending. When five o'clock on Friday rolled around, we were faced with the disappointing and embarrassing situation of having only six rowers and our coxie to board the bus the following morning. Neither Daniel nor Dima were able to travel. Having paid for our entries, our transportation, and accommodation, we weren't about to cancel the trip. This was not a regatta where you simply called up the organizers the day before and explained that you wouldn't be able to attend, regardless of the circumstances.

The lottery for this regatta was enormous. If we provided any good reason for the regatta chair to question entries from the School, crews would be hard-pressed to earn a spot in the coming years. Given all of our options, we really only had one—go down there and find spares.

Jesus Serrano was a lightweight who had been with our rowing program for a number of years. Fortunately for us, he was agreeable to making the trip as a last-minute substitute for one of our empty seats. Although he lacked the size and subsequent erg score of our missing rowers, he was as technically proficient as any of them. He certainly wasn't going to slow us down.

With one more seat to fill, upon arriving at Henley Island that morning to board the coach that we had booked with the St. Catharines rowing club, I asked one of their coaches if they had a spare that we could borrow. Lucky for us, they did.

I introduced myself to the young athlete and asked if he wouldn't mind sitting in as a spare for our crew. Knowing his other option was to travel all of that way to watch from the bank of the river, it felt good to offer him a chance to race. To my relief, he appeared excited at the idea of racing with our crew. Relieved, I made my way to the back of the bus and my seat knowing that at the very least we'd be able to fill every spot in the boat. The weekend wasn't going to provide us with much feedback going forward, but we'd make the best of it and ensure the boys had as good an experience as we could manage.

When we arrived at the rowing site on the bank of the Charles River ten hours later, we had little time to waste if we were going to get a practice row in before the course was closed for the day. With the boat rigged and everyone changed and ready to row, Winston and I gathered the oars and we made our way to one of the designated launch docks.

Sandy was as good as any coxie that I had ever worked with in terms of steering. He understood the subtleties of controlling the rudder to guarantee a smooth race and a fast time. However, when you add the component of having additional crews in front, behind, and beside you into the mix, the game gets considerably more interesting.

Part of the attraction of the HOTC was the drama created when you had multiple crews passing under a bridge at the same time with a fixed amount of space. With young cocky teenage boys at the helm, many of them unwilling to back down from any opponent who challenged them for right-of-way, regardless of what the rules stated, you were bound to have some added excitement.

Given that, I made my position very clear. "If ever in doubt, protect the boat. It's not worth it."

Any time you make a line-up change in a crew, not surprisingly there's an adjustment period. In a perfect world, we would have had a week to fine-tune the rigging and allow new members a better chance to blend in with the others. Instead, we had one row—about forty-five minutes to be exact. The point of the row was simply to get the boys' travel legs moving and come off the water feeling better than when they went out.

Although taller, our St. Catharines spare was a lightweight just like Jesus Serrano. With the spare in four seat and Jesus two seats behind him, the crew shoved off. Given how well our boat had moved in the training sessions leading up to this weekend and the level of experience in our athletes, there was a good chance they would be able to adjust quite quickly and have a decent showing the next day.

As well as being a top academic performer, a School prefect, and a good athlete, Jesus was about as polite a young man as one could imagine. Whether you encountered him in the halls of the School or just coming off the water after a hard training session, he always met you with a smile and a warm greeting. When I asked Jesus about coming down to Boston as a spare, he immediately phoned his parents and told them about the trip. His dad, being an enthusiastic supporter, decided to fly up from Mexico City and surprise his son.

The morning of the race, as we were standing outside the bus that would take us to the course, his dad snuck up on Jesus and tapped him on his shoulder. It was very touching to see Jesus's excitement when he turned around and saw who it was. Everyone was struck by his dad's genuine playfulness and smiled as the two laughed and embraced. It was the perfect tone with which to start the day.

As Winston made the final adjustments to the boat, I gestured for the athletes to gather around. We still had about fifteen minutes before we were due at the dock.

"I'm guessing it comes as no surprise to any of you that given the new members sitting in this boat, we've basically disqualified ourselves from this event. Therefore, you truly have nothing to lose here. We want you to go out and have the best race you can no matter what's happened or where we are in our training. That's it. That's all we'll ask for, and that's all you can really expect. Control what you can. Stay focused in the boat. Have fun with it. Any questions?"

They had heard that message from me often enough to know what was expected. I wasn't much for last-minute rah-rah pep talks, anyhow. My thinking was if the work wasn't done by race day, no amount of macho bravado-laden speechmaking was going to hide that fact. Go out and race. Let the work show up. Simple.

"Oh, and you'll need one of these," I said, smiling at our new member from St. Catharines as I held up a shiny new Ridley uni-suit. I always brought extras. When you coach teenage boys, you learn these things.

Everyone went quiet. "I'm sure you're going to get an earful for putting this thing on. But the rules state every member of the crew has to be wearing the same stuff. So, you can tell your friends back home that you *had* to wear it." He smiled and took hold of his orange and black racing kit. His new Ridley teammates-for-a-day laughed and patted him on the back.

I was struck by how well this had worked out. By no means was I okay with the gong show that had transpired at Ridley before we left, but the crew's ability to adapt and move forward reaffirmed that our approach to competition was the right one.

Trust—always trust. It's a tough one to embrace sometimes. Especially when you're a teen. This wasn't what we envisioned, but everyone was doing their utmost to keep this experience positive and not get hung up on what had gone wrong. Instead, they were making the best of what we had been dealt. Impressive.

Trust was a lesson that I had learned from Robyn years earlier. When you compete on the world stage for seventeen years, odds are you're going to have a few occasions when things don't go as planned. It took watching a number of her races, but eventually I noticed and, more importantly, learned to appreciate that when Robyn experienced setbacks, she always looked for the opportunities within them.

What I now understood and tried to pass on to the boys I coached was that trust was really the only way out of hardship. Granted, easier said than done sometimes. However, at this stage of my life I had finally realized how well this approach worked. It is undeniably the most effective tool for moving forward in a shit-hits-the-fan moment. If we're completely honest with ourselves, the only other option is self-pity. Hardly a competitive strategy for achieving high performance.

For me the acid test was my slowly evolved perspective on Seoul. If someone had found me in the moments after our Olympic final, in my cloud of disbelief and, well, self-pity, and told me in an upbeat manner, "Ahhhh, chin up, Jase. It's all good. Someday you'll look back on this race and think, *Wow, what a gift—this was the best thing that could have ever happened to me*," I would've—well, I don't even want to think what I would have done. But today—I get it. I understand that thinking.

In my heart, did I wish I'd won an Olympic gold medal that day? Stupid question—of course I did. But you get my point. Losing that final pushed me down a path of self-discovery that I wouldn't have had reason to venture down if we had won. Furthermore, winning that race would've reaffirmed that a combative strategy in sport is *the* only way to compete.

It had been a fifteen-year journey that I wouldn't have necessarily chosen given the struggles and hardships that I encountered. But what I learned on that path—who I became on that path—has undoubtedly made that dark ugly stuff I went through well worth it.

When I think about the coach I would be today if we had won, I can't even imagine the level of crazed dysfunction I would be passing on to my athletes. At twenty-five, I was an asshole. I have no interest in ever knowing the fifty-two-year-old version of that guy—no thanks!

CHAPTER FOUR

TIM COY HAD been a lifelong friend from my childhood days on the Ridley campus. His dad, an Old Ridlean, had been a teacher and coach at the School. Tim grew up knowing the Ridley that I had, and relished in it as an athlete. Fortunately for Tim, he inherited his mom's height and matured into the perfect size for a coxie.

Once in Upper School, he went on to jockey some of Ridley's fastest crews during the mid-1980s, winning more medals than anyone else in the School's rowing history. In 1983, after a quiet, almost reluctant beginning, he developed into one the feistiest and competitive coxies I ever rowed for. Now, as the head coach at Shawnigan Lake School, he had imbued his crews with those traits and had the results to show for it. After many years of coaching together at Shawnigan, this would be the first year our crews would be racing against each other. I didn't see it as a big deal. I had long since moved on from the antiquated strategy of seeing opposing coaches as the enemy.

Tim was a good coach, and we had both learned from Neil that you don't travel long distances unless you have a good crew to race. The crew that he was bringing to Boston had won the Junior Boys' heavy eight on the basis of their time in the heats at the previous year's infamous 2013 Canadian Schoolboys. True, they'd be a younger crew. But one of the fastest eight's I had ever coached was made up of predominantly grade eleven athletes. This year we may have had some older, more experienced rowers, but nothing was going to be a done deal, especially with Tim's crew in the mix.

It was a glorious autumn day in Boston. With our eight shoved off and headed to the start line, I ventured out to meet up and watch the race with some of the parents. Normally, I wasn't much for hanging around anyone while my crews were racing, let alone the athletes' parents. But, aside from the safety of the boat and the crew in it, there really wasn't a lot on the line that day.

Standing on the Eliot Bridge, the last one over the Charles River before the finish line, we watched the Ridley and the Shawnigan crews come around the last major bend and make their way underneath us. Surprisingly, as our Ridley crew came into sight, they looked quite respectable. The blade work was decent and they were actively passing crews.

Shawnigan, which had started seventy-fifth, finished forty-eighth. Our boys, who started sixty-fourth, finished forty-ninth—two seconds behind the Shawnigan boat. With both crews having begun so far back in the mix, it was hard to take too much information from that result. There were so many variables in a race like this. Forget about the circumstances surrounding our crew. Our takeaway from that weekend was that our boys were adaptable and able to rise above challenging situations. At the time, we had no idea how significant this one attribute would be in serving this crew through the coming months.

The events that had transpired leading up to the weekend presented Winston and me with the perfect teachable moment on accountability. If just one of us had chosen not to honour the group and what we had committed to as a team, the ripple effect of that choice would have been enormously detrimental. Boston made that clear to everyone.

We re-emphasized our commitment to one another and the goal we had laid out in August: to produce the fastest eight we could by June 8, the day of the Canadian Schoolboys. If we were committed to that as a group, the chances of us reaching that goal were greater.

In the weeks following our race on the Charles, our strategy hadn't changed—focus on what we could control. At this stage of the game, that meant continuing with small boat rowing to ensure our technique was still optimal. Aside from the adaptability the crew displayed in Boston, their results showed that size and pulling aside, technically they were able to come together as an effective crew regardless of who was in the boat. The mechanics of the stroke that we had begun to focus on two months earlier were clearly paying off. I wasn't about to throw that out and persuade Winston to return to a hammer-style crew, my previous default. Winston had convinced me we could have both—relentless aggression with disciplined finesse. I still believed that combination was our ticket.

The next week, we were back in the weight room. Paul's program was having its desired effect: the boys continued to not only gain size and strength, but also transfer that new strength into the boat. We were beginning a new phase with Paul, and the boys were excited. They'd bought into his routine and could feel the positive gains from the hard work.

Part of what was helping us train at such an intense level was a nutritionist who we were now working with. It was all part of building that supportive team on our bus. One more like-minded person to contribute to our desired goal. We were intent on reviewing every aspect of the boys' day and looking for opportunities to make positive changes that would result in a better performance for each of them.

Lowell Greib was a naturopathic doctor and a certified sports nutritionist. More importantly for me, he was still active as an athlete and worked with some very high profile national team triathletes and runners. He obviously knew his stuff because the prescribed diet changes and new supplements the boys were taking were helping tremendously.

With the HOTC over, we were looking at roughly three to four more weeks of on-water training. The mileage that we were putting in at this point in the year was higher than that of any crew I had coached previously. The boys were fit, and getting faster—all without breaking down. Very good indicators. If we kept up this pace, we'd have something to show for it in the spring.

With limited local crews to race, we looked to the upcoming Ontario University Championships. Their annual regatta took place on the Henley Course in St. Catharines the following weekend. Knowing Brock's head coach, Peter Somerwil, from my national team rowing days, I asked him if there'd be a chance our boys could race as an exhibition entry in an outside lane. Pete, being supportive of what Winston and I were trying to do, agreed. When we told the boys, they were genuinely excited to finally have some serious competition other than one another.

My old coach, Neil Campbell, was always looking for opportunities to race us "up." He knew it would make us faster. And, as much as it initially scared the crap out of us, we simply got used to it each year until we welcomed those chances to race older and bigger crews. For young athletes, there was no better feeling than beating an older crew that was *supposed* to beat you. The lessons doing so taught us were lessons worth passing on to these boys. Nothing is impossible—and don't ever decide your fate until you've tried your absolute hardest to accomplish the challenge that's been laid out in front of you.

If we were going to race the best crews in the world, these young boys would experience moments when they were forced to redefine their limits—physical, mental, and emotional. Racing bigger and stronger athletes was our strategy for creating those moments.

In Boston, I had met up with an athlete that I had coached when I was at Shawnigan. He was racing in a throw-together master's crew from California. Max Wyatt, or Big Max as we lovingly referred to him, was part of an exceptional group of young men that I had worked with in 2003/04. That group of boys had helped me solidify the idea that winning was the by-product of solid conscious process.

It was such a pivotal year for me as a coach and, quite honestly, as a person. From 2000 until that crew in 2004, as a junior coach I had never made winning the goal. Instead, it was all about the journey, the idea I'd learned from Robyn. Yes, with those junior crews we won a lot of races, but I never saw the strategy of not focusing on winning as the effective competitive strategy it was proving to be. Instead, I simply saw it as doing the right thing as a junior coach. The fact that those crews were successful was simply a bonus. But I never put the two together. Their accomplishments were born out of my personal agenda to prove to myself that one could *win* without focusing on winning. Nothing more.

Now, having evolved and honed that approach, I fully recognized that regardless of how I arrived at that personal challenge I had embraced a decade earlier, focusing on winning was a distraction from accomplishing the very thing. A paradox, to be sure, but true.

I still wanted to ensure that the athletes I worked with had healthy experiences in rowing, and not focusing on winning accomplished that. And now I also realized that our approach to competition helped us win more often.

Any time you draw a line in the sand as a reference to when and where good enough is, you subconsciously inform the mind that this particular moment in time and all of the work that it's taken to get here is somehow *good enough*. The by-product of that is a body that physically backs off and stops striving. I believed there was no such thing as good enough. In fact, I would ask my athletes, "Where's the fun in *good enough*?" Let's see if we can go faster, farther, harder, longer—you name it. Let's see what you're truly capable of each and every day.

With Big Max and the rest of his crewmates, I was determined to maintain the philosophy that we had established as a successful junior crew, not necessarily because I thought it would help them win, but instead because I wanted a clear conscience with regard to how I was motivating them. When I moved up to coach them as seniors in that 2003/04 year, I was pleasantly surprised to realize that I was onto something.

As an athlete, my motivation had always come from outside of me. Everything was an extrinsic experience—something I chased. Winning being, of course, the end target. I chased the satisfaction of knowing that I was better than my competitors. I chased the relief of not having lost. I chased everything in life. If something wasn't worth chasing, it didn't interest me.

Using that form of motivation, which worked on many occasions, eventually lost its attraction and eventually lost me. The result was some confusing days trying to find my desire to train when the desire of winning, and all that I thought it would bring me, died.

With the boys, I purposefully encouraged them to be motivated from within, to use intrinsic motivation—a form of motivation that we're all hard-wired to experience from birth but lose touch with as we grow older and are taught to chase external rewards.

"You can't have dessert until you finish your vegetables" seems harmless enough, but that's how it starts.

I found as I continued to coach after 2004 that when I could connect a young athlete with the simple joy of getting better, that became a powerful, sustaining form of motivation. Far more motivating than either convincing them that winning was a feeling worth chasing or, conversely, that losing was one worth avoiding. Both of those had been integral parts of my playbook when I was competing.

What I had begun to understand was that my main goal each day should be to ensure that when the athletes arrived at 4:00 p.m. and left at 6:30 p.m., they felt better about themselves than when they had arrived. Sure, the physical training and technical aspects of rowing were essential, but if I built this foundational experience into their daily practices, we'd not only improve at a faster rate, but also reach higher levels of achievement for longer periods of time.

After years of producing consistent winning crews, I no longer needed convincing. It was now the backbone of my coaching philosophy for achieving high performance.

Big Max, having gone on to win multiple national championships at the US collegiate level and even a gold medal for Canada at the U23 World Championships, was an example of just how long that motivation could sustain itself.

As we wrapped up our visit, he asked, "Are you doing the same thing with your guys now that you did with us? You know, the 'not focusing on winning' thing?"

"Of course, I am. Why would I have changed?" I answered smiling.

"Good to hear—because it works."

We both laughed as I got up on my toes to hug him goodbye.

The winning aside, what I cherished most about my time at Shawnigan was the relationships that I had today with those grown men. What they achieved that year as a crew was remarkable. Accomplishments aside, what it meant to each of us as individuals all of these years later was unique. And yet, arriving at the pinnacle required a journey that touched each of them as individuals in similar ways. Our combined efforts resulted in a very fast crew.

I loved hearing about what they took from those years. Those conversations were the acid test of our approach. Invariably, they remembered winning the races, but the lessons, memories, and friendships appeared to always resonate more for each of them.

With my Ridley crew, regardless of the lifelong friendships that I recognized I was in the midst of helping to build, there was still one thing everyone associated with the School wanted this crew to do in a few months' time—and that was win.

For me, the expectation that this group of athletes be fast was omnipresent. For a guy who had spent the better part of fifteen years coming to terms with an obsession with winning, it was a delicate dance. Of course I wanted these boys to win. In many ways, that's why I was hired. However, the fallout of my relationship with winning had led to a constant touchstone: "how" we became a winning crew was as important to me as whether or not we won.

When you line up six boats at the start of a race, and one of the crews consists of younger and less experienced athletes, there's an expectation that young crew will lose. When they don't, it can put a few noses out of joint. I knew that if our guys did what they were capable of, there was a good chance they would surprise a few university coaches. Knowing that, I made sure the boys understood clearly that regardless of how the racing went, it was important to maintain the composure and maturity that we had established as part of our team's culture. Meaning, race knowing the results you achieve will reflect your preparation—nothing more. And, if those results mean you win, understand that it's simply a positive indicator and, like always, don't shove it in anyone's face.

Ridley's motto for competitive sport, "If you lose, say nothing; if you win, say less," became the School's modus operandi with its second headmaster. That sentiment was about as Canadian as you could get—polite to the core.

It had been sixty-five years since Harry Griffith instilled this code into the ethos of the School. Times had obviously changed, and with them how athletes celebrated triumph. Humility was still an important virtue of sportsmanship, and a significant life lesson that most coaches aspired to teach their athletes. But humility wasn't as palpable as it might have been back in the days of "Well played, old chap!"

When I was at Ridley, I felt the significance of that message on many fronts. Not only was it pervasive around the campus, both my dad and Neil oozed it. If I wanted to please either of them, a frequent pastime of mine, I knew I had to ooze it as well. Now as an adult coach, I certainly appreciated the value in what I was teaching these young men, but there was a part of me that wanted them to have more fun than I did in celebrating their achievements. My aversion to rejoicing in my victories as a young athlete came from a strategy of maintaining motivation as much as wanting to appear polite and appease my adult mentors. I'm not sure how or even when it all began to pervade my inner dialogue, but somewhere along the way I became my own hard-ass gatekeeper of what was considered acceptable praise.

I had convinced myself perversely that if I celebrated winning, I would somehow lessen the desire to push on and win more often. If I was good enough to win a race, then I was good enough. No need to train harder and more frequently—right? In fact, when others would congratulate me, I would respond inwardly, *It's bullshit, Jase—don't listen*, constantly telling myself to ignore the distracting approval.

I knew there was more to achieve, and I knew that I had more in me to give. I figured that somehow others would jeopardize my drive to find it. That drive resulted in some impressive accomplishments, granted. But it also contributed to my premature demise without ever achieving my truest potential.

Undoubtedly, if there was a bitter pill to swallow from my Olympic experience, it wasn't necessarily just that we had lost. It was that my motivation to win was in some ways a contributing factor to that outcome. When you have that humbling conversation with yourself—that you contributed to your own undoing—it's a moment. One that solidified my commitment to never passing on my limiting belief that the end result, winning, justified all means of getting there—no matter how destructive or devastating the route.

Robyn frequently reminded me that part of establishing a strong relationship with my athletes meant accepting who they were as individuals, even if that meant accepting someone who didn't think like I did. Knowing now the importance of diverse team chemistry, having a boatload of young Jason Dorland's—intensely driven athletes, was not our ticket to success. We needed balance.

Recalling that feeling I had as a young boy—that winning meant those around me were happier—I didn't want our rowers to feel that my acceptance of them was conditional. I knew that in order for our crew to achieve our potential, my acceptance had to come first. It was the most challenging part of being their coach. Being awake to my tendency to show approval as a form of encouragement. I will like you—only if you work hard, do as I say, and win. That strategy is all too common in sport, and for me deeply engrained. It was my personal work, and I struggled to manage it every day. With this our first test of the season, I set out to remain as even-keeled as I could possibly be. If we won today—terrific. If we lost—that was okay, too. It didn't change how I felt about our young athletes as people; their performance was separate.

Having laid down our heaviest week of practice thus far, Winston and I knew we had ramped up an already daunting challenge. We were curious as to how the boys would now respond to racing with such a high level of cumulative fatigue in their system. The weekend's racing would test more than their speed; it would also give us an indication as to how well their bodies were managing the workload.

Normally, going into a major regatta we would execute a strategically planned taper to facilitate optimal performance. Even for lesser regattas, at the very least we'd back off the intensity of their work the day before; however, for today's races, we were pushing right through. If the results were positive, we knew that with a taper they'd be capable of much more.

Standing on the bank of the Henley course waiting for our coxed four to race down in the first heat of that event, I recognized an elderly woman standing beside me. She was an old friend of my mom's. I introduced myself. She was surprised at how much I had grown up. It had been at least thirty years since she had last seen me. I'm not sure what she was expecting. She was there with a friend whose grandson was racing for one of the universities. She introduced us and we continued to visit as I kept an eye on the course.

"I had heard from your mother that you were living back in St. Catharines and coaching at Ridley."

"Yes, we moved back three years ago."

"Well, I'm sure Eleanor is loving having you home. It's must be a terrific help for her."

"I hope so." I smiled. "It's been great to spend time with family, and for Mataya our daughter to get to know her grandparents."

"Yes, I'm sure."

As our race finally approached, the conversation went quiet. We were standing just shy of the 1500-metre mark—almost three-quarters of the way into the race.

"Now which crew is that one?" she asked, pointing at the lead boat in the far lane. "They're not listed on the program? They're quite a ways out in front."

"That's our Ridley boat," I said. "We were allowed to enter as an exhibition crew."

"But, they're high school? And I understand that this is a university regatta?"

Just in case her friend's grandson was in our race, I kept still.

"Oh my." Her proper British accent finally broke the silence as she turned to look at her friend. "Well, you must be doing something right, Jason—continued good luck," she offered as I waved and said my goodbyes. Old habits resurfaced as I quickly downplayed her comment and quietly returned to the dock to join Winston and wait for the boys.

The rest of the day went similarly—all positive indicators. We were extremely pleased with the results. Although the four had easily won their heat, their qualifying time was the third fastest. Given their lead, we recognized they might have fared better if they had been in the faster heat and been pushed.

With hockey season ramping up, Steve was unable to race that day. Therefore, given the job that Jesus had done in Boston, we returned him to the line-up in both the quad and the eight. The quad raced in another coxed four heat, as there was no quad event at this regatta. They won that race, as they should have. A good quad should always beat a good coxed four. Regardless, they looked quite strong from my usual vantage point. We then combined the two boats to race the eight where the boys rowed a 6:08 time in their heat and finished third overall—a decent time for October.

After the disappointing experience of the previous weekend, we were happy that the crew had finally had a chance to test their speed. Winston and I had a pretty good sense of the progress that we were making, and now the boys did as well. For young athletes to know that after a heavy week of training they were still able to race hard and beat crews that perhaps they shouldn't—that would do wonders for their confidence. It was great to see, especially given the exhaustion that they must have been feeling. This was exactly what we needed as our autumn on-water training was coming to an end.

Driving them back to the School, I could feel their satisfaction. There was a lightness to the group. They were playful and excited despite being tired. Parking the van in front of the School, I turned around and said to the boys, "It's a nice feeling isn't it?" They all paused from gathering their backpacks, looked up, and smiled. "I want you to take a moment before we meet up again on Monday morning to really let that sink in. We're not done by any means. But think of how far we've come in two months. Imagine what we can do between now and June—I hope that excites you. It sure excites the hell out of me!" The van was silent. "Have a great weekend, boys. Get some rest."

Moving forward, it was vital that we make the next few months about simply getting better—as individuals and as a group. Our next official competition wasn't for more than three months. This is where the usefulness of our approach to motivation paid off.

If we started our next phase of training with, "Okay, boys, we've got three months to get ready for our next race, let's get at 'er!" that's a long time to hold anyone's attention and focus. Instead, this next phase of our training would continue to be about the task of improving. Strength. Technique. Aerobic fitness. Flexibility. Focus. Competitive grit. Discipline. And within all of those components, we would continue to build in each of our rowers his *why* for showing up each day. From that *why*, their cohesive bond would flourish—the final intangible ingredient of our success.

With hockey season now in full swing, Steve's commitment was wavering and, with it, a question was growing in the minds of everyone about whether we would in fact have an eight. As good as the job Jesus had done for us was, he wasn't a viable option. He was planning on rowing the lightweight single that year, and at 5 feet 6 and 138 pounds, he was simply too small to sit in a boat with other boys who clocked in north of 6 feet and over 190 pounds. His efficiency was impressive, but we needed more length and power than he physically could offer.

Regardless of the future of the eight, we had to stay focused on our goal—pursuing the best races we could manage come springtime. The process that spoke to was clear, and the boys did their utmost to show up for each part.

CHAPTER FIVE

WITH NO IMMEDIATE races in our future, our plan was to spend every on-water practice in smaller boats until Mother Nature decided it was time to head indoors for our winter season. It had been a beautiful autumn thus far with great weather and calm water. The long-range forecast suggested we would get at least another few weeks out of doors. With winter on the horizon, we were determined to make good use of our limited time.

Transparent competition was a huge part of our philosophy and the culture we had established. Whether we were doing timed pieces on the ergometers or on the water—it was a race. The boys had heard enough from me—*every day is a seat race*—to know that any time they lined up against someone else, it was an opportunity to see how much speed they could generate and for how long. The more we could replicate that competitive pressure cooker, the more prepared we'd be come May.

Luc Brodeur was a local boy who had come to Ridley in grade nine. As his advisor that first year, I was responsible for meeting with him and my other advisees once a week. My role was that of a support system for any and all issues those students might have been experiencing in all aspects of life at Ridley. At my first "meet the creature" day in 2010, I was sitting at my table waiting for my next parent meeting, when I looked up and noticed Luc and his parents heading toward me. As I watched them get closer, I thought Luc's dad looked familiar.

"Hi Jason, I'm Paul Brodeur—Luc's dad."

"And I'm Kathy—Luc's mom."

"Nice to meet both of you," I replied as we exchanged handshakes. "Now, why do you look so familiar to me, Paul?"

"We went to Edith Cavell together," he answered with a knowing smile. "And then we rowed against each other when I was at West Park."

Crazy—after almost twenty-five years on the coast, one of the first parents I meet upon returning to Ridley was from my childhood, and I would eventually be coaching his son.

Luc rowed his first two years with our juniors and then moved up to our senior program in grade eleven. Now, in his final year, he was a strong member of our team. Luc was the quintessential optimist. He saw possibility in everything. There wasn't a single time that I could recall from my three years with Luc when I had ever heard him question his ability to achieve the goals he had laid out for himself.

When I met with each of our athletes in September of this year, I asked what their goals were. What universities or colleges were they looking at? What were their rowing goals? And in that vein, what were they thinking was a realistic time for their ergometer scores?

"Well, Jason, I've been giving this a lot of thought," Luc answered, but not in a sheepish manner, or as a delay tactic while he searched frantically for a reasonable number after being put on the spot. No, instead, I knew that he meant it. Luc had been thinking long and hard about this year's erg scores. "In order for me to make the Junior National Team, I figure I have to row sub-6:10."

Scoring 6:10 was an ambitious goal for any rower—in university. Luc's best score to date was 6:17, a very impressive score for a high school rower. He had pulled that at our training camp in Princeton, New Jersey, five months earlier. To take another seven seconds off his personal best wasn't going to be easy. When rowers managed to get their scores under six minutes, they were getting close to Senior A National Team material. Therefore, the closer Luc tried to get to six minutes as a seventeen-year-old, the harder those one-second decrements became.

Upon hearing his response, I simply looked him straight in the eye and said, "Okay, Luc. We've got some work to do, then."

"We sure do," replied Luc, smiling.

He showed up every day and quietly went about his business in an unassuming, but intensely purposeful manner. If there was a workhorse in our group, Luc was it. No drama. No fanfare. Just head down, and straight ahead. Having Luc on our team was an essential part of what made us so powerful and fast. The bar that he set for the others was high. While he passed no judgment, his teammates respected him and did their best to follow his example.

In their singles, the boys were starting to establish a pecking order. Daniel, Mathew, and Luc would exchange the top spot every day with each subsequent piece. Although teammates and close friends, they raced hard each outing and tried to unleash a performance that kept them in the lead as they raced up and down the course.

Steve was a good boat mover, but his inconsistency in attending practices was beginning to affect his fitness and thus his ability to keep up with the leaders. Cosmo was a good sculler as well but hadn't much experience in a single and, therefore, spent most of his time in a double with Dima or another one of his teammates who was also putting in the miles required to perfect their sculling stroke.

Josh Gatcke was one of those teammates. He was new to our senior group. Josh had been part of our junior boys eight the previous season and was a positive addition to our group. Technically, he had a decent stroke. He was a fair size, and he liked to pull—always a good attribute.

What he had going for him the most was his sense of commitment. There was nothing that he wanted more than to be a contributing member of this program. He smelled of it. That translated into a remarkably mature presence that kept showing up every day and putting in the effort. He was surrounded by some impressive athletes, and he knew it. He respected his peers and knew that if he were going to row with these boys, he'd have to in turn earn their respect, also.

Josh was indicative of the bottom-up culture that we were building. It wasn't enough to have superstars. In rowing, one guy couldn't make a boat go fast on his own, but he could sure make it go slower. Given that understanding, each athlete had an equal place on the team. At every opportunity we encouraged our rowers to push from the bottom and pull from the top. With that team paradigm, they were constantly inspired to strive for more.

As we began our next phase of a long journey, it was time to back off and restart the fitness-building process again. I liked to work on a six- to eight-week cycle that increased in volume and intensity with each week until finally, at eight weeks, we returned to a level that was more challenging than where the previous cycle had begun but allowed the athletes a period to rebuild and recharge. Given the scheduling of holidays within the school year calendar, the cycle fit nicely into those inherent breaks.

Having just finished our first cycle, we began our initial week of long-distance pieces that focused on efficient boat moving as well as continuing to build each individual's aerobic base. Paul's weight-training program mimicked our on-water schedule. Therefore, during these recovery transitions, and as their fatigue dissipated a bit, the boys became a little more mischievous. That mischievousness played out as spirited banter during our travels in the van more than at any other time. In many ways, it was my favourite part of my coaching day. Driving the boys back to the School from practice knowing they had just survived another challenging session from the schedule that I sent them every Sunday.

I remembered that feeling from when I was their age—riding with my crewmates as Neil drove our exhausted bodies back to the campus for dinner. It was a brief reprieve from the craziness of life at Ridley. The sense of belonging—brotherhood even—was our comfort, like a childhood blanket. It soothed away the stress of teenage life at a demanding school and in an exceedingly demanding sport.

That old black and orange van had held so many young Ridley rowers before us—all of them united in the pursuit of being faster than the previous year's team. The stories and legends were many. We had no sense of it at the time, but our own contribution would be shared someday in the very same van with the very same reverence we had for the rowers that had come before us. Our role in that tradition, although unspoken, was hard to deny. It helped weave the unifying fabric that made us so close.

Part of that fabric was constructed from the healthy teasing that flew around the van with boyish charm. Although there were times our discussions lost all charm and went straight to the proverbial locker-room as we ganged up on one another. A new girlfriend. A failed test in math. Bad gas. It didn't matter. It all fuelled our unstoppable urge to outdo the story or playful comment we had just heard. One can only imagine the hilarity of our adolescent comments—however inappropriate. My guess was that it was everything Neil could do to stop from driving off the road at times as he quietly listened in.

Now, as I took the wheel of a new black and orange van, I reflected that nothing had changed in thirty years. The same stories. The same jokes. The same obsessions. Insecurities. Dreams. Fears. All of it, exactly the same. There was something so comforting and reaffirming in knowing that the transition from boy to man was travelled on a similar bumpy road each passing decade.

Yes, the players were different, but the lessons weren't. I felt privileged to be welcomed along their journeys—one that could be so unforgiving at times. It was in those moments that I appreciated my role as their coach more than at any other time. True enough, we all wanted this year to be memorable with regard to our success. But I knew that what we accomplished that year would be so much bigger than just winning races. The remaining eight months together would forever transform these boys.

I loved that about coaching.

Listening to those boys share their lives as we had with Neil was beautiful. I was vicariously reliving my teenage years through these ambitious young men. There wasn't a day that went by when I wasn't reminded of how precious our time was together. Sure, coaching them was my job, and the responsibilities were many. But, above all, it was a privilege to be handed the reins of influence that came with such an enormous role. As long as I kept that understanding at the forefront of my decision making for the remainder of the year, I could live with any outcome.

Siobhan was doing a wonderful job. She had taken a women's coxed four to the HOTC and implemented physiological testing along with other assessment standards she had used as a regional coach at the training centre in Welland. The shift in attitude, focus, and accountability for her crews was palpable. I knew they and future women's crews were in good hands. Also, she and I had established a routine of meeting at a local coffee shop every Monday morning. Over our steaming beverages we would discuss all things Ridley rowing. Our meetings ensured that the lines of communication stayed open between the men's and women's teams, and provided us a chance to brainstorm around growing the program as I transitioned out.

With our first term of rowing over for the majority of the crews, we organized an intra-squad regatta that first week in November as a way to mark the end of the season for the novice rowers that had joined in September. With experienced senior athletes sitting in the stern of the shells, we lined up four eights and let them race one another.

The afternoon ended as a fun and positive experience for everyone. I had reminded our boys that "every rower was novice once, including you" as encouragement to be patient with the athletes behind them. As frustrating as rowing with a boat full of newbies can be when you're used to what these boys were, it was a good exercise in developing leadership as they assumed the role as the top members of our boathouse. Come springtime, the tone that our seniors established would help solidify the culture we were working so hard to maintain.

Peter Yates had played a pivotal role in helping me transition from life as a full-time athlete to a teacher and coach. We had known each other for almost twenty-five years. He had hired me as a coach when I was blindly scheming my comeback for the 1992 Barcelona Olympics. Seven months into my pursuit of that elusive Olympic gold medal, my motivation began to falter. In 1989, he had been the director of rowing at Shawnigan as well as a full-time teacher and housemaster.

When I realized I had come to the end of my rowing journey, it was Peter who encouraged me to find purpose outside of athletics. Quiet and constant, he was always available to listen and to provide kind and supportive encouragement. There's an expression, "We listen to reply." Not Peter. He listened to understand me. Only when he knew his wise words would be of service did he offer them.

In the years following my first stint at Shawnigan, he would regularly check in with timely phone calls to see how his young mentee was doing. During my second run at Shawnigan as a coach and a teacher, he was an enthusiastic cheerleader for my newly developed coaching philosophy. The phone calls continued even after I returned to Ridley. He loved that we had garnered so much success so quickly using what he referred to as an athlete-centred approach.

It was on one of those phone calls that he had told me about his illness. Being Peter, his approach was to remain positive and pragmatic as he set out to first understand and then defeat the "invader" as he called the cancer. His voice changed with the chemo; however, his support for me, as well as my coaching, never wavered. It was always the first thing we discussed.

Invariably, each phone call eventually landed on the topic of his unwelcome trespasser. I didn't even like to use the name. It sounded so caustic and aggressive. Peter spoke openly about the procedures and what the days following his treatment were like.

The first time he told me, he knew the silence on the phone meant my throat had locked and I was unable to speak. Peter knew I could so easily become a bucket of sobbing tears, and therefore he would speak for me. When I had regained my composure, I would share my thoughts in strategic bursts until another wave of emotion rendered me speechless.

The thought of losing this man, my friend, who had given me and so many others the gift of thoughtful, life-changing perspective, was enraging. As one does in these instances, I thought of all of the selfish and destructive trash in our society that was more deserving of this unbiased predator. I knew that sort of thinking wouldn't serve Peter, so I kept those thoughts to myself.

The first time Peter was sick, he battled back, won, and promptly returned to the life he had known. This time, however, his invader had returned stronger and less agreeable to a fair fight. Daily updates from a mutual friend indicated that Peter was losing his second battle. Halfway into November, we received a call: "Come as soon as possible."

Landing in Victoria on a sunny Saturday afternoon provided mixed emotions for both Robyn and me. It was wonderful to be home, but our reason for being there was heartbreaking.

Mataya, our daughter, was simply excited to be back on Vancouver Island closer to her "bestest" friend, Maya. We had called ahead and told Maya's parents that we would be in town. Naturally, an afternoon play-date for later that week was scheduled. But death is a big concept to grasp when you're eight years old. Mataya was doing her best to understand why this would be the last time she saw Peter.

We drove straight to the hospital.

Understandably, Mataya was nervous about seeing Peter. He had a procedure done earlier in the week that allowed him to breathe through a tube in his throat. He was still able to speak, but only in short bursts as he covered the hole in his trachea to force air through his vocal chords.

As we rode the elevator to Peter's floor, we told Mataya that she didn't have to see him until she was ready. Armed with books, crayons, and paper, we arrived on the palliative care floor of the Royal Jubilee Hospital. To our amazement, he was sitting in the lounge, with Joanne, his wife, at his side. His girls, Aly and Lizzie, along with other caring friends and family, were nearby.

Everyone expressed their appreciation of our being there and welcomed us warmly. Peter and Mataya locked eyes immediately. Peter, ever sensitive to the needs of others, made sure Mataya wasn't upset by the change in his appearance. Now hairless, pale, and gaunt, Peter smiled. "Well, Mataya. Look at how much you've grown!"

His new and strange-sounding voice caught Mataya off guard. She sunk into me.

"How was the plane ride?" Peter continued.

"Good," answered a curious and pensive Mataya.

"I'm glad. And I'm so happy that you've come to visit me!"

My eyes began to fill as the enormity of the situation settled in. Hugs and handshakes were frowned upon with Peter's compromised immune system. Instead, with glistening eyes, Robyn and I smiled warmly at Peter and said our hellos. What else could we do? Peter's smile answered everything: *I'm doing my best with what I know is coming and, more importantly, I'm glad you're here.* We shared the goings on of life in St. Catharines with him. We talked about everything that we could think of. At first, the conversation was slightly awkward and forced as we struggled to keep light with family news while simultaneously considering his future.

It was now past the dinner hour, and the waiting room was quickly filling. Friends and family were showing up in droves to see Peter. Joanne came in to signal it was time to wrap up our first visit.

"Okay, Goose! Time for you to leave," she announced, as she burst into the room and put her arm around me. Goose was a nickname Peter had given me at Shawnigan. It stemmed from an incident years earlier on the ski slopes at Manning Park in British Columbia's southern interior.

For decades, Shawnigan would close down for one week during February's rainy season and ship everyone off to a ski lodge for the better part of a week. The idea was to escape those grey wet winter days on the West Coast and create an opportunity for students and staff to experience nature and one another outside of the School's gates.

Our routine had been to ski down a run, ride back up the mountain on a lift, and then gather at the top before heading off on another run. One day, just after lunch, a few of us were riding the chairlift. When my chair reached the top, I skied over to join what I thought was the group I was with. As I approached everyone, I came up and stuck my ski pole between what I thought were Peter's legs and pulled back in order to catch his "boys" with the basket of my ski pole.

When the voice that uttered "Whoah!" reached my ears, I realized those "boys" were not attached to Peter. Needless to say, I apologized profusely. No matter how many times I tried to explain that his outfit was the same as that of one of my friends, his puzzled, unimpressed look said it all: *Go away, weirdo!*

When I looked around, I saw everyone, including Peter, bent over in hysterics. That night, back at the main cabin and in front of all of the staff, Peter recounted the day's events and pronounced me, forever after, as "Goose."

The next morning, we returned to the hospital in Victoria. This time, we had Peter all to ourselves. We had been encouraged to bring photos, artwork, poems—anything to brighten Peter's hospital room walls. Mataya had been busy drawing the night before and was excited to tape up her artwork.

Robyn's gift was her Reiki. In fact, each night for the entire week we were there, she would go back to the hospital after everyone had gone to give Peter a Reiki treatment as he went off to sleep. Peter was always amazed by the heat and the energy he could feel coming from Robyn's hands. She was quick to clarify that the heat and energy were coming through her, not from her. Peter would smile at her modest clarification.

I chose to bring a poem. Not being one to write poetry, I hoped it would at the very least provide me a way to express what I appreciated about Peter, and to thank him for his gift.

My Friend Peter

In all my time I've never claimed to be a wordsmith or a poet.
Simply read on a few lines and you, too, soon will know it.

But, if you have a moment, I do have a true story to share.
About my friend Peter that might raise a hair.

I met him 24 years ago it was 1989.
Picked me up in old blue Land Cruiser not much shine.

His smile was warm; his handshake firm and strong.
A soul I could trust right out of the gates; that didn't take long.

I will never forget that first day we met.
He had a handsome golden named Carlson who smelled; that much you could bet.

He hired me to coach rowing; he was actually my boss.
I was determined to please him; there would be no loss.

I arrived with a wall of bravado to keep others at bay.
My friend Peter, he saw through that the very first day.

My bruises and sorrows would be hard to keep.
Not with Peter around, you know what they say, "still waters
run deep."

He always had time for me no matter my concern.
When Peter spoke, it was clear to me, I had much to learn.

A friendship developed, although to me he was more.
"Big brother" isn't too far off. Something new to explore.

I told him my dreams of revenge and winning gold.
He questioned the value in that. Shit, he was bold!

My world was spinning, my life's goal turned on its head.
What would I do? What more could there be instead?

Peter challenged my purpose, kid gloves gently guiding.
He pushed me to face that in my life from which I had been hiding.

In time I saw the meaning of Peter's caring way.
I began to feel lighter, even excited with each new day.

I have much to thank him for all he has given.
His wisdom, his time, and his love all helped me find a life
I can live in.

How do you say thanks? How do you pay back a gift of such size?
With my friend Peter, my contentment from afar was his only prize.

We all strive for a grand legacy to leave when we're done here.
My friend Peter has left one with me that much you should be clear.

That soul who Peter met all those years ago was one lost pup.
"People come into our lives when we most need them" pretty much
sums it up.

He has taught me to dream big and look beyond what at first might
seem real.
To consider every path when venturing out that was his deal.

That coaching is never about the prize, the result that you
have earned.
But instead, what you have taught your charges, what they
have learned.

I can truly say that I am a better person because of our meeting.
Clearly, the gift is all mine.
My friend Peter, I promise never to forget you and allow all that
you've taught me to shine.

Love always,
Gooseman.

By now, I was a sobbing mess in the chair at Peter's side. At this
stage in our friendship, Peter had seen me cry many times. There
was no awkwardness. No apology. Just Kleenex—lots of them. When
I was done, I folded up the poem and laid it on the bureau along with
all of the other photos and gifts he had received. There was nothing
more to say. The poem said everything, and Peter's smile said he
heard it.

That week became a rhythm of morning hospital visits followed
by afternoon get-togethers and dinners with friends. The Friday
before we left, a crowd filled the waiting room and spilled out into
the hall. Given that the majority of the people who had travelled
to see Peter knew one another, it ended up being an enormous
Shawnigan Lake School reunion. When the noise became too much,
we were asked to move downstairs to the cafeteria.

The next morning, during our final visit at the hospital, Peter
asked me if I had ever been awarded a Shawnigan rowing pin.

"No," I answered. "I didn't even know there was one."

"Old award. You deserve one, of all people." He then motioned for me to pass him his travel bag. After shuffling around inside for a moment, he pulled out a clear miniature baggie with a small sterling silver tiepin. It had "SLSRC" covering a horizontal oar attached to a pin.

"This is my last one. I want you to have it." I took it from Peter and removed it from the baggie. It was tiny, but beautiful.

"Thank you, Peter. This means a lot coming from you."

Peter nodded.

After a long pause, I said, "I was wondering if you wanted to row down the Henley-on-Thames regatta course one more time." Peter pursed his lips, squinted one eye, nodded, and gave me the thumbs-up.

"I figured as much," I smiled. "Good. I'm going to put you in five seat. Okay?" We both laughed. "Course, ya know? If we lose by an inch, I might live to regret this moment."

There was a warm, glowing smile on his face. I could tell he was thrilled at the idea that he would race Henley once more.

The next morning, it was time to say goodbye.

"Not afraid. Travelling to light. Not darkness. All good, Gooseman," he managed to say.

"I love you, Peter. I'll see you again some time."

His eyes were glistening as I reached out and took his hand. It was warm and strong like the first time I had held it. I gave it one last squeeze.

A few weeks later when Peter passed, I shared the news with the boys following our afternoon session. I was visibly shaken. On my way home, my phone began to chirp and chime numerous times. When I got inside the front door, I checked my messages. They were from the boys. All of them, sending their condolences and support in the loss of my friend.

In that moment, I knew we were creating the right team. We were a rowing crew. But we were so much more. I was their coach—true enough—I was also someone they knew cared deeply for each one of them. They were becoming a family of exceptional young men, one that looked out for and cared for its members.

CHAPTER SIX

———┤ ├———

WHILE I WAS away in Victoria, the crew's on-water training had come to an end. Given that December was closing in, I figured we had done pretty well. The boys were more fit, bigger and stronger, and rowed better than they had when we began the year in August. Each a "positive indicator" of our progress; that is a term I constantly used with the boys. Now, it was time to build on what we had started and arrive in March with further gains in all of those essential components.

Training indoors for five months through an Ontario winter can be a challenge for anyone. In designing the program upon which our young athletes were going to embark, I remembered my indoor training year of 1987/88.

It was the year before the Olympics, and I had chosen to put school on pause and move back to Ontario to train with my pair partner. After rowing on the water all four seasons for two years on Vancouver Island, I knew this training was going to take some getting used to. My days consisted of gruelling ergometer sessions, heavy weight lifting and, when the weather allowed for it, long difficult outdoor runs. What I achieved that year was my highest level of fitness ever. My ergometer score ranked me with the top rowers in the country and helped me earn a spot on the men's eight going to the Olympics. However, the price had been mind numbing. I had spent hours upon hours sitting on an ergometer. Worth it? No question. But as a coach with that experience, I wanted to accomplish the same outcome without the drudgery that indoor winter training season had been for me.

Furthermore, in hindsight, I believed that our 2012 crew had spent too much time on the erg. Yes, the boys had been fit and strong come June, and it showed up in spades on race day. But that same drudgery manifested as nagging injuries and burnout by the time we got to England. I knew this year's boys had to have variety if I was to achieve my goal of balancing their training without compromising racing potential. I decided that for the next few months we would develop each boy's athleticism first, and let the rower grow from that. With that in mind, we set out to become as fit as we possibly could, while trying to keep each day engaging and fun.

As it turned out, Luc's mom, Kathy, was a spin class instructor at a local fitness club. Part of our Tuesday afternoon's aerobic training fell under her leadership. Having the team hear a different voice was an important part of the variety. When a team hears only one voice, one perspective all year, that voice can become monotonous and, consequently, ineffective. Besides, Kathy's style was more playful and energetic than mine. That too was a great way to create variety. Not surprisingly, her workouts involved loud music as part of the motivation for each class. It may not sound like a big deal to most people, but for someone who had come from an era when music was seen as something "soft athletes" used as a distraction from the pain, it was a huge departure for me. I bit my lip and let Kathy work her magic.

From those bike sessions, Kathy then led the team through a fifty-minute callisthenic routine targeting the all-important core strength of our athletes. Then, we would finish every Tuesday's workout in the pool. When I had rowed at Ridley, I was a member of the School's swim team. After one of Neil's punishing weight workouts, swimming was extremely challenging, but in the end, I was stronger for it.

With the boys, I used a combination of flutter board drills for their legs, arms-only pulling drills, underwater swimming, and water aerobics. At the end of thirty-minutes we would mix up teams and have relay races—they loved it! Those days, despite being some of the longest, were their favourites. Overall, by mixing up the venues, we created all-important variety without compromising the benefits of improved aerobic capacity and core strength and avoided the drudgery and possible injury that a two-and-a-half-hour erg session might have caused.

In my rowing days, athletes weren't always known for their flexibility. Consequently, their injuries were many. Incorporating a yoga class once a week proved an invaluable addition to our routine. Jay hired a local yoga instructor to work with all of the high-performance teams throughout the winter term. It was another way to facilitate variety, improve flexibility and continue to develop core strength.

As a bonus, our instructor incorporated mindfulness and meditation—two words you wouldn't readily find in any of their classroom textbooks. This approach was a chance to open the door to the notion that reaching potential as athletes and students required more than just being a willing cog in the machine of a training regimen and rigorous academic studies. Again, it was a new voice, a new perspective: all good stuff for the future of the team.

Our rowing tank remained an essential part of each week. Of our ten scheduled training sessions, we spent two of them in the tank to master a stroke as close to perfect as possible. Just running through mindless drills wasn't enough. They had to execute them as if each stroke were their last.

In addition, we showed real-time video on a large screen TV at the front of the tank so the athletes could see the changes they were making to their strokes in the moment. With the help of my iPad and an app called Ubersense (now called Technique), we could take time to break the sequencing of each stroke down to one one-hundredth of a second. It's one thing for a coach to point out areas where their athletes can progress. It's something altogether more powerful and long-lasting when the athletes can see where their technique is compromised and then coach themselves. That provides a huge opportunity for improvement.

While we continued our sessions with Paul in the weight room, the final piece of each week's training puzzle was the ergometer. It's a nasty machine, really. There's no way to properly participate in what it has to offer without a vast amount of excruciating pain being part of the mix. Many rowers will concede, however, that the sport really is a contest of who can manage the most pain for the longest period of time. And the best way to mimic that is with the erg.

Each of our ergometer sessions targeted a specific training zone, and most of those zones involved pain. There was a noticeable difference in the van on the days when I picked up the boys and drove them to our off-campus tank and erg facility. They were quiet and focused as they transitioned from the requirements of the classroom to that of the ergometer. I tried to engage them in conversation as a strategy to move them out of their heads. So much of the discomfort of the each erg session was the buildup to hurting.

My guess was that each boy's first waking thought was the workout that was scheduled for the day. On afternoons that involved the erg, it began with a shot of adrenaline as they entertained the inevitable.

For many reasons, those intense erg sessions were the most frustrating part of my coaching days. When VO_2-max (measures oxygen consumption during intense exercise) or race pace specific work was scheduled, I invariably found myself fighting back tears numerous times throughout each session, tears that forced me to quickly leave the room at the end of each piece. Disappearing served two purposes. I didn't have to watch the agony each of the athletes experienced, agony that was the result of what I had prescribed, and they didn't have to see my eyes tear up.

Being present at, and perhaps more importantly responsible for, those painful moments stirred emotion deep inside me. When you ask athletes, especially those much younger than yourself, to willingly push their bodies to heights of effort and pain that most of their peers would back away from, that's a big ask, one that I never took for granted. I remembered well the pain of the training sessions of my youth and the trust I put in Neil Campbell.

I purposely remained awake to that ask every single day. Not a moment went by when the power that I held over these young men escaped my mind. When I drew up the schedule each Sunday night, copied it to an email and hit the send button on my laptop, I did it knowing the week's workouts were going to enable gains in boat speed, but those gains would come only if the boys had felt a remarkable amount of trust and belief in me.

Watching them find the strength to push through moments of self-doubt during excruciating sessions on the erg and find more self-confidence and a greater inner knowledge was a privilege. They understood it wasn't about being tough or macho. It was bigger than that. Their reasons for enduring had to do with understanding that finding their best race as individuals and as a crew would require an inordinate amount of time spent in pain. As bizarre as it may sound, knowing that guy beside you is hurting as much as you were is as inspiring and motivating as it is comforting.

With hockey season in full swing, Steve's ability to attend training sessions on a regular basis was compromised. Which meant we were teetering on the edge of having either a viable eight or not. Nick Lam, the final member of our crew, had rowed with us the previous year and had returned in grade twelve with the hopes of joining his crewmates at Henley. He was a "legacy student," which meant he was the son of an Old Ridlean. Being from Hong Kong, he hadn't been at all familiar with rowing when he joined us but was an exceptional rugby player. He had a muscular physique, and he'd picked up the sequencing of the stroke relatively quickly.

Nick was also clearly a thinker. The conversations I would overhear between Nick and his fellow rowers told me that he approached the world differently. He wore his emotions out front for everyone to see and didn't really care what anyone thought, and the compassion and care that he showed toward his teammates were obvious. Besides his book-smarts, my guess was that he would score quite high on any emotional intelligence assessment. Nick was always concerned with how everyone in the boat was doing and was the first to cheerlead when others were struggling.

Sometimes, however, in a sport like rowing, overthinking the training or the mechanics of a stroke can be a detriment. When athletes spend too much time in their heads as opposed to just being and letting the motion and effort of the stroke show up, their ability to reach their potential can be handicapped. Nick had a tendency to do that.

When that happened, I would encourage him to surrender to the effort that was required instead of overanalyzing every little aspect of the workout. When he did that, he was an effective boat mover. When he didn't, not surprisingly he found it difficult to reach his potential. Every athlete has a challenging characteristic that is simply part of their package and that a coach manages in order for the athlete to contribute his best to the team.

Knowing we were one seat away from not having an eight, Nick had, unbeknownst to me, been sharing our predicament with his roommate Chris Anderson. Chris, like Nick and Cosmo, was a school prefect, which meant they were students the School's administration recognized had leadership skills. Along with their other school commitments, prefects were required to help influence the culture of the student body in a positive and supportive manner.

I knew Chris only because he was a member of Arthur Bishop House, the house in which I was on duty once a week. He, like Nick, was a good athlete. Gifted with a strong build, he had participated in the previous year's rugby team. One night while I was on duty, Chris asked about joining rowing.

"Why on earth would you want to do that?" I asked him.

"I dunno know. A challenge?"

We both smiled. "Okay. It can be challenging. I'll give you that. But only if you do it right! Why else?"

"Nick tells me if you don't find someone to fill in Steve's spot, you won't have an eight."

"True. We're down to the line here. If someone doesn't step in soon, there's no way they'll be able to handle what we have planned."

After a moment of further consideration, Chris continued. "Well then, I want to be that guy."

I looked at him intently. "You would join our program so that your roommate would have a boat to row in?"

"Sure. Why not? Rowing means a lot to Nick. Besides, I think it would be cool to be as fit as he is."

I smiled again. "Chris, you realize the workload will be like nothing you've ever experienced. Your hardest day of rugby training will compare to one of our warm-ups. You understand that, right?"

"Nick said the same thing."

"Well, I'm not going to stop you. But it's going to be ugly for a bit. The guys you'll be training with have had a year to get used to our current volume of work. It's going to hurt a lot. You're going to get frustrated. Your initial scores will be way off the others' scores, but if you can hang with it for about two weeks, you'll start to see some small improvements."

"Sounds good. I'll see you tomorrow," he replied with a confident smile.

"Perfect. Nick knows where to be. Just show up with him."

The next morning, sure enough, Chris walked into the weight room with Nick.

I wasn't surprised. But I wasn't counting on him lasting. I had worked with athletes who had joined rowing late in the year before, but they had been athletes with a tremendous aerobic base they had built through another sport. Chris had little idea of what was in store for him. Perhaps that was best. Because if he had known, there's no way he would've shown up that morning.

As I expected, all of the boys shook his hand and welcomed him to the group. I imagined they were all thinking, *This guy's nuts!* But, if nothing else, we all admired his courage to try.

At first, his progress was as expected: painful and slow going. Winston was impressed with Chris's gumption but unimpressed with the scores that he was producing in his initial erg sessions. Perhaps Winston was more realistic than I was about the likelihood of our new crew member catching up to the others and becoming a contributing member. Regardless, I was determined to help Chris remain focused on just simply getting better. There was no denying, we needed an eighth guy. And, for the time being, he was it. It wasn't long before we began to see some improvements—small ones at first, but then as his new-found fitness and strength kicked in, Chris's scores improved with greater momentum.

Long before he joined our group, we had decided on a date at the end of November for our first two-kilometre erg test of the year. Although two kilometres was the international standard distance for indoor racing, I gave Chris the option of rowing half the distance. I knew that the information that I could garner from a one-kilometre test could tell me a rower's capacity for raw strength and determination. In other words, take that score and double it, and you'll have a ballpark idea of what they could do if more fit. Not surprisingly, Chris insisted on testing the full distance. He didn't want any special concessions.

The erg is an inanimate machine, a tool that gives feedback, from which athletes and coaches take meaning. It's in that meaning that your ego can run rampant with stories of either grandeur and victory, or weakness and defeat.

The pain of an erg test is hard to explain, both in terms of the magnitude with which it rips through your body and the resulting turmoil that infuses your mind. You're often left to wonder why in hell you voluntarily participate in such a brutal experience. But you do time and again, hoping that the work that you've done will result in a test that leaves you momentarily incapacitated, but encouraged.

I remembered well the feelings that owned me on the day of an erg test. Butterflies became bats. The gnawing at your stomach was inescapable. No matter what tricks you played with your mind, you always came back to the fact that an extreme dose of all-consuming pain was in your near future.

I knew all too well that what the morning and afternoon had felt like; the stress of waiting was omnipresent in everything you would do that day. So when the boys showed up at 4:00 p.m., I tried to be everything I would've wished for on my test days. Positive. Playful. Supportive. Understanding. Quiet. Strategic. Any and all of it. Each of the boys had his own method of mental and emotional preparation, and it was my job to be sensitive to each one and act in a way that mirrored what they needed to find their best effort.

For me, watching an erg test was never fun. There is no joy in witnessing the inner goings on of an athlete conveyed through their facial expressions. Behind them and clear of their line of sight, I would move from one athlete to the next, watching intently the numbers on each machine's monitor, which displayed real-time 500-metre splits, along with a predicted final score. The key for each of them was to find that edge between too much and not enough effort. If an athlete can produce optimal power output, where the resulting lactic acid is manageable, they could garner a good score. If, however, they produced so much lactic acid that their bodies were rendered useless, the resulting score would be compromised.

For the last two months, we had pushed that edge each week. Now, the challenge for each of them was to let that training show up without blowing up. Too often, overexcited athletes start with ambitious aggression only to crash two or three minutes into the test. As

I always said to our rowers, "Remember, 'the erg always wins.' There is no outsmarting this machine. No matter what you do, the erg is a heartless measuring device."

When the test was over, the scores indicated that our training was working—personal bests all around. Some boys showed greater gains than others, but the main thing was we were moving forward as a team.

Luc was the standout. He had improved his score from his 6:17 in May 2013 to 6:08, two seconds under the 6:10 goal he had set for himself, which also happened to be the world standard for junior rowers. That was impressive. But as an eight, we averaged 6:30 without Chris. Nowhere close to being fast enough. We had to be under 6:20 as a crew if we were going to compete with the best in the world. Although Chris had faired relatively well for a first attempt, he was still close to a minute behind Luc. The question remained: could we shed more than ten seconds off our collective time with only seven months to go?

When we weren't training, I was in meetings with coaches, parents, athletes, administration, and alumni, each representing important needs that require constant attention. It was the part of the job that I enjoyed the least. My "happy place" was in a coach boat, not sitting around a table.

The coaches met every Monday during the lunch hour. We reviewed the facility assignments for the week. Discussed any issues that existed with our athletes or administration. Provided an avenue to keep communication lines open while we were off the water and didn't readily run into one another.

Each Tuesday, Siobhan and I would sit down with Jay in his cramped office. When you're an athletic director, sports equipment and team jerseys can easily overwhelm a small space. Jay's office was no different.

Our meetings were always positive and productive. We would discuss concerns we'd heard from the other coaches and plan upcoming travel for regattas and training camps, and purchasing new equipment, or chat about the progress of our program and any challenges we were facing within the day-to-day operations of the School.

I couldn't have asked for a more supportive administrator than Jay. A talented athlete, he wasn't a rower himself, but he understood what we were trying to do. He knew that building a high-performance program in any sport required hard work and commitment. In one of our meetings in early December, I shared with Jay and Siobhan what I had been dreading from the beginning of the year: that some of our athletes might struggle to balance their commitment to rowing with their commitments to academics and other responsibilities to the School. In particular, I was worried about the athletes enrolled in Ridley's new International Baccalaureate (IB) curriculum.

With the Christmas break approaching, I could sense Nick beginning to falter. He was questioning whether or not he could continue with rowing. Knowing the thinker that he was, I imagined this had been brewing for a while. We had chatted on a few occasions when I was on duty during the fall term. Each time, however, I left the conversation believing that Nick was just tired. The pace at Ridley was relentless.

As an IB student and a prefect, Nick had a very full calendar. What seemed to be pushing him over the edge, however, was a girlfriend who wanted more of his time and didn't understand Nick's commitment to rowing or to his teammates. She was a great girl, and they made a cute couple; you could tell that they genuinely cared for each other. But each time Nick and I seemed to have sorted out his dilemma, it was undone by one conversation with her. Finally, on the first Friday night of December, Nick called me on my cell and said he needed to talk.

He was visibly shaken when he came through the front door. I gestured toward our living room. "Can I get you something to drink or eat?"

"Um. Actually, some water would be nice."

"I'll be back in a sec."

As I filled Nick's glass with water, I thought back to when I was twenty-five years old and knocking on Peter Yates's front door in search of someone to talk to. It was March of 1990, and I had been training at Shawnigan Lake School since September. I remembered feeling so lost. Waiting for Peter to answer his door, I wasn't really clear about what I was going to say to him. All I knew was that my motivation for going to Barcelona for the 1992 Olympics had gone sideways. Knowing I couldn't sustain my training given the shift in my gut, I felt that my rowing days had come to an end. And, like Nick, I needed someone to share my disappointing realization with. Peter's questions that day made clear to me that my life as a rower was over. I knew Nick was no different. In his heart, he was done. Like me, all of those years earlier, he just had to convince his mind.

In my last year of rowing, I remembered playing every head game I could imagine trying to get through the next day's training sessions. It was a living hell. I used every motivational carrot I could think of just to get one more training day checked off: redemption, revenge, validation, and, of course, seeing myself on the podium in Barcelona with an Olympic gold medal around my neck. When those didn't work, I grabbed every negative stick within reach—pussy, undeserving, quitter, and on most days the one that worked the best: *just like I thought, you* are *an Olympic loser!*

In the end, I was rowing for the wrong people. Racing for the wrong reasons. And I still had three years to go. Nick had just over six months. But I wasn't going to be that coach who pushed him to do something he didn't want to do. Or worse, be someone he couldn't be. I had to let this go. It was best for Nick. And, perhaps equally as important, it was best for our team.

"Jason, I've been thinking," he began "You know how you tell us that the fun is in finding more . . . that there's always more to give? That we should never be satisfied with our best effort today because you can find more tomorrow? Well, I'm having a tough time with that. My girlfriend and I have been talking about this. I've been sharing your philosophy with her. And she believes that thinking like that prevents me from ever feeling good about what I've accomplished."

I struggled but managed to contain my frustration with him as I'm sure Peter had with me.

"That's not quite what I say, Nick. We've talked about this before, but you keep misconstruing the message. Yes, I believe there's always more to give. But I've never said that what you accomplish each day isn't good enough. When I talk about the exciting thing that could happen tomorrow what I mean is that you can build on what you've discovered today. It doesn't mean you can't be proud or happy with what each day brings, as long as you're learning and moving forward. There's an important distinction there, Nick."

"Oh. I guess so." He took a sip of water.

I sat quietly and waited for him to continue. After a few moments, tears began to well up in his eyes. I grabbed the Kleenex box at the end of the coffee table and placed it in front of him. He blew his nose and continued.

Looking at the floor, he said quietly, "I don't think I can keep rowing, Jason."

"I know."

There was nothing else to say. No convincing to be done. No new strategies. No compromises. No nothing. As much as we both wanted him to continue rowing, we both knew it was over. You can't row with a gun to your head. If Nick didn't want to continue, there was no amount of talking that would change that.

Nick insisted on telling the rest of the boys himself. It didn't seem to come as a surprise to many of them. Most of the guys, like me, had seen it coming. I think it was the finality of it that was hard to accept. The question hung in the air: now what? The trouble was that neither Winston nor I had an answer. We were hanging onto hope that Steve would have a change of heart and start showing up for practices. All we could do was keep on track. We had come this far; there was no way we were going to pack it in now.

No sooner had we lost Nick than I noticed Cosmo was starting to show signs of distress. One afternoon he arrived late for spin class looking exhausted and out of sorts. Normally punctual and vibrant, Cosmo had been quiet, moody, and unengaged with the others over the past week. Not his usual MO.

At the end of the class I asked how he was doing.

"Okay," he answered. Usually an intelligent conversationalist, it was obvious he didn't want to talk. Naturally, I took that as my sign to continue asking questions.

"How's school going?"

"Not bad," he said, avoiding eye contact. He knew I wasn't going to let this go.

"How's IB treating you? Do you have many projects due?" I prodded.

"What are we going to do about the eight? Who are we going to get to fill Nick's spot?" he asked in return, which told me he had something to hide.

"I'm not sure. Maybe Steve? Maybe nobody?"

He looked at me sideways. "Nobody? What do mean, nobody?" he snapped. "We can't row an eight with only seven guys."

I paused a moment, then leaned in. "Keep this between you and me, okay? No one's ever won the coxed four and the quad with the same four athletes at Schoolboy. We've been thinking that might be something fun to try."

Cosmo looked right through me as he processed that alternative.

"The events are a little over an hour apart. That's a huge challenge and most coaches recognize that they'd need an impressive boat to even attempt it. But Winston and I think we have the athletes to give it a shot." Knowing how much he liked a challenge, I let that settle in for a moment.

"Hmmm," he finally responded.

"Question is . . . will you make it to June?"

"What do you mean?"

"Cosmo, you look like hell. You've been pissy all week. You were late today. You missed yesterday morning. Something's up." I paused, stared right at him, but this time he didn't look away. "So, back to my question, how are you doing?"

With eyes beginning to glisten, our steely young rower showed signs of cracking. And then he confessed that he was exhausted. It was a heavy workload time of year for IB assignments. He had seven due, one for each course. No wonder he was struggling. Together, we came up with a plan to get him through to Christmas. We also agreed that something had to change with regard to all of the obligations he had outside of his academics and rowing.

I felt his relief. I could tell this was important to him. Normally, he was unshakable. He always appeared to have everything in his life under control. Regardless of his numerous commitments, his discipline and time management skills allowed him to thrive within the pace of Ridley. But the last few weeks had been too much, even for him.

The next day, I arranged for a meeting with Jay and all of the other players with regard to Cosmo's many commitments at Ridley. A week later we all met. After a long discussion, it was agreed that academics and rowing more than anything else were what was going to help Cosmo get into the University of Pennsylvania and, more importantly, finish the year off positively.

I was relieved. Finally, we could take many of the other activities that were taking up so much of his time off his overladen plate. With that potentially devastating game changer averted, we finished off the 2013 indoor training season without any further incidents.

CHAPTER SEVEN

———┤ ├———

WITH IT BEING our last year at Ridley, I wanted to host our family Christmas dinner. My parents were now both in their late eighties; an opportunity like this one wasn't going to come around again any time soon. In 2001, Dad had had a heart attack and was given three months to live. Only trouble was no one told him. It was now almost fourteen years later, and he was still kicking life's tires; I loved that about him. There was no fear with this man. You did what you did to the best of your ability. And, as long as you believed in and stood by your convictions, that was good enough for him.

I could vividly remember the excitement of celebrating Christmas Eve when I was a child. Those were magical times. Sitting in our living room beside a cozy roaring fire while crisp white snow blanketed the empty campus outside, a sweet-smelling pine tree lit with shiny bright lights and surrounded with colourfully wrapped gifts, and the savoury aroma of dinner spilling from the kitchen as Bing Crosby's soothing baritone voice oozed out "Jingle Bells" from the hi-fi.

We would sit around the table sometimes joined by a member of the Ridley staff who didn't have family nearby. Mom and Dad were always good about opening our home to others. After dinner shortly before 9:00 p.m., we would walk across the courtyard to the School's chapel. There we would gather with other members of the Ridley community for a Christmas Eve service conducted by the chaplain.

Built in the 1920s to commemorate Ridley students killed during the First World War, the chapel was an impressive building. As children, we believed ghosts were living under it. During our summer nighttime play we would never consider venturing through or even near its creaky old wooden main door. On Christmas Eve, we felt safe and willingly dashed inside to find our seats.

After singing classic Christmas hymns and listening to the chaplain's message, we made our way over to the headmaster's house for treats and something to drink. For me the cakes, brownies, and other goodies were the attraction.

Once home, I eventually managed to fall asleep despite the excitement and the truckload of sugar that was speeding through my veins. Come morning, and only after Dad had checked to make sure that Santa had arrived in the night, we would storm down the stairs and find our stockings overflowing with presents.

So, for me, having Mom and Dad over for our final Ontario Christmas dinner was a big deal. All of us gathered around the table: Mom and Dad; my two brothers, Scott and Paul; Scott's wife, Rose; and their children, Ryan and Kaylyn. It was so cool to use technology and add our sister Wendy to the mix through FaceTime. Watching Dad blow Wendy a kiss that night made our move east and all of the challenges that we had experienced thus far so worthwhile.

My dad was my first coach. In a word, he was a jock. In his university days after the war, he played on multiple varsity teams while studying at McGill. He taught me how to swim. How to skate. How to throw a football. How to play tennis—all of it. He even taught me how to box. I didn't realize my fortune at the time, but as far as coaches go, he was a good one.

Sadly, as a national team rower I had lost touch with some of my early childhood experience. In this and my final year at Ridley, I was finally beginning to understand just how much my dad had influenced me. Helping him to the car in the biting winter night's air, I was reminded that this man, who could easily carry his sleeping boy from the car to his bed, was now a frail old man. He had experienced so much in his life. I took time to hug him a little longer before he got into the car; I knew these moments were numbered.

There was nothing like a few weeks' rest to recharge the batteries and return fresh to training and ready to go at it full bore. At Ridley, the busyness of the place resulted in athletes being chronically sleep deprived. It was always a challenge to balance a training schedule with a required amount of sleep. We tried to rely on weekends and Wednesday sleep-ins to bank as much as we could, but it was a fine line. So far we had avoided sickness and injuries within the group, which indicated that we were managing okay.

For their two weeks at home at Christmastime, we had assigned the boys aerobic recovery work on the ergs as well as maintenance work in the weight room. Enough to keep them active and engaged while allowing their bodies to rebuild and repair. Now, we had eight weeks until the March break. Winston and I planned on making them intensive. This was our last cycle of indoor training before we hit the water and tested our boat speed against the West Coast crews at our rowing camp at Shawnigan Lake. Before that, however, we would have two erg championship opportunities that would assess our fitness.

In the first week of January it was clear that the break had done exactly as we had hoped. The boys were fresh, playful and energetic. It was time to get back to work. However, just when I thought all was well, Dima started to question his future with our team. It was clear to me that he was getting pressure from home. He had enrolled in the IB curriculum, and his grade eleven workload was steadily increasing. His challenge was how to maintain his commitment to the team and keep his academic work a top priority.

Finally one Wednesday afternoon, he showed up to the gym late, and I knew by the look in his eyes that he had some news he wasn't too keen to share. He looked pale and frightened standing before me.

"Jason. I'm going to stop rowing."

I knew there was no convincing or negotiating to be done. And I knew how hard this was for him.

"It's all good, Dima. I understand," I answered, trying to relieve the stress that was pent up inside him.

"I want to thank you for my great experience. You have been a great coach. I have learned so much from you." Hearing his words, I smiled and moved closer to hug him. With that he began to cry.

I tried to remain compassionate toward Dima, but at the same time there was a part of me that was furious that activities like sport-for-life could well be the future of my old school. Gone could be opportunities like the one Dima was now walking away from: an opportunity that would have changed his life. Instead, replaced with an academic focus that, although important, should not have been at the exclusion of experiences like this one. I felt sorry for Dima. I knew in his heart that he wanted to stay with his crew, but it was not for him to decide.

Daniel was the first athlete I came upon. "Oh, so now Dima's quitting?" He was obviously as upset as I was at what had just transpired. "What now? This is bullshit!" He said throwing his extra shirt to the ground. His reaction was a fair one.

I turned and walked to the fountain. I was in no shape to answer him. We'd seen it coming with Nick, but not Dima. Since the day he had joined, he'd been a hard-working team player. And he had improved tremendously. He was bigger, stronger and, as far as we could tell, seemed enthusiastic about getting to Henley. Winston referred to him as the Russian Bear because of his strength. Pound for pound he was a boat mover we were now going to miss.

At the end of our weight session, we gathered around as a group.

"Look, this is not about Dima. I don't want any of you taking this out on him. He's still one of us and deep down I'm sure he's just as upset as you are." I paused, took a deep breath and gathered my thoughts. "Yes, this obviously changes everything. We're now down to six athletes. Regardless of what Steve decides, the likelihood of us having an eight is remote at best. So, here's what we're thinking."

Now was as good a time as any to share what I had with Cosmo before the Christmas break. At this point, we all needed a positive option to latch onto. As I told them about our idea of competing in the coxed four and the quad at Schoolboy, I could feel the energy in the group shift.

"What about England? Could we still race at Henley?" asked Daniel. He was not completely buying into the change in direction.

"We could. There's a quad event for youth clubs. Which means we'd be racing a little over our heads. And there's a coxed four event for university junior varsity athletes as well. Which means we'd be racing a lot over our heads. We'd simply have to decide which event. But Winston and I both feel you guys are capable of competing in and holding your own in either event."

"What about Sandy?" he asked.

"Yup. Fair question. Well, it would depend on which boat we choose. Regardless, he'll still have the US Schoolboy and our own Canadian Schoolboy here at home. But he may not have England. And that's just the shitty fact of where we are. I'll speak with him tonight and give him a heads-up as to what's happened. Okay?"

I looked around at our group. They were obviously caught off guard. Their dream of taking an eight to England was crumbling away; however, they could see there was a legitimate out. Regardless, one issue remained: we now had six athletes and a coxie with four seats to fill. Josh and Chris weren't stupid. They both knew the pecking order. And neither one of them was in the top four spots.

I spoke with both of them after practice and explained that they would continue to train with the hopes of them filling a competitive double. I also mentioned that one of them would travel to England as a spare, regardless of what boat we ended up racing in. They completely understood. The news had not come as a surprise; both seemed okay with their redefined roles and opportunities. By the end of the week, while I was thinking we were now back on track, Chris informed me he was quitting.

I really couldn't blame him. None of us could. We were all genuinely touched when he had shown up in December and helped us fill that remaining seat. The courage and commitment that he had demonstrated thus far were impressive. There were absolutely no hard feelings.

Now, we were five rowers and a coxie going forward. Sandy took the news in stride. Not surprisingly, it required a lot to get him rattled. He knew one thing for sure: the coxed four that he would eventually back into the starting gates in a few months' time would be an incredibly fast boat. And he was looking forward to it.

As for Josh, the youngest of the group, his maturity and composure were exemplary. Not once did he show any sign of resentment or bitterness to the ones who'd quit and left him in a difficult position. He refused to be the victim. We talked about the role he would play and the challenges he could embrace. He reassessed his situation and continued to show up as the athlete that we had gotten to know thus far: focused, supportive, and driven. Exactly what we needed.

Although all the guys knew only the fastest of them would sit in the boat, the discrepancy between Josh and the other four rowers was substantial enough, at the time, to identify easily who would sit in those four seats. Even though Josh respected the guys, he wasn't about to back off and not try to challenge any of them for a seat. The top boys wouldn't have had it any other way, and they too took on the challenge of what Winston and I had laid out. They wanted to go to England, badly. And no one else was going to get in their way. For them, nothing really had changed. The training was the same. Our goals were the same. The only thing that was different was the boat class they would eventually race in.

Saratoga Springs is a picturesque little city in upper New York State. I loved the old architecture and charm of the downtown, as well as the running trails located on the edge of the city. Most years, a magical snowfall blanketed the old buildings and made the downtown core look like a Norman Rockwell painting.

Of all of the conferences to attend throughout the winter, Jimmy Joy's was my favourite. His conference, aptly named "The Joy of Sculling," attracted quality presenters from all over. Jimmy, an ex-university and national team coach was passionate about his craft and upon retiring from coaching rowing decades earlier created an opportunity for coaches to gather and share the latest research and ideas about high performance and rowing. Today, his conference is among the best in the world.

Knowing Robyn's background as an Olympian and now as a counsellor, Jimmy asked her to present at the conference and sit on a discussion panel the opening night. One of the biggest trials for me as a coach was the time away from my family. Although Mataya would be hanging out with Grandma, having Robyn along for this weekend to experience three days of "rowing talk" was a treat.

To begin the conference, Jimmy had compiled a panel of coaches, former athletes, and experts in the field of emotional well-being and its effect on high-performance athletes. It was a diverse group, and it was fascinating to hear the opinions of sports psychologists and others, all of whom shared research and information on what I had had to figure out the hard way. It was reaffirming to know that our coaching at Ridley was in keeping with the latest research on the link between healthy emotions and high performance.

Along with Robyn, one of the panel members was David Meggy-sey. He was an ex-National Football League (NFL) player and author of the book *Out of Their League*. *Sports Illustrated* calls it one of the one hundred most important sports books ever written. It exposes everything that is broken and wrong with sports today even though it was written forty-five years ago.

During the 1960s, David played college football for Syracuse University and then went on to play professionally with the St. Louis

Cardinals, now the Arizona Cardinals. At the age of twenty-eight, after playing for seven years in the NFL, he wrote his book, a tell-all one that chronicles the events and circumstances that led him to Syracuse, St. Louis, and then retirement. His reason for writing the book, as he puts it, was to expose the inequities, mistreatment, and exploitation of young players and inspire change within the National Collegiate Athletic Association and the NFL.

Meeting David at the conference was a joy. Here was a man who loved sports: the physical and mental challenge, the strategy, the comradery, and the all-in united purpose of moving a ball one play at a time down the field. Now in his seventies, he still had a youthful glow when he told stories of his days on the gridiron. However, his tone changed when he spoke of the politics and craziness of what we all know can ruin a good thing. He believed that if we didn't move sport beyond its current interpretation of just being competition between teams and athletes, its days would be numbered. We both felt that sport was a vehicle to a higher state of consciousness. Through sport, individuals were afforded the opportunity to move beyond just the physical experience and learn what it was to be fully in that moment: mind, body, and soul all integrated as one.

Speaking with David was a reminder that I wasn't crazy. That there was more to sports than just competing, and winning and losing. That sport was an experience not only defined in our physical bodies, but in our spirits and souls as well. Similarly, David saw the information that I had shared at that conference during my presentation earlier in the day as essential not only for an athlete's fullest development, but also for the future of sport itself, not, as some said, as flakey and New Age.

Robyn's presentation encompassed her work as an athlete and now clinical counsellor. In her sessions, she shared the benefits of a supportive relationship between the coach and the athlete, and how that reinforced her highest moments on the track. Furthermore, she talked about valuable tools such as tapping and the Emotional Freedom Technique as useful strategies that would enable coaches to help their athletes augment what is referred to as their "optimal state of arousal," being in *flow* or in *the zone*. In other words, these tools could help an athlete avoid becoming overwhelmed with stress during high-pressure moments.

Jimmy's conference was light years ahead of any other conference that I had attended. He wasn't afraid to let his progressive ideology shine through in his choice of presenters, regardless of how others felt about it. He knew that science was beginning to back up what he and many other pioneer coaches had believed for decades.

Yes, the physical and technical components of every sport were important in order to reach high performance. Equally as important—perhaps even more so—was the mental and emotional state of every athlete while they inhabited that physical and technical realm.

I knew that to be true. I didn't need the science. I had seen it through my own experience as an athlete, watching Robyn for all of those years on the track and now as a coach. I recognized that aspect of our athletes' development was the foundation upon which we did the physical and technical work. To neglect it would be to neglect the boys, their potential and the entire season.

CHAPTER EIGHT

OUR NEXT STOP would be Toronto and the Canadian National Indoor Ergometer Championships. This would be our first test on a national stage. Our first public debut since Boston. That in itself caused a bit of anxiety for Winston and me. There had been a fair bit of chatter about our boys. Coaches from everywhere would be watching here and online to see what kind of numbers our crew was spinning.

The boys were ready to show the fitness they'd achieved.

Rowing isn't exactly spectator friendly. For the most part, onlookers watch from the finish line while sitting on hard metal bleachers that are 2000 metres from the start of the race. Sometimes those bleachers are covered. Other times, not. If the weather's lousy, yuck.

In addition, given the distance from the start, unless you know which crews are in which lanes or you have really good binoculars, you are hard-pressed to tell who is winning. The boats are basically dots on the horizon for a good chunk of the race. But it's still exciting, especially right at the end. And it's exciting for the athlete too. With hundreds of cheering spectators at the finish line, it's quite a feeling.

At an indoor ergatta, as they're known, spectators watch the athletes sitting on ergometers and rowing as hard as they can for anywhere from six to nine minutes. What organizers have done to make these events more exciting is develop software that translates the scores on each of the ergometer monitors into little boats on a huge screen for everyone to see. You don't really watch the rowers;

you mostly watch the screen that tells you how those rowers are doing, and this creates a relatively exciting sporting event.

These championships were set up like almost every other ergatta with rows of perfectly spaced ergometers a few feet from one another and coaches and other supporters cheering from the sidelines. This particular event was in a large hockey arena with plenty of seating and a great vantage point. It was a sight to behold: rowers pushing themselves to their utmost limits in front of hundreds of screaming onlookers.

It's difficult to watch at times. As you can imagine, especially with the younger athletes, you sometimes see rowers who aren't physically prepared and end up barely surviving the 2000-metre race. Hence some nine-minute times. Others end in a ball of flames: quitting in tears or vomiting on the machine. Yes, it can and does get nasty sometimes, but it's also a remarkable display of human strength, endurance, and grit.

After watching a few of the junior races, it was time for our senior boys to warm up. They had been through this process often enough they could do it in their sleep. Our race-day warm-up was our training warm-up, minus the extra starts they would do in preparation for the explosive beginning to the race. The work was done. They had slept and were fed and hydrated. All they had to do was sit on those unforgiving contraptions and let all of their hard work shine.

Moments before their race was called, we gathered quickly in a small huddle. "As you all know, this is pretty simple. Jump off the line and take advantage of those first strokes. They're free. Get that wheel spinning as fast as you can and then start nailing the splits we've trained for. When it comes time to go, empty your tanks. But remember, start sprinting before you think you can. That will ensure those tanks are empty. Any questions?"

Their eyes said it all: let's get this done!

As I watched our boys walk over to their assigned ergometers, my butterflies began to flutter. But that was okay. Regardless of how many years I had been doing this, I still got nervous at these events. I had told Robyn, "the day I stop getting nervous would be my last day coaching."

I climbed into the stands to watch and took out my camera to get shots for our rowing website. If nothing else, taking photos was a good distraction. I was able to take in the race but not get too worked up knowing I had to gather pictures of all of our athletes. With our rowers spread out on the different ergs, I would have to remain mobile during the entire race to get some good action shots. I had already spent most of the morning taking photos of our junior athletes during their races. I had some good spots sourced out.

Luc was lined up beside an athlete from St. Catharines named Dan de Groot. The two of them had been racing each other since their junior years. Dan was an exceptional athlete and an extremely gracious and polite young man. I had watched him develop in the four years that I had been back in St. Catharines. I remember congratulating him after he won the junior category in 2012 at this same event, beating Luc and Daniel (Tkaczick), who finished second and third

That year, he and his dad spoke with me about coming to Ridley for grade eleven and twelve. After the shit-storm that resulted from athletes coming to Ridley to row in the two previous years, I simply passed them on to admissions and left it up to them. Sure, I wanted him to join our program—why wouldn't I? He was strong, he rowed well, and he was a good student. Who wouldn't want that sort of individual on their team; however, knowing the pushback that would result from him leaving his school, I wanted the move to come solely from him.

A few months later I received an email from Dan informing me that he had been admitted to the School and that he was very excited to be joining our program in the fall. Hell, I was excited, too. He was one more outstanding athlete to add to our mix on which we could continue to build our program as we aimed toward this year's goal. Then later on, in June, while we were in England racing, I got word that Dan's teachers, coaches, and rowing friends were, as it was described, "putting the boots to him." He was being pressured to withdraw from Ridley and return to his current high school in September.

By the time I got home, Ridley's admissions confirmed that Dan had withdrawn his acceptance and wouldn't be joining us in the fall. I knew there'd be some flak from the local rowing community, but I didn't expect it to end with this. Needless to say, I was disappointed. Not just because we wouldn't have Dan to contribute to our program, but because I was sad for him. His long-range plan was to row at an Ivy League school in the States. Ridley would have provided the perfect opportunity for him to get used to the academic rigor that those schools would expect. When I saw him again in the fall, it was a bit awkward, but I completely understood.

Now, two years later he was still at his school and doing just fine. He was rowing the single and was anticipating another terrific upcoming season. Our boys continued to remain in contact with him through Facebook and other online social media. It was no sweat off their backs. Dan was still Dan and they treated him as they had before this ordeal ensued.

As the automated starting commands silenced the crowd, I raised my camera and began to shoot. Halfway into the race, Luc was leading with Mathew in second and Dan de Groot in third. As they approached the last few hundred metres, Luc was still holding onto the lead, and Dan was closing quickly. As the crowd cheered them on, I put my camera down to watch the sprint to the finish.

When they finally stopped, Dan had finished one second behind Luc's winning time of 6:12, the fastest time in the country that day for high school boys. Mathew had finished third. Although, Daniel had led for the initial part of the race, he eventually faded and finished tenth with a time of 6:37, followed by Josh in 6:39.

Daniel's performance was indicative of what was becoming a rather large monkey on his back. He was capable of being up with the leaders, even winning. His maximum-power tests on the erg reaffirmed that. Trouble was he spent too much time in his head worrying about his final score, and that was undermining his preparedness. This was the third time this year that Daniel had tanked an erg test.

My concern was that once athletes started to struggle with performance anxiety, especially on the erg, it could be hard to break that cycle and it would begin to feed into a self-fulfilling prophecy. The more they feared a lousy performance, the more they contributed to it. It was time to start having some conversations about what was going on with Daniel.

Cosmo finished fifth, with a 6:27 time, a personal best effort that gave us a combined score just south of our 6:20 goal. Despite Daniel's slow time, both Winston and I knew that if he had pulled what he was capable of, he'd be up around 6:10. Which put us well under 6:20, and in February, with no taper.

Josh's time was a personal best as well. It was the first 2k in which he had gone under 6:40. He was thrilled, and rightly so. The gains that he was making were tremendous. All of his hard work and commitment were beginning to pay off. In fact, all five of our guys were in the top eleven positions at the event. And when we compared our times to the ergattas that were happening simultaneously across the country, no other school had come close to doing the same. All of this was a good indication that how we'd been training was indeed working.

The bonus for the day was that Siobhan's girls had won the senior and junior events. She had some big powerful novice girls to work with, and she was definitely bringing them along. Things were looking up for the girls' program as well.

As much as we didn't like to back off training for smaller racing events, both Winston and I believed in careful transitioning out of physically demanding tests like the one the boys had just experienced. Over the next few days, we provided enough activity to maintain a training effect while still allowing them to recover and recharge adequately. The Ontario Erg Championships were four weeks away and would be our most important test to date. With only a few weeks to get ready, it meant they would head into the most intense training to date. Our job going forward was to manage the workload optimally between now and the first of March, the day of the championships. That would require striking a balance between concentrated periods of race preparation and the right amount of recovery.

A steady-state row on the ergometer could be mind numbing. It was the equivalent of going for a very long run but on a rowing machine. The purpose was to build an athlete's aerobic base and the bigger, the better. Therefore, rowers were encouraged to maintain a pace that they could sustain for an extended period of time. In our day, we were told to keep our hearts beating at a rate that allowed us to just barely talk aloud. Anything harder and we'd be training a different aerobic system. Anything lighter and we were wasting our time.

The other potential fallout from extended work was the chance of reinforcing poor technique. Given that in a ninety-minute session of steady-state rowing an athlete could take upwards of two thousand strokes, you wanted to make sure that he was taking good ones. The best trick that I had found for preventing poor technical strokes was having our rowers do long pieces with their feet out of the foot straps. I considered that drill the equivalent of rowing on the square. If you struggled with keeping your blade squared and the boat balanced, it was probably because your technique was compromised. The same went for rowing on the erg with your feet out. If you struggled with that drill, it was probably because your posture and power application weren't optimal.

If you've rowed on an erg without your feet being strapped down, you'll know how hard it is to not focus on maintaining good posture without the sensation of going ass-over-teakettle. Therefore, when our boys did long pieces, we made sure their feet were out. It all played into the plan of optimizing our indoor season. We didn't want to just clock long steady-state rows on the erg. We wanted to put in those long sessions while reinforcing the way we were going to row on the water—effectively. It had taken them a few weeks to get used to it, but now they rowed on those ergs better than we ever did.

Under Paul's direction in the weight room, the boys transitioned into a power stage that was all about improving the explosive force of their legs during the drive phase of the stroke. Paul happened upon a workout called the "German Leg Day." It was nasty—ten sets of ten reps—but the gains were almost immediate. We could see the change in their stroke during our tank sessions. Furthermore, their erg scores during our race pace erg work were improving as well. I loved stuff like that. It reaffirmed my belief that there were always ways to improve. You just had to care enough to go looking.

As we continued to train for the Ontario Championships and began to piece together the logistics of our spring camp at Shawnigan, one thing became apparent: with five athletes and one coxie, how would we train side by side with a quad or coxed four and a single? The simple solution was to bring in another rower. The easy choice was Jesus, not only because he deserved it, but also because he had done such a great job for us in the fall that training with Josh in the double would be an easy match. Jay had no problem with the idea, so we moved ahead with those seven athletes along with Siobhan's four travelling to the West Coast in a few weeks' time.

With February came the 2014 Winter Olympics in Sochi, Russia. The Olympics were one television event I truly enjoyed watching. It wasn't just about the sports or the competition or the fact that Canada did much better during the Winter Games than the Summer Games. It was the stories behind the athletes and their journeys.

Maybe it was because I was getting a little older and more nostalgic, but I loved hearing about the athletes and their families and the challenges they'd overcome to get there. I planned to enjoy my obsession for the next fourteen days straight; however, during the first week, the phone rang late at night. When Robyn answered it, I knew right away what had happened. Her mom had been ill for a number of months and her sister was calling to say that she had just passed away. The Alzheimer's that she had been diagnosed with a few years earlier had aggressively deteriorated her health. Regardless of the blessing this was, it was a hard moment for Robyn. She had just lost her dad a little over a year earlier. The next morning, I drove her to the airport. She was off to spend time with her siblings on the East Coast. In the meantime, I had one more conference to attend before the end of the month. I was presenting a keynote at the Ontario Coaches Conference in Kingston.

Overall, it was a fun conference. Part of what made it so enjoyable was that I was able to sit in on more sessions than normal. I was pleased to hear that the trend had clearly shifted toward a process-centred approach for coaching. That was encouraging.

One of the other keynote presenters, Vicki Keith, shared the work she was doing with para-athletes. An ultra-distance swimmer in her day, she had some crazy records: longest swim, farthest swim, and multiple crossings of various Great Lakes. Along with all her impressive accomplishments, she was doing outstanding work as a swim coach. We both had many of the same concerns. Vicki understood that, given the nature of her athletes, the only way she could be successful as a coach was by using a holistic approach. She didn't just worry about their training; she worried about their entire well-being. She embraced the notion that individuals who are emotionally and physically healthy make the best athletes. And her success as a coach confirmed that. My question was, why not for every athlete? Why do we somehow feel that able-bodied athletes can skimp on the emotional part? It made no sense to me. As upbeat as these conferences tended to leave me, I knew there was still much work to be done.

In the midst of the organizer's closing remarks, I got an email from Sandy that indicated the boys had lost some direction during my absence. The scores from the weekend's session were positive, but some of the boys had chosen to do the workout at separate times rather than together, which they knew I wouldn't have been okay with had I been there. One week to go until the Ontario Erg Championships was not a good time to create new personal agendas. This had to be about team and nothing more.

The next day we sorted out the choices that were made on the weekend that resulted in separate training times. The crew owned it, and we moved on. One of the things I'd learned about coaching teenage boys was that when there was stuff to be dealt with, the most effective way to do that was head-on. If they appreciated anything, it was honest dialogue. No games. No bullshit. Just the truth. We identified what had led to some of the choices that took them off track, and then had a conversation about where that could lead us if it continued. They got it. Lesson learned.

With three days to go, Cosmo was complaining of some knee pain. He had mentioned it earlier in the week, but now it was preventing him from rowing at full pressure. Some chiropractic maintenance work had been necessary throughout the year for some of the boys, but this was the first major injury any of them had sustained. Cosmo was pissed. Understandably. We had trained all year, and this was the event that we were gunning for in terms of erg scores. It was a chance for them to compete in front of their friends and family and finish the indoor season on a high note before they began rowing on the water after spring break.

Lenny, the School's physiotherapist, began treatment immediately in an attempt to settle the inflammation and hopefully allow Cosmo to race. Lenny was another great member of our "bus." He was always available and worked long hours to ensure our athletes were in good health. If anyone could have Cosmo ready, it was Lenny.

The rest of the boys seemed good. As we backed off the workload throughout the week, both Winston and I could feel the difference in the crew. We went over the individual race plans time and again with each of the athletes to ensure they knew exactly what splits to hit. The work was done. Everything from here on out would be rest, recovery, and execution.

We talked about the importance of sleep leading into the championship, and not just the night before. We discussed diet and how to ensure that "gut grief" didn't undo all of the good work we'd done during the last number of months. Then on the Friday, the day before they raced, we rehearsed the warm-up, followed by a steady-state pressure 2k on the new ergs that were now in place. They were ready.

CHAPTER NINE

THE RIDLEY GRADUATE Boat Club had been hosting the ergatta at the School for decades. More than a thousand people came through the School's new sports complex that day, mainly rowers, along with their contingent of family and other supporters. Athletes came from all over southern Ontario and upstate New York. If you wanted to test yourself against some tough competition, this was the place to find it.

I arrived well before our senior boys were slated to race. Just like in Toronto a month earlier, the junior events went first. I wanted to get some photos of our younger athletes and see how they fared. As I stood behind some local coaches, my camera at the ready, the junior girls were about to begin.

With the race underway, the usual instructions that one might expect came spilling from the mouths of the two coaches beside me. They encouraged their athletes to sit up taller at the catch. To use their legs more effectively. To watch their pacing. All of these commands were good ones, but none of them produced a change in their athletes' performance. How could they? For one, there was no way their athletes could hear them. Once these races started it was hard to hear anything, let alone expect your athletes were going to hear some instructions from their coach. It was so loud, in fact, that many of the student volunteers who sat beside the ergs and recorded scores wore earplugs. As well, the athletes were young kids who were so caught up in the noise and craziness of the race that no amount of reasonable coaching tips were about to register.

With about three hundred metres to go, things got ugly. That same coach beside me started to yell at the top of his lungs, "*kill 'em*! Come on, *kill 'em!*" Yes, by this point, our zealous coach had truly lost it. He was screaming with his hands cupping his mouth, and jumping up and down, telling his young female athlete to kill someone. Figuratively, true enough, but if this guy had been up on the big screen and seen himself, I don't imagine it would've been a proud moment.

Of all of the emotions that came up for me, compassion was what resonated. I knew exactly how he'd got there, because I'd been there myself. Although I may not have jumped up and down or screamed at the top of my lungs twenty-five years earlier, I'd be thinking the same thing. "Kill that son-of-a-bitch!" It was what I'd been taught. It was what I'd learned. It was what I believed won races. That sport was a war. And the point of war was to kill and win.

The paradigm of rowing being akin to war was as old as the sport itself. I, like so many other young athletes, had been raised to believe that seeing our competition as the enemy would further stir our motivations to new heights, and that would enhance our wills to win. There was merit in it. And it could work. Hell, it did work for me many times. But to what end? What was the final lesson in that? That hatred was the key to high performance? That in order to find our utmost potential we had to spin ourselves into a crazed state of rage? That's what I used to think. That's what I used to do.

I didn't believe that bullshit anymore. Now, thankfully, I saw it for what it was: archaic, destructive, and ultimately limiting. The crazy part of it is that coaches who still hang onto the notion that sport is war are really doing it for the implicit message in that comparison: that an athlete is as tough as a soldier. Athletes sacrificing the same as a soldier going off to battle? Absurd. And incredibly disrespectful to the soldier.

When we, as coaches, use hate for the competition as a means to inspire better performances in our athletes, we do a number of things. First, we teach them that it's not only okay but also effective to do so. We vindicate redemption as a chosen model for competition, and this, in turn, supports the out-of-date war paradigm that so often is used as a motivator for athletes.

We also reduce sport to a simple grudge match and disable the athlete's connection with the full power of sport to transform his or her life into something greater than that of just being a winner. Sport is supposed to be about improving fitness, developing skills, supporting personal growth, and acquiring important life lessons. And when we choose to instill this competition-as-war strategy in our athletes, we impede their ability to perform to their potential. We shift the focus from what the individual athlete is responsible for—their process—to focusing on their competitor, which, paradoxically, doesn't help them perform. It's outrageous when you think that coaches who embrace the hate model actually prevent their athletes from possibly winning.

It was that persona of implied toughness that ultimately made it so hard for me to leave rowing. If I rowed, therefore I was tough. That was my badge. At that time, the description registered as important to me. It was all part of creating an identity based on what I did. Not on who I was. When I realized that badge was a lie, I was able to move past competition that existed on the surface and move onto one that occurred much deeper and at a more meaningful level. The machismo element will eventually be sport's undoing. Until enough people speak up as to what should be the highest purpose of sport, it will continue to reside in the basement steeped in egoist strategies.

We tried to show our Ridley athletes that by competing for the sole purpose of "killing" their competition they create an impediment to their best performance. Our boys learned that focusing on the destruction of the guy beside you was a waste of their time and energy. They learned that they were better served by following Robyn's lead and embracing their competition as an invitation to find out what each of them had to give in the moment. That was their ticket to high performance and the possibility of winning. The best part for me was seeing how performing with that attitude made them better people.

Over the past four weeks, during race simulation workouts, Winston and I had emphasized positive self-talk with the boys, Daniel in particular. The whole purpose was to provide strategies for preventing self-defeating stories taking over their minds during the race. Athletes, like anyone, can fall victim to their own self-sabotage in moments of low self-esteem or lack of confidence. For whatever reason, they can concoct a story that convinces them that they are unworthy of challenging their competitors, or not fit enough, or not deserving enough.

As crazy as it may sound to an outsider, those tendencies are all too common in high achievers. The critic in each of us can be hyper-vigilant in high-performing athletes. That critic, who pushes them to be better, to strive for more and more, can sometimes kick into overdrive and tear them down. Our strategy was to quiet their minds before an event and then create opportunities for them to feel good about themselves during the warm-up and then the actual race. Often crews that have great warm-ups have great races. When they felt strong during the warm-up, we told them to emphasize that strength through a series of positive affirmations. If the erg still felt light halfway through the race, convince yourself it's because you're so fit. Capitalize on any positive chatter and make it the dominant conversation in your mind. "You're writing the story, so write a great one," was my advice. Try to delay, or even prevent, negative talk from taking over.

Finally, if and when some derogatory comments presented themselves, we suggested that our athletes confront them with pointed commands. Tell the voice making the negative comments to leave. Follow that with comments that are supportive and true. Get yourself into a place of positive self-talk early and build on that. Easier said than done, mind you. The power our mind holds over our body's ability to perform is staggering. But like any exercise, it took practice. Telling yourself supportive things about your ability to race isn't enough. You have to live it. Therefore, with each training session, we focused on not letting the mind take over when the pain became oppressive.

Mental toughness alone is limited. Sure, on some level as an elite athlete you have to possess a high degree of mental toughness in order to push through extraordinary levels of pain and reach new heights of achievement. After meeting Robyn, I realized that being able to work with the pain from a relaxed and focused place allowed athletes to reach beyond their established levels that they had reached using mental tenacity alone. Again, it came back to rethinking the notion that pain was something you had to overcome or defeat. I didn't see it that way anymore.

As a rower, part of my identity was wrapped up in the mystique of being tough. I loved that people thought I was a bit crazy, able to tolerate extreme levels of pain. But that approach got me only so far. Had I been willing to let go of what my ego used as fodder, I would have performed at levels I had never achieved before. Now, I encouraged our rowers to relax into the pain. I wanted them to invite it to flow through them as opposed to pushing it away. The expression "that which you resist persists" is apt; the more they resisted the pain, the longer it would hurt. We told the boys to give in to it. Embrace the pain. Sit in it, and demystify it. Play with it on a mental and emotional level. Talk to it. Make it your friend. "You're not going to die!" is what I would tell them. "It may feel like it, and your mind might want you to think that way, but you won't. Trust me!"

Daniel knew this chance was the last one to show us the athlete we all believed he was. Aside from the pressure he most surely created for himself, he knew there was a coach who had come up from Boston University to watch him. Daniel had been in touch with a number of US schools. If he pulled the time that we believed he could, my guess was that would seal the deal. There was a lot riding on this for him.

Daniel blew out of the start like he had in practice in the weeks leading up to the race. Almost five hundred metres into it, he was first, Luc second, and Mathew was third. If we could manage a one-two-three finish, that would be outstanding.

Unfortunately, just as it had happened four weeks earlier, Daniel began to slip. We could see the panic and fear in his eyes. He was in trouble. Then, coming up on a 1000 metres to go, he simply stopped rowing, released the oar handle, and took his feet out of the straps, just sat there while the others raced on beside him.

I watched in disbelief. He'd almost had it. He had been on his way to finishing his first 2k at the level he was capable of, and possibly winning. He had been on track to taking back the controls, putting to rest once and for all the self-destructive mind games that had haunted him this year.

My emotions morphed. Anger. Frustration. Then, empathy. I walked over to him. He was sitting completely still; his head hanging. My first task was to make sure he wasn't hurt.

"Are you okay, Daniel? Physically?"

"We can talk after."

"But you're okay?"

"We can talk *after!*" replied Daniel with a little more fire this time.

I turned and left him. As Daniel sat motionless, the race continued on around him. Luc had overtaken first place and was on track for a sub-6:10 time. Mathew, right behind him, was also heading for a personal best. Having Dan de Groot come storming back in the end was not a concern for Luc today. Dan had pulled out of the competition with an injury.

Cosmo, as well, was watching from the sidelines. His knee was still sore, and it was not worth compromising his ability to train at the camp in less than two weeks' time. As much as he would have preferred to be in the thick of it and break that elusive 6:20 score, he knew it was wise to sit this one out. A few spots farther down the line of ergometers, Josh was having a great performance. A new-found confidence, combined with our taper, had him racing the last 500 metres for a top-five finish. Luc finished first with a time of 6:07, five seconds faster than what he had pulled four weeks earlier and three seconds under his goal of 6:10. Mathew, finishing second, took another two seconds off his previous personal best, clocking in at 6:15. Although he finished seventh, Josh took ten seconds off his personal best, breaking the 6:30 barrier by one second. Amazing. These boys had confirmed what I constantly reminded them: "You get the performance you deserve."

Winston and I knew we had the sub-6:20 crew we needed. Based on the numbers, Cosmo was as close to pulling sub-6:20 as he'd ever been. Daniel could have been up with Luc had he finished. We knew that, but our knowing didn't matter. We needed Daniel to know that, to believe it. With the gym cleaned up and everything put away, we met as a group on the bleachers. Even though we had seen three outstanding performances earlier that day, everyone was aware of the beaten elephant in the room. They were quiet. Daniel's struggles were the crew's struggles. If we didn't sort this out, it would hold back all of us, not just Daniel.

Winston and I had pushed them hard, and now their bodies and their minds needed a well-earned break. We went over the schedule that would take them to March 12, the day we left for the West Coast. There was plenty of rest and recovery in store for this tired lot. Steady-state rows and maintenance in the weight room were the order of business for the next ten days. With everyone clear on our next steps, the boys made their way back to their houses while Daniel and I sat alone. It was time to talk. Time to see if there was something we'd missed in the weeks leading up to this race.

"So, how are we doing?" I started. Daniel hadn't said a word since I'd spoken with him during the race.

"How do you think?" he answered, his head still down, his eyes fixed on the dusty floor.

"I don't know. I wouldn't have asked if I did. I'm guessing you've been better. But I want to hear it from you. What happened out there, Daniel?"

"I didn't want to disappoint my dad. I'm here because of him. I wanted to phone him afterwards with a time that he'd be proud of. I didn't want to have to phone him like I did last time with some piece-of-shit result."

I waited a moment before pointing out the obvious. "Okay. But now you have to phone him and tell him you quit. That you didn't even finish. If you thought your shitty result was going to suck, how do you think this is going to feel?"

He looked at me. Not pleased. Sometimes you have to point out the truth of the matter regardless of how ugly it is to look at.

"I don't imagine good," he said in disgust as he gathered his stuff and left.

I watched him walk out of the gym. This incredibly gifted young athlete was lost. Lost in what he was doing with his rowing. Lost, more importantly, in why he was doing it. He had to sort that out. What was his *why*? Until he got clear on that, it didn't matter how gifted he was or how hard he trained. He needed a powerful *why* to sustain him.

I was left alone in a huge empty gym. The whirring overhead fans began the task of clearing out the exhausted air, stale from thousands upon thousands of gasping breaths—the place reeked of it. A buzz of excitement still remained from the vast amount of energy that had been spent there that day. Sweat dispensed. Goals achieved. Some not.

In my frustration, it was hard to hold onto what we had been using all year long to get us through these moments, to trust that everything was happening exactly as it was supposed to. "How could this be the best thing that ever happened?" Screw that—I'd had enough. In all my years of coaching, sure, there had been some challenging moments, but never before had so many of them been crammed into one season. If there was a purpose for this, if this was our intended path, I was either too tired or too pissed off to see the reason, at least in that moment.

I tried to sort out how we could get through to Daniel. I wanted to shake him, scream "Stop overthinking this. Let go of all of the fear that you have wrapped up in what losing or failing might mean, and just start showing up because it's fun. It's fun to be as strong and as talented as you are. Start feeling that. Start enjoying that. Start loving that, Daniel!"

Lying in bed that night, I replayed the day. There was a lot to be encouraged by, including three personal bests from the boys and two wins from the girls; Siobhan was doing what we'd hired her to do. Cosmo's knee would heal and Daniel would come around. We were making progress and getting better each day. That's all I asked of the boys. What I needed to do was embrace my own teaching and not resort to my tendency to find what was wrong right away and fix it. It was okay to enjoy what the crews had accomplished that day.

CHAPTER TEN

AFTER A FULL day of travel, it was wonderful to arrive on Vancouver Island and the shores of Shawnigan Lake. It was dusk. The lake was black and still, the sky an eerie grey. The last remnants of a disappearing sun provided enough light to make out the shores, our stage for the next ten days. I walked toward the beach and took in a deep breath of West Coast air. It felt cool and wet as it filled my lungs.

What I learned out on this lake about coaching, about life, and about how I wanted to be remembered was transformative. The coach I was in 1990 and the coach I was now were vastly different. Gone was the obsessed, screaming madman that hounded young athletes up and down these waters in pursuit of the justification of my worthiness as a coach. Replaced now with, well perhaps the obsession was still there, but the pursuit was about finding ways to get faster, ways to get better. That was the rush for me. What methods could we discover that would result in more boat speed? If I had learned anything in my years as a coach, it was that process and patience were instrumental in achieving any goal. Our process was working. My patience was holding. And we were making ground. The next few days would be the start of the final stage of our intended process. One day at a time. One row at a time. One stroke at a time. As the day's light faded to black and the moon and stars came out, I took in one last deep breath, turned, and made my way back to the building where we were staying. I was tired and my bed was calling.

The next day began with a short bus ride. Although we were staying at a camp situated on the lakeshore, it was still too far to walk to the campus where we would be having our meals. As we went through the gates of Shawnigan Lake School, more memories rushed in. The bus dropped us off before the little apartment I'd had in 1990, my first year. I looked up at the window and smiled as we passed. It had been almost twenty-five years since I had lived in that small room. I'd gone through a lot of turmoil in that small space. Of all those memories, the one that came back in that moment, funnyily enough, was the time that I got chicken pox during an outbreak at the school. I had never been so sick. There were also some big life moments tied to this place for both Robyn and me. We were married in the front gardens. Mataya was born here. It was where we said goodbye to our "first born" as we liked to refer to Ike, our golden retriever of nine years. It felt nice to be back.

Tim was all smiles as he welcomed Winston, Siobhan, our athletes, and me to Marion Hall. The dining room had been the gift of an alumnus. The space always reminded me of Harry Potter's Hogwarts. The vaulted ceiling was three storeys high, and the room had floor-to-ceiling windows and walls of West Coast cedar.

Tim showed the athletes where to get their meals and how to clean up when they were done. After years of hosting teams on a regular basis, the kitchen staff knew the drill and served up breakfast with enough calories to fuel our hungry athletes through the morning's row.

John Bomans had been the school's boatman since 2006. I had met John many times before at previous camps and in St. Catharines when he travelled with Shawnigan to the Canadian Schoolboys Championships. He was warm and welcoming, and, after introductions, he showed us which boats and oars we'd be using. I recognized many of the boats from my time as a coach at Shawnigan. The one boat that was new was the *Peter Yates*. It was rigged as a pair and slung on the deck in stretchers. *Synchronicity*, I thought. It reminded me of why we were here. I ran my hand along his name and gave a quiet affirmation. *Don't worry, Peter, we'll have these boys ready for England.*

One of the great things about rowing camps is the repetitive nature of the training. Given that the motion of the rowing stroke doesn't change from one race to the next, having three outings a day stimulates the muscle memory of your athletes, and with that, you increase the likelihood that they will progress at a quicker rate.

The scientific term for it is "myelination." It's how the body builds a sheath around nerve fibres that allow electrical messaging from the brain to travel more effectively to and from the muscle. It's sort of where the expression "you can't teach an old dog new tricks" comes from. Once the myelination is established, it's hard to rewire it. When muscle memory is engrained, it becomes resistant to change. With repetitive rows, you ensure that the athletes are either building or rebuilding the most effective sheaths to support a proper stroke right from the get-go. I've always felt that I could accomplish in a ten-day rowing camp what might take weeks to do at home with once-a-day rows.

Once our assigned boats were down from the racks and in stretchers, Winston kicked into action. I followed his instructions as he methodically ran numbers through his head based on the measurements he was taking. I had a sense of the rigging that we wanted and how we were going to set up each of the athletes. But it was times like this when I appreciated Jim Collins's approach of working with people who know more than you. I was quite content to relinquish complete control to Winston. It was easy. I trusted him.

Before shoving off for our first row, we gathered on the dock to recap our purpose for the next ten days. The boys were very excited to be moments from getting back on the water. Since they had lived on ergometers and in a tank for four long months, the thought of being back in a boat was a welcome reprieve for them, but I wanted to make sure we all knew what the plan was for each day and what we wanted to accomplish during our time here.

Our goals were simple: take the technical focuses that we had incorporated throughout the winter months in the tank and transfer those into the boat. If we could do that while allowing our fitness to show up, we would be well on our way to achieving our bigger, more challenging racing goals for the year.

Tim Coy's crew wouldn't be showing up for another few days, which gave us the run of the place. We had the boats and the oars that we wanted, and the space that we needed on the water. Knowing we would be racing his boys a number of times over the next week or so, having a few rows to get the cobwebs out was perfect timing for us.

Back at the camp later that night, with the boys in bed, Winston and I sat up and talked over a beer.

"What do you think? Do we have something here?" I asked.

He replied without hesitation. "No one is going to touch this crew. No one!"

If there was anything that I admired about Winston, it was his confidence. He smelled of it. I, on the other hand, didn't. I had inherited my mother's worrying tendencies and spent too much time trying to stay a few steps ahead of what might go wrong. I appreciated having his reassurance in our corner. And, on the basis of our first day, I knew Winston was right. The boys came back to the dock after their first row like they'd been rowing the entire winter. The way we'd approached our time in the tanks had worked.

The next day was more of the same: long miles at low rates. Establishing some good rhythm and flow at this point of the season was a must. There was no point banging the rates up too high too soon. They'd get their belly full of race pace work when we got home. For now, it was about establishing a strong base built on a fluid stroke cycle while exerting maximal pressure.

For the afternoon row, Aalbert Van Schothorst, the University of Victoria's new men's rowing coach, came out in the coach boat with us. Aalbert had been handed the ropes from a program that had once been a dominant force but had struggled of late. He had his work cut out for him. And, not surprisingly, Aalbert had also identified building a healthy high-performance culture as his biggest challenge. He was perfect for the job. He was knowledgeable, keen and, as an added bonus, young and single. The hours that he would have to commit to pulling off the turnaround that he had planned would be substantial. With professional coaching being the title champion for divorce rates, Aalbert was wise to leave marriage and children off the table for a few years.

After two days and six rows, we chose the coxed four for the last outing. We headed into the west arm, a long, narrow body of water that jutted perpendicularly from the lake. The conditions were perfect. The water was like glass. The temperature was cool but not uncomfortable. And there wasn't a sniff of breeze.

As we made the corner, Aalbert pulled out his video camera. "Do you mind?" he asked.

"Mind what?" I answered.

"If I video them. I want to take this back and show the varsity athletes how it's done."

Winston quietly turned around and gave me a smile from the side of his mouth. Maybe he was right: no one was going to touch these guys.

As Aalbert filmed our crew, Winston and I remained silent. By this time in the day, we liked to leave the boys alone to figure things out without us nattering away at them. By now, they knew what a good stroke felt like, and they had the wherewithal to create one. When coaches spew endless amounts of commentary and corrections at their athletes, they become more of a distraction and frustration than anything else. Knowing when to offer critical feedback is equally as important as knowing what to say and how to say it. At turnaround points during the row, while the boys were rehydrating, I asked the three questions that were the foundation of our coaching: What's going well? What's not? What do we need to change to make things better? Any other information was mostly surface fluff and, therefore, useless. During practice, after practice, and especially after races, these were the questions we counted on to reveal the work still to be done. They also helped with our other goal: to have the boys take ownership of the challenges we'd laid out for them. Yes, Winston and I could control every aspect of the day, but we knew that was limiting. Allowing the crew to have input about what was going right and, more importantly, what needed to be fixed, was imperative to achieving the results we all wanted. Performance aside, it also helped create an environment in which our athletes were invited to the table as equals because their ideas and opinions were not only welcomed, but valued. In my day, "Because I said so!" was reason enough to jump when told. In this instance, we wanted to create a team of rowers who saw themselves as problem solvers and were not just robots that did what we said. When it comes to developing the relationship between coach and athlete, this is one of the best ways to start.

Shawnigan Lake is about seven and a half kilometres long. It's ideal for extended low-rate pieces. When I was training on this water in my single, depending on conditions I could cover the course in under thirty minutes. For an eight, anywhere from the high teens to the low twenty-minute range was a decent time.

If our coxed four could come down in under twenty-five minutes, we'd be off to a good start. So, on the first day of competition, Tim Coy and I agreed that a "head-of-the-lake" piece was the best way to get things going. Once the crews were warmed up and waiting at the top of the lake, we explained the order of racing and put ourselves in a position where we could see each boat properly. We had three coach boats following; Winston and I were in one, Tim in another, and Siobhan was with the Shawnigan women's coach in the third.

Given the race was as long as it was, we would send the smaller and slower boats off first thereby creating a situation in which, if we planned it properly, the boats would finish closer together. That was the thinking, anyhow. Josh and Jesus had been progressing well in the double. They were moving the boat about as efficiently as we could have hoped given the limited amount of time they had been rowing together. In the previous two days of rowing, they'd been able to keep in touch with the coxed four during the shorter pieces. This was a good indication of their rowing and fitness. We were curious as to whether or not they might surprise some crews. With everyone in place, we began to send the boats off in timed intervals. We had decided that the Shawnigan four would go before our crew. Both Winston and I wanted to see how Sandy and the boys would manage in a "chasing" situation.

The interesting and challenging thing about rowing is that if you are behind in a race, you're unable to see your competition. You are facing *backwards*, so once a faster boat is out of view, you no longer have a visual reference for how you are progressing. You are essentially racing blind. It was up to Sandy, the coxie, in the bow of the boat to make sure the crew was following the straightest, most efficient course. The rowers would have to rely solely on the information he provided; hence the importance of a coxie who knew not only how to steer, but also inform and motivate the crew.

Winston and I were curious to find out how our boys would manage the challenge of racing from behind. Mind you, they could still win the piece on the basis of time and not pass the other crew, but that's not what we had planned. We wanted them to race full-on, aggressively from the word go, and reel in Tim's boat as fast as possible. Yes, you have to pace yourself to last a twenty-plus-minute race, but the idea is to arrive at the finish line having spent everything that you have.

With all of the boats gone, and their start times recorded, I hit the ignition and chased after the armada of boats. As we pulled in behind our crew, we could tell that they had made up some distance on the Shawnigan four, but not as much as either Winston or I would have expected or wanted.

At the halfway mark, our boys were making only incremental moves on the Shawnigan crew. This wasn't making sense to me, and I could see the frustration on their faces. They knew they were having a good row; the boat was moving well, and their technique appeared to be just fine, but it wasn't translating into the speed they had shown over the previous two days.

Finally, as our boys pulled even with the Shawnigan crew, I shouted to Winston, "Look at how fast our blades are going through the water compared to the other boat's. That doesn't look right. We're not getting the same bang for the buck that the other crew's getting."

"I measured the oars. They should be good," answered Winston. "But you're right, those blades are ripping through the water."

With the two boats side by side and rowing at a controlled rate of twenty-two stokes per minute, it was easy to compare the run that each boat was producing. Clearly, ours wasn't what it had been.

By the time both crews reached the finish line, our boys had managed to pull away from the Shawnigan crew, but their relative positions were far closer than they should've been. Especially given that this wasn't Tim's top four. After adjusting all of the times, it was clear that we had won that piece, but our performance left me wondering what, if anything, had gone wrong. Maybe we just didn't have the speed that we thought we did? Maybe Tim's boat was a lot faster than we had expected? Either way, it wasn't the start to the week of racing that we had hoped for. On the other hand, the double crew had done exactly what we thought they would; they had beaten some of the other bigger crews and were feeling very positive about their row.

Unfortunately, Siobhan's quad had a tough start to the week. The Shawnigan girl's crew had beaten them handily. Even our double had beaten them. The Shawnigan crew was an experienced group with some exceptional athletes. They'd be a hard boat to catch this year. Siobhan had her hands full if she planned on getting to the podium in June with her girls.

Top | Ridley College's 2012 senior men's heavy eight crew stands with the Calder Cleland Memorial Trophy after winning their final at the Canadian Schoolboy (Canadian Secondary School Rowing Association, CSSRA) Championships in St. Catharines, Ontario. L–R: Aaron Kirkey, Jordan Meyers, Jonathan Chisholm, Mac Copp, Nicole Venditti, Connor Boyd, Austin Bald, Owen Kemp-Griffin, Igal Flegmann. STAN LAPINSKI, GOLDMEDALPHOTOS.COM

Bottom | Cosmo, Mathew, and Luc race alongside Dan de Groot at the 2014 Canadian Indoor Ergometer Championships in Toronto. JASON DORLAND

Top | Cosmo, Luc, Daniel, and Mathew enjoy ideal conditions during an afternoon row at training camp in March 2014, on Shawnigan Lake, BC. JASON DORLAND

Bottom | Winston and Jason having a chat with the boys before their quad race at the 2014 Mother's Day Regatta in St. Catharines. FRASER MACKAY

Top | At the UPenn boathouse in Philadelphia, Rob Silk joins in on a team photo with the boys at the 2014 Stotesbury Cup Regatta. L–R: Jason, Rob Silk, Cosmo, Daniel, Josh, Sandy, Mathew, Jesus, and Luc. UNKNOWN

Bottom | Sandy, sitting up, brings his crew back to meet us at the dock after winning their heat in the coxed four event at the 2014 American Schoolboy (SSRA) Championships in Mercer Lake, New Jersey. JASON DORLAND

Top, left | Sandy gets the traditional toss into the drink after winning the 2014 American Schoolboy (SRAA) Championships in the coxed four event. JASON DORLAND

Top, right | Winston and Jason, along with the boys, stand around Jason's mother (Eleanor Dorland) and father (Carl Dorland) moments after Carl christened the coxed four in his name, in St. Catharines. PAUL DORLAND

Bottom | During their final at the 2014 Canadian Schoolboy (CSSRA) Championships in St. Catharines, the coxed four does exactly as we instructed them—get out front and stay there. JASON DORLAND

Opposite, top | The Ridley boys, having just won the senior men's quad event at the Canadian Schoolboy (CSSRA) Championships in 2014, enjoy a moment together at the grandstand. STAN LAPINSKI, GOLDMEDALPHOTOS.COM

Opposite, bottom | Sandy Morrison joins his Ridley crew (Cosmo, Daniel, Luc, and Mathew) as he accepts the trophy for the senior men's coxed four event at the Canadian Schoolboy (CSSRA) Championships in 2014. STAN LAPINSKI, GOLDMEDALPHOTOS.COM

Top | Winston Cook gets a workout in while keeping an eye on the boys as they push through another erg session in the boathouse in Dusseldorf, Germany.

Bottom | After a morning row, Josh Gatcke heads back to the boathouse in Dusseldorf.

Top | Forever positive, Luc Brodeur gives the thumbs-up after another morning's training session in Dusseldorf. JASON DORLAND

Bottom | A morning row in the heart of Dusseldorf. JASON DORLAND

Top, left | With five strokes to the finish line, the Ridley boys struggle to hold off Nottingham Rowing Club in Ridley's second race at the 2014 Henley Royal Regatta, in Henley-on-Thames, England. TONY HOLMES, HRRPHOTO.CO.UK

Top, right | Moments after releasing Peter Yates's ashes into the Thames River, Jason joins Joanne Yates (Peter's wife) along with his two daughters, Lizzie and Ali, for a commemorative photo. UNKNOWN

Bottom | The final team photo in Henley-on-Thames after getting knocked out in the semi-finals by the Windsor boys. L–R: Luc, Mathew, Daniel, Jason, Winston, Cosmo, and Josh. UNKNOWN

Back on the dock, with the boats still secured in the water waiting for the second row, the boys stretched and refuelled with the snacks that had been brought down from the kitchen. While I was talking with our crew, I noticed Winston disappearing with a tape measure. He had that "I'm-on-a-mission" look about him.

As the boys went to get changed into some drier clothes for their second row, Winston came over with a relieved look on his face.

"I measured the oars. They are way too short."

"What happened? They were fine yesterday," I asked.

"Yes, before Tim's guys got here," he answered with a smile.

"What do you mean?"

"Tim's guys took the blades we had been using because those were their blades. The only reason we were able to use them yesterday was that Tim's guys weren't here. I guess when our boys went looking for blades and saw that the ones they had been using were gone, they must have grabbed the women's blades. That's why they struggled so much. I've lengthened them as much as I can. They won't be perfect, but they'll work. It's all good, my friend." Then squinting his eyes and shaking his head, he added quietly, "Our guys would've doored them if we had had the proper load. But don't say anything to them. Let's wait until we can use this little bit of information to our advantage. Agreed?"

I smiled. "You're not just a pretty face, Winston. I knew there was a reason we brought you along."

"You better believe it. I've earned my scotch for the day."

That night, after dinner, we joined the Shawnigan and Brentwood crews at a bonfire on the other side of the lake. It was a way to show what we coaches believed: you can be friends with your competitors.

Back at the camp, just before heading off to bed, Winston, Siobhan, and I talked about the day with two of the parents from the girl's crew. Tim and Elaine Toffolo had given up part of their March break to travel out west with us, help out, and watch their daughter row in the quad. They'd been at previous camps in the US. Tim was a real estate agent and a hockey team owner who had a passion for sports. Elaine was a nurse and equally passionate about their daughters' sporting endeavours.

Both were a shining example of most of the parents that I had met in my four years at Ridley. In fact, I considered becoming friends with the Ridley parents to be one of my favourite perks from being back to coach at the School. They were an incredibly positive and supportive group of individuals. Everything from purchasing boats and equipment to getting behind fundraising, assisting with travel, or making meals, you name it and they got involved. I found having them around inspiring and energizing.

"Those Shawnigan girls are *fast!*" said a very tired Siobhan.

"True. But you have novice rowers in your boat; Shawnigan doesn't. You know as well as I do that when your girls start to figure it out, the boat speed will come quickly," I replied.

"Yeah, I know. It's just that we got beat by so much out there today. It's going to be hard to keep the girls from getting discouraged throughout the week."

"Come on, Siobhan. That's why we pay you the big bucks, right?"

We all laughed. She was right though. She knew she had some work to do if she was going to come anywhere close to Shawnigan's crew. They were the fastest boat on the West Coast and would provide an ideal benchmark for our women's progress. They'd have a few more chances throughout the week to claw back some distance. And I wasn't kidding, with two novices in the boat and Siobhan's coaching, they'd improve quickly.

In the end, it was an ideal week. The weather held. No one got sick or injured. The accommodations were perfect. Even the food at Shawnigan was, as the boys put it, "way better than at Ridley." Crews were tired but pleased with the work that they had put in and how well they had come together as a team. They were champing at the bit to get home and start racing. Before that, we had one last row. We had arranged to race as the quad against Brentwood and the Victoria City Rowing Club. Tim's crew wouldn't be joining us. His boys were feeling the effects of three-a-day rows and had opted out of our session for a row on their own.

The plan was to do ten one-minute pieces at higher rates. It would be the first time we allowed the boys to push the rating up to a range that was closer to their racing pace. Given the level of fatigue in their systems, I was interested to see how well they could handle the rate increase.

Winston had left for Vancouver the day before to spend some time with his girlfriend before continuing on to Toronto and then home. It was just Sandy and me in the coach boat. He was running the clock, which allowed me to call out the start and finish of each piece while keeping an eye on our progress and not the time.

With different boats joining in on the training session, we staggered the crews according to boat speed. We had the women's crews lined up, as well as our double, followed by the two quads and an eight. We would do three pieces in one direction and then spin around and come back the other way, repeating that pattern until we were done.

Brentwood College had been a powerhouse in rowing for decades. No other Canadian school had been as successful as it had at producing top-level high-performance crews. In fact, Brentwood had put far more athletes in Olympic rowing shells than any other high school rowing program in the country. And most of their athletes had come back with Olympic medals. Now, closing in on their hundredth national title, they were experiencing what many programs did after a successful year. In 2013, their senior boys had won the national championship eight easily, but six rowers from that crew had graduated. Now, in a rebuilding year, Brentwood was hard-pressed to repeat the win.

The Victoria City Rowing Club also had a strong rowing program that attracted athletes from right across the lower part of Vancouver

Island. The club had an impressive history and its rowers would be a considerable challenge to our boys.

For the girls, the row was an important one. It would be Siobhan's final chance to garner a sense of how well the crew had progressed over the last few days. As for our quad, the boys had been sorting out their roles in the boat all week. Mathew was sitting in stroke seat. His undeniable strength, fitness, and even-tempered tenacity made him a natural for it. He had a solid stroke cycle, and the boys now trusted him to manage the rates. So far, he had done an exceptional job.

Daniel was sitting behind him in three seat. The day after his erg meltdown at the Ontario Championships, he'd gone back the very next morning and re-rowed it. He texted me that he'd pulled 6:22 with a member from the previous year's crew there to verify it. I was pleased that he had completed the race on his own terms, but that wasn't how ergattas worked. You didn't race when you were ready; you had to race when you were told. He was back to his old self now: confident, aggressive, and contributing in a big way to the pace of our group.

For the entire week, Luc had been the steady performer we had grown used to. Given his happy-go-lucky nature, it was always interesting for me to witness his commitment to getting better. In my time as a coach I had worked with only a handful of athletes who were capable of pushing themselves to the levels of exhaustion that Luc could. He was a huge part of why this boat could go so fast. Never one to talk much in or out of the boat, he just loved to pull.

Cosmo's knee was as good as new. The time off had proven worthwhile. His no-nonsense leadership style made him a natural for the bow seat. It also helped that he was our lightest crew member. If your bow seat guy was too heavy, he could cause the bow section of your boat to be submerged at certain parts of the stroke, hardly ideal for reaching optimal boat speed. Cosmo had risen to the challenge all week and had seen for himself that, in the heat of a race, he could manage the higher rates while still calling focus pieces and maintaining a straight course.

With each one-minute piece it became clear to both Sandy and me that we definitely had something with this crew. They were not only beating the other quad outright, but holding off and even moving away from the eight on a consistent basis. That generally didn't happen with two evenly talented crews. Given our crew's level of cumulative exhaustion, they were still finding a way to generate enough boat speed with each progressive piece to come out on top.

What I loved about it was how much the week had forced the boys to get clear on their *why*. Why had they given up their March break to row in this cold, damp weather? Why weren't they on a beach with their friends or skiing in the mountains? Instead they had a sore ass, bleeding hands, and every muscle in their aching body pleading to stop and just lie down. Why were they continuously pushing themselves to exhaustion? As a coach you hope it's because they want to do it more than anything else because they love it. They love that, when they have nothing more to give, they can always find more. They love that the other guys in their boat feel exactly the same way they do. They love that they would row into a tsunami together if that's what was required to find their absolute potential.

With the boats put away, we gathered our group of tired athletes on the dock for a photo with the Shawnigan girls. Then they turned around and dove into the frigid waters. No sooner had they hit the lake's surface than they were dashing their numb bodies off to the showers to warm up.

I returned to the dock on my own for some quiet time and to ask myself the same question: *Why?* What was my *why?*

OF THE FEW legendary rowing coaches in Canada, Jack Nicholson was one of them. As a young man back in the early 1960s, he began working with local rowing crews. Now in his eighties, he still spent most days sitting in his beat-up old coach boat chasing athletes, young and old, up and down the Henley course.

In the year before Seoul, he helped coach me on my quest to make the Olympic team. I have no doubt that without his training regimen I may not have earned a spot in the eight. He was knowledgeable, detailed, and passionate and, more importantly, understood his athletes. He was the consummate straight shooter: no superfluous fluff with Jack.

In 1972, he joined Neil and the other Ridley coaches when the program was still in its infancy. Jack brought many attributes to the new club, but it was because of his experience as a sculling coach that he offered the most insight and eventually made a name for himself.

Along with coaching high school and local club athletes, Jack took many elite Canadian rowers to dozens of World Championships and multiple Olympics. But, as is the case with so many coaches, eventually the incessant politics of the national team spoiled the fun for Jack, and he opted to focus solely on his Ridley athletes. After a career chock-full of numerous highlights, he was now content to spend his days coaching rowers who loved rowing as much as he did.

Jack had agreed to work with Jesus as our lightweight single, while Steve would join Josh in the heavyweight double. It wasn't ideal for Josh given the discrepancy in their fitness, but with Steve's boat moving skills, at the very least Josh would be able to row in a boat that would support his continued development as a sculler. Under Jack's watchful eye, Josh would only improve between now and the time we left for Henley.

Winston and I had decided that it would be the quad that we would take to England. Therefore, along with racing in the double at local regattas, Josh would assume the role of spare for the remainder of our season.

With the rest of the crews in our program set and their boats and coaches assigned, we began the final stint of our journey toward the Henley Royal Regatta. There would be plenty of racing stops along the way, but for the month of April there would be some heavy slogging. Knowing that our spare was in good hands with Jack allowed us to focus on our quad and coxed four.

All indications were pointing us toward several months of exciting racing. The key would be to not get caught up in that excitement. The boys knew they were fast. They had bought into what we were selling; the fun was going to come from the challenge of finding ways to improve. They also knew they could get faster. And, quite honestly, they'd have to. Tim's crew may have been the best on the coast, but the Americans would be quicker. As for England, the crews at Henley would be world class. We still had a lot of work to do. That belief would ultimately be our best strategy to accomplish our racing goals, but holding firm to our commitment to process would be the focus.

Along with the racing results, one of the highlights of the week at Shawnigan had come from a moment I'd shared with Josh. Following the double, Winston and I pulled up beside him and Jesus to see how things were going. It was near the end of the week and everyone was tired. The look in his eyes said that something was up. I could see that he was on the verge of tears. "What seems to be the problem?" I asked.

"Jason, I don't know if I can finish this row," he said, clearly apprehensive about revealing his self-doubt.

He peeled his hands away from the oar and lifted them to show me. They were shaking and not just from his exhaustion. Even with the tape and bandages his hands were bloody and causing him some genuine grief. I don't imagine there's a rower anywhere who's pulled on an oar the way it's supposed to be pulled and not experienced the pain of blisters. Now the stress of asking to stop was causing him even more.

I smirked. "Well Jesus, looks as though you're going to have to lug Josh's ass back to the dock. You okay with that?"

"I think I can manage," Jesus said. Ever positive, he began to readjust their course before taking his first stroke of the trip back to the boathouse.

"Think of it as some resistance training, Jesus!" Winston yelled out.

We all laughed. Josh was relieved.

Years earlier, I would have been surprised if any one of my athletes had said halfway through a session, "Jason, I don't know if I can finish this row." It's not that they were tougher back then, or that we put in less mileage. Nothing about the rowers had changed. What had changed was me and, with that, their perception of me. The athletes I'd worked with back then would have been too afraid to tell me they couldn't finish a workout. That somehow they weren't mentally tough enough to be in one of my crews. It bothers me to say it, but on some level, they were scared of me, anxious about how I might react.

As I described in *Chariots and Horses*, my own experience rowing for Neil Campbell had been laced with fear. In those early years, I would've cut my hands off before I'd complain about blisters to Neil's face. It felt good to know now that one of my athletes trusted me enough and felt safe enough to tell me exactly how he was feeling. I took it as a commentary on my evolution as a coach. It was an acknowledgement of just how far I had come in changing from the coach I'd once been.

For me that short exchange with Josh reaffirmed that we were doing it the right way. We were achieving high performance without compromising the emotional well-being of our boys. That was my answer to *why?*

CHAPTER ELEVEN

————— ¦ ¦ —————

ACK IN ST. Catharines, we resumed the ten training sessions per week routine we'd established in the fall before winter set in. Only now, half of those would be on the water. The trouble was, our water was limited. It had been a brutal winter. Martindale Pond had frozen over. Now, in April, only a small portion of the course, just over 1000 metres, was free of ice. It was what we had. There was no way we could control the weather, but we could get creative about choosing our time at the course. We could also spend more time than usual in the tank and on the ergs.

Even once the ice completely melted, we continued our weekly tank sessions in search of that elusive perfect stroke cycle. We also chose to dedicate our most intensive workout of the week to the erg. There was nothing that held athletes accountable more than results. The boys continued to race one another each week during those workouts, pushing themselves to their utmost limits.

Luc managed to maintain his role as the leader of the pack; Mathew, Daniel, and Cosmo took turns with the second, third, and fourth places. On occasion, Josh began to sneak into that fourth position. His steady progress did wonders, not only increasing his confidence, but also keeping the top four boys on their toes.

We also maintained our weight training with Paul at least three times a week. He tweaked the boys' lifts and repetitions slightly to continue developing explosive power within the group. I had never worked with a crew that could come off a starting line the way these boys could. I was convinced the weight training with Paul contributed.

On the days we were on the water, we used long pieces in small boats to facilitate that all-important "will to race." Even though we were going to be racing in a four-manned crew, we rarely spent time in it. The majority of our rows were spent in the doubles and singles, and only two or three rows a week in the quad or the coxed four. When I used to row for Neil, he would have us rowing in fours for the majority of the season before stepping into the eight a few days before major regattas. Neil knew that having us in the smaller boats was an effective strategy for mimicking a racing environment and creating greater boat sense by having us master the more sensitive shells.

In addition, I continuously changed up the combination of the crews on the days that we did race in the doubles. Racing with the same partner all the time could sometimes lead to a divisive crew. Changing partners prevented smaller teams within the larger team from possibly adopting a combative, "us-against-them" mindset. By continually rotating the line-ups, every athlete had to adapt to racing with new partners. It mimicked the long-standing tradition of what was called "seat racing." Simply put, it's when coaches line up two identical boats and race them side by side over the same distance. Then, after recording the times of the two crews, they switch one member from each crew, usually the ones sitting in the same seats. A row back up to the start would get the athletes used to one another, and then the crews would race again over the same distance. Once more, and the coach would record and compare the results. The athlete with the combined faster time was the winner.

This process was usually reserved for times when coaches had more athletes than spots to fill. Since we had our top four athletes selected, the motivation to "win" your seat was gone. Embracing the seat racing environment as part of our process created a competitive atmosphere that the boys loved. Some coaches feel the head race style is the fairer of the two because of the perception that everything is about the times recorded. Many of those coaches are concerned that, with side-by-side racing, athletes pick and choose the races in which to try their hardest on the basis of whether they think they are going to be switched or not. Some coaches even feel that rowers are more likely to race harder if they prefer one partner to another. I've always believed that if you have to worry about your athletes favouring their friends, you had bigger culture issues than seat racing would ever solve.

I also liked watching the side-by-side races unfold. I believed that's where the truly important information was revealed. Not so much in the times. I wanted to see whether, with 750 metres to go and two seats down, an athlete would pack it in or dig in. In those moments, true character was exposed, the kind that made or broke crews. If an athlete assessed his situation and determined it was time to race harder, I wanted that guy on my team. Dogged determination was hard to find and even harder to coach.

The late Easter break that year provided us our last long weekend of extra training before our first race of the season. Normally, the Early Bird Regatta fell on the first weekend of May, but this year it was a week early. Winston and I weren't too fussed about it, given how well the training had gone since getting back on the water. We knew the boys were not only prepared to race, but eager to race as well. The only problem was that, due to a scheduling conflict with an event at the School, Cosmo would have to sit out.

Ridley was the only independent school in Canada to still have a cadet program, and because Cosmo had a significant rank, he was unable to miss what was called the "Church Parade" in which students would march through downtown St. Catharines to St. Thomas's Church and then after the service march back to the School. In my day, we would march in the morning and be back in time to race later that afternoon. But now, the race schedule didn't line up enough for Cosmo to do both.

We used Cosmo's absence as an excellent opportunity for Josh to race in the coxed four. We had known for some time that Cosmo wouldn't be able to race with us at the US Schoolboy Championships because he would be in the midst of his IB exams. Given that we had planned on racing the coxed four there all along, it was a great way to give Josh a big international event.

Being a spare can be a lonely job. You train just as hard as your teammates, but your chances to race don't always come along. Now the boys were as excited as I was to give Josh a shot. They figured it was the least they could do for him. Having Josh row in the Early Bird Regatta would put one race in the four under his belt before heading to the States. It was better than none at all.

With a slight change in rig, Josh was able to row in Cosmo's bow seat position. Josh was just a little smaller than Cosmo, meaning there really wouldn't be any noticeable change in the boat in terms of weight and height. Of all of the athletes to switch, these two were probably the easiest. Once the rigging changes were made and their pre-race erg warm-up was complete, Winston and I called the boys in.

"Okay, Sandy. We're just looking to get Josh down there in one piece. Nothing too crazy off the line, Mathew. Just let the rate go where it wants to. Don't force anything, okay? What we do want you to focus on is that third 500 metres. Let's see how much space we can open up with just power through the water—not rate. Got that? This race isn't the time to blast that thing down the course. Just get off the line clean and go to work. If it's feeling smooth, Sandy, you can let them bring the rate up a bit in the end. But do it in the water first. Any questions?" Nothing. "Okay, they should be calling us any moment. We'll get your oars."

As a coach, any time you walk your boat to the dock with your crew's blades on your shoulders just before a race, it's a nerve-racking experience. It was for me, anyhow, especially the first race of the season. It was like working on a clay sculpture for eight months and then placing it on a table at an art gallery for everyone to see and critique. These boys were an extension of our coaching—the way they raced, how they carried themselves, how they behaved, how fit they were. Both Winston and I had influenced all of that. Now was the time to see if what we had prescribed in all of those areas had worked.

Just before the boys shoved off, I leaned into Josh and put my hand on the back of his neck. When I was rowing for Neil, he would always do that: put his warm leathery hand on the back of my neck, give it a gentle squeeze, and say something assuring. It was his subtle way of adding that little bit of extra connection. It was one trick that I had borrowed from him years ago and used at Shawnigan. Now it was automatic.

I could tell Josh was a bit more nervous than the others. Understandably. "Look, it's all good. Just let the training show up, Josh." I squeezed his neck. "Got it?" He nodded. "You'll be fine."

After the boys rowed away, Winston and I walked to our perch just shy of the 1500-metre mark. Less than thirty minutes later, and right on time, the race started. It didn't take long to see that our boys were out front. As they came by, they easily had a three-boat-length lead on the top local crew: Governor Simcoe. More importantly, they looked okay. Josh was doing a fine job. For Winston, I'm guessing it was no big surprise. For me on the other hand, it was a relief. We both watched his blade work going into the last 500 metres of the race.

"You'd be hard-pressed to tell this was his first row on port," Winston observed.

"You bet, not bad at all," I answered.

Josh had rowed starboard side the year before in the junior heavy eight, and we had planned on leaving him there when we raced in the US Schoolboy. For Early Bird, Winston figured he was a good enough sculler that switching sides wasn't going to kill him. So, instead, we opted to throw him into the fire and see how things went.

As Winston had predicted, he'd adjusted without any trouble. Josh and the boys were happy that they'd made it through their first race unscathed. After the race, during our debriefing, the boys were quite pleased with their effort and happy that they'd clicked as a crew and won so easily. They knew, however, that the competition would heat up as the regattas progressed.

After training for eight long months, this was the time of year that all rowers desperately longed for. May not only brought flowers, it also brought racing: 2000 metres of gut-wrenching, full-on, side-by-side racing. And our boys were desperate to get started. It was one thing to compete against your teammates or strive for personal bests, but lining up beside another crew and pounding down the course at race pace was the rush we all lived for. It was time to see if all of the preparation thus far was on track.

The quad hadn't really had a chance to go toe to toe with anyone since our Shawnigan camp. We had raced in doubles and singles often enough to know that the boys certainly knew what to do, but it couldn't replace the challenge of dealing with the distractions of an unknown crew in the next lane.

A week earlier, as a tune-up, we did a high-rating workout with Brock University's lightweight men's eight. Ten-by-two-minute pieces were on the schedule. Lightweight crews are generally quick off the line, especially eights. Our boys came away having met the challenge and then some. That session confirmed what they knew: they had some viable boat speed. Now they just wanted to race a group of boys that were their age and sat in a quad next to them.

Ridley was adjusting to the new IB curriculum and corresponding timeline by having the entire student body write their exams in early May. Keeping the boys focused on their training while having to write their finals had been paramount. I believed in what Neil had told us years ago: "If you can't hack your studies, you can't hack rowing." We knew their work ethic and discipline would see them through. Our boys had gotten this far; they would manage.

Jay had assured us that training time would be made available each and every day. And, sure enough, every afternoon we made our way to Henley Island (referred to simply as "the Island") for our on-water session. In the end we only had to shuffle around the line-ups a few times. The bonus for us would be that once we left for Philadelphia, everyone, with the exception of Cosmo, would be finished their exams. If there was going to be a silver lining to the new schedule, this was it.

In 1977, Neil had his heavy eight stay in Princeton between the Stotesbury Cup and the US Schoolboy, which were held one week apart. It just made sense. To load up the boats and travel all of the way down there, race, and come home, only to turn around and do it again four days later, was crazy. I ran the idea by Jay, and he agreed.

Greg Hughes, the head men's coach at Princeton, was a Brentwood graduate. When I called and asked if we could train on Lake Carnegie, Princeton's training site, for the week in between the two regattas, he agreed. Now, four years later, that training camp was a major part of our preparation for both the US and the Canadian Schoolboy. And something the boys and I looked forward to each year. This year, Josh would be racing the double in Philadelphia with Jesus and then joining us in Princeton while Cosmo and Jesus returned to Ridley to write their remaining IB exams. It presented some logistical nightmares, but Lori, Jay's assistant, was on it.

At our first weekly coaches' meeting in May, Jay told me they'd hired Dereck Schwandt to coach next year's senior boys. I had coached against Dereck numerous times when I was at Shawnigan. Currently, he was a teacher and rowing coach at Vancouver College. He'd done an excellent job of building a successful rowing program, especially with the lightweights. His accomplishment was a perfect example of capitalizing on a challenging circumstance.

Vancouver College's Fighting Irish varsity football team had a tradition of winning championships, partly because the majority of the large athletes who attended the school played football. That left

CHAPTER TWELVE

RUNNING HAD LONG been essential to my sanity. When I quit rowing in 1990, I turned to running as a way to manage the void left behind. Although not exactly a speed demon, I had the capacity and fortitude to go for long distances. That's when I began entering ultra-marathon events. Training for those races allowed me the hours that I needed to process all of the leftover crap from Seoul that was causing such chaos in my life. It proved my saving grace. Now running, along with other strategies focused on self-care, allowed me at the very least to function.

During the hours that I would disappear into the woods, I would think. Think about everything. Life. School. Family. Rowing. My future. If it was in my immediate world, it came up on those long runs and I tried to process it. It worked. Now, I no longer disappeared for hours, but I still did my best thinking on trails.

May in the Niagara region could be spectacular. Katie and I set out for our usual midday sixty-minute run along the twelve-mile creek through the heart of St. Catharines. It was a beautiful warm day. The sun was shining, and I had lots on my mind that needed sorting. Ten minutes into the run, on a long decline, I felt something snap in my heel. At first, I thought I'd landed on a large stone. My foot hurt, but I kept running. By the time I got home, it was really sore. I thought I'd bruised my heel and assumed it was only a temporary setback. Two days later, it had settled down, and I figured it was on its way to mending. I donned my running stuff and took off with Katie once again. When I got home from that run, I could barely put any weight on my foot. *Not good!* I thought. During regattas, I walked upwards of a few miles, depending on how many races our boys had in the day. Carrying oars and shoes and walking to and from my viewing spot was going to be challenging.

When Sunday arrived, the pain really hadn't subsided much. If I could get through the weekend, the injury would start to clear up by the following week for sure. In the meantime, I would just have to limp and get used to people asking what I had done. For now, I was going with the bruised heel.

Once again, Robyn awoke on Mother's Day to an empty bed. By 6:30 I had made my way to the Island to set things up and be at the clerk's booth for the coaches' meeting. We listened in as the race scratches were announced for the day. As I looked out over the course, I was reminded of the late Craig Swayze, a sports writer for the *St. Catharines Standard*. Rowing was on his beat, and in one of his columns he described Martindale Pond as having "sun-dappled waters." If coaches were hoping for good conditions to test out their speed, we had it in spades. There was no breeze to speak of, and the water had barely a ripple. Mr. Swayze would have been in his element that morning.

In the early 1980s, this regatta had been a mere 1000-metre sprint, a rinky-dink event with only a handful of entries. Since then the regatta had grown so much that some heats had to be run in the morning. That was a testament to the growth of the sport and how well the St. Catharines Rowing Club ran regattas. The volunteers were a well-oiled machine. If there was one thing this club could do, aside from produce some fast crews, it was to send races off on time. If the weather conditions remained good, the races were certain to run seamlessly all day long.

Our boys would be racing the coxed four and the quad. Siobhan would have another shot with her quad, while Jack's boys would race the lightweight single and double. In addition, our junior crews, which had just finished their sixth week on the water, would have a second try at covering the 2000-metre racecourse while striving to improve on their performances from two weeks earlier at the Early Bird Regatta.

After finishing second in their heat, Josh and Steve advanced to the final. The girls, who had lost to Governor Simcoe at the Early Bird, closed some distance and finished three seconds back in their heat to advance to their final. The boys in the quad won their heat by five seconds over E.L. Crossley. Our Ridley crew would have three races that day. Winston and I instructed them to get off the line quickly and then lengthen out to a comfortable rate that maintained a good lead. They did exactly that.

With five hours until the coxed four final, we sent them back to Ridley to refuel, study, and rest. There was nothing worse than sitting around a regatta site waiting for your race, especially in the hot sun; it could suck the life out of you.

After lunch, the double struggled to hold the pace that the other crews established early in the race and finished fourth in their final, eleven seconds back from the leaders. Fitness was the issue. Steve had been joining us for our weekly erg session over the last few weeks, and it was making a huge difference. But he still had some work to do.

Next up were the girls. As we had predicted, given the amount of room there was for improvement, the decrements would likely be big ones. Sure enough, they finished second to Simcoe again in the final, this time losing by only half a second. If they kept this up, there was a chance they could be in the hunt for a medal at our Schoolboys in a few weeks' time.

The event organizers decided to make the coxed four race a straight final with eight boats. Although six was generally the norm, we were just fine with avoiding another heat. The Governor Simcoe crew would be our main competition just like they had been two weeks earlier. Our instructions were the same as always: establish a lead quickly and then sit on it for the entire race. That would be the strategy for Schoolboy, so we figured our boys had better get practised at it. The reason was that at that Schoolboy, where there were less than fifty minutes between finals, they would have to learn how to control the race from the lead position in their race while conserving energy for the quad event, where we would let them open up the throttle a little more.

Right on time, the fours began racing down the course.

"Holy shit! Things are lot closer than they should be," I said to Winston as the crews raced by.

"Yup. That Simcoe crew is putting up quite a fight. Our boys look rattled. There's no rhythm or run to the boat. They don't look like they should," Winston replied.

I was trying not to panic. "What the hell happened? They should be miles out front."

We were both quiet.

"Wait. There they go. Something just happened. Now they're starting to open up," he said.

As they crossed over into the last 500 metres, it was evident they would win, but not by much. When we met the boys at the dock, they were quiet.

"Let's not worry about what happened in that race just yet," I said. "Let that one go and refocus on the quad. Okay? We'll talk about it later. Agreed?"

They all nodded.

Winston and I grabbed their blades and followed them up to the boat bay. As soon as the boat was back on the rack, the boys grabbed some food and liquids. They knew this was a trial run for our School-boy. We would have more recovery time in a few weeks, but for today we had only a few minutes to eat, visit the washroom, and then race again. With everyone ready, we gathered around one more time.

"Now I'm guessing you've had better rows before. But use this quad race as an opportunity to see if you can change your mental game. Something didn't click out there in the four. It's not like you forgot how to row or you lost all of your fitness. Some part of our mental component was off. So let's see if you can refocus and show up the way you're capable of in the quad. Got it?"

"We can do this, boys. Here we go!" shouted Daniel as they moved to the racks to get their boat.

By now, my mom and dad, my brothers, Scott and Paul, and Scott's wife, Rose had shown up on the Island to watch. Robyn, Mataya, and Katie had come down as well. It was nice to have the extra support and enjoy a brief visit, but I still felt distracted by the coxed four race. After spending a few moments with everyone, Winston and I walked over to our usual spot to watch.

"What the hell happened to you? Why are you limping so much?" asked Winston as we walked to the bank. "Robyn kick you?"

"It's a bruised heel. That's what I'm telling everyone, anyway."

"What's a bruised heel?"

"I have no idea. But it shuts everyone up. I did it running. And now it hurts a lot!"

We went silent as we both arrived in time to see the boys come by.

"Now, that's better," I said with a sigh of relief.

"Would you shut up? No one's going to touch these guys. Christ, you worry too much," Winston said shaking his head.

"What? It's my job to worry."

The quad looked like a new crew. This time, they raced as the boat we knew they could be. Long. Powerful. Fast. They were well out in front and looking quite comfortable. It was a better way to end their day. On our way back to the dock to meet the boys, we swung by my family to say goodbye. Everyone acknowledged our crews' efforts and shared their well wishes for the future.

If there was ever a rowing mom, ours was it. Between growing up in Port Dalhousie and then being married to Dad, she had seen more than a few rowing races in her day. She had endured three boys rowing for Neil in high school and then racing internationally. She knew the sport inside and out. What amazed me the most was the critical eye she had developed. In the years I would bring Shawnigan crews back to race at Schoolboy, she would often comment on their technique. Never general remarks as in "they looked good" or "they're a nice-looking crew." Partly because they didn't and they weren't! I wouldn't have described any of those crews as being pretty. Instead, Mom would comment on their blade work or their run or something more substantial.

Today was no different. As I hugged her before heading back to the dock, she said, "Those boys remind me of your Shawnigan crews. The way they put their blades in the water. They look very powerful."

"Thanks, Mom. You're right. They're a strong crew. But you know what? They're faster than those Shawnigan crews." We both laughed.

When the boys finished their cool-down on the ergs, we gathered around to talk about the races.

"So, that was a better race?" I started.

Their looks said it all. "Much better. And I know we have another gear," added Cosmo.

"Good to know. Now, how about that four race?" I asked.

Mathew answered. "It's weird. The warm-up was really good. The rates came easy. I think we all felt ready. But once the race started, we couldn't find any rhythm."

The others nodded in agreement.

"Why do think that was?" I continued.

They were quiet. Then Daniel spoke up. "Honestly. When we came off the line and didn't drop Simcoe the way we did last time, I think we all started worrying about why that Simcoe boat was still there with us. I mean, those guys hate us so much, especially after what happened at Early Bird. So, when they were still with us at the 1000-metre mark, I think they just kept throwing everything they had at us because they wanted to beat us so badly. Finally, with 500 metres to go, Sandy got us to focus in on the boat and called some pieces. That's when we took off. If it wasn't for Sandy, I'm not so sure we would've won that race."

Everyone looked at Sandy.

"What? We had to do something," he said. Everybody laughed.

"Nice one, Sandy. Thanks, for that," added Winston.

"Okay, great lesson there. When we focus on the competition, it takes us out of our boat and what we're supposed to be doing. When we worry about the other crews, we're limited. You've heard it from Winston often enough. Take care of your own three feet in the boat. Agreed? Okay, I think Jesus is coming down soon. If we can get out to the bank and cheer him on, that'd be great."

Jesus was in a tough spot. The lightweight single was a challenging event at the best of times. What made it even more difficult for him was that he weighed a good twenty pounds less than his competitors. Pound for pound he was a good boat mover. But you just couldn't give away that much muscle mass and expect to be in the hunt. Despite that uneven playing field, Jesus still managed to finish fifth in his final and, according to him, have a good race. Jack, who admired his grit, was pleased.

CHAPTER THIRTEEN

THERE WAS A reason that the Stotesbury Cup Regatta was the largest high school regatta in the world. It was well organized. The setting was beautiful and centrally located so other schools on the East Coast could attend. Perhaps more importantly, the attraction for so many was that you could feel the history of rowing when you stood on the banks of the course. The famous American painter Thomas Eakins chose the banks of the Schuylkill River for his famous paintings because, according to some, it was the birthplace of rowing in America. The history along Boathouse Row, situated on the east side of the river, was palpable.

There was a lot of personal history there for me as well. Heading off to Philadelphia with Neil and the rest of our young crew was a moment I cherished. Driving down to the States to race the best American crews had always been a big deal. Neil used to call in a favour each year from Ted Nash, then legendary head coach at the University of Pennsylvania. We would boat out of UPenn's boathouse instead of from the public docks that most other crews used. It afforded us the comforts of our own washroom, showers, and a place to get away from all of the noise and distraction that came with launching from the public sites.

We'd look at the historical photos on the walls while we waited for our race. One could spend days admiring all of it. There was even a photo of Neil stroking the St. Catharines Rowing Club's men's eight at an international regatta on the Schuylkill. It was a great photo:

a bunch of youngsters and Neil, flying down the course at breakneck speed. That crew would eventually become the Canadian boat for the 1968 Olympic Games in Mexico. Neil was thirty-eight by then. They chose him not because they couldn't find anyone else for that seat, but because Neil was that good. That tough.

There were other items of memorabilia from Ridley. In 1981, Neil asked me to hand over my racing singlet to Ted after our final that year. Truth be told, I didn't want to part with it. I loved that thing. I had worked so hard to earn the right to wear it. But, with Ted and Neil standing there, I wasn't about to say no. UPenn had a tradition of stapling rowing singlets to the wall. They had an incredible collection. I took comfort in knowing that my singlet would hang there.

When I returned in 2010 with my first Ridley crew, it was gone. In its place was an old Ridley T-shirt with Chris Ferguson's name attached. Chris had stroked Neil's young 1978 crew that won against a heavily favoured and stacked crew from St. Catharines Collegiate. My brother Paul was in that Ridley boat. Winning the Stotesbury Cup with his younger crewmates was one of his favourite rowing memories

After an eight-hour trip, we pulled into the city and eventually made our way to the Schuylkill. Tim Toffolo had once again volunteered to drive our boat trailer down with us. It was no simple task: it was loaded with suitcases and supplies in addition to hauling a long steel-framed trailer packed with boats, oars, and everything else we needed to rig our boats. With easily over a hundred thousand dollars of equipment behind him, he managed to get the trailer there in one piece.

In the two days before leaving, we had pushed the boys hard. Sitting in a van for eight hours wasn't exactly the most effective recovery. We knew they needed a long row to move the blood and stretch out their muscles after the day's trip. The course was going to close in a few hours, so we wasted little time in getting our boats rigged and ready.

The regatta had grown so much in recent years that now the organizers had to run time trials to eliminate crews in the first round. It was the most efficient way to take twenty, thirty, or even forty crews in one event and whittle them down to six crews in each of two semi-finals. If you didn't finish in the top twelve of your time trial, you were heading for the "boat trailer finals," as we used to call them. It was quick and dirty. But it also meant that there was little room for mistakes. You had one shot. And if you screwed up, it was a long trip home.

Just like in the year before, heavy rain and high winds were expected in Philadelphia. Unfortunately, the weather forecast turned out to be right. And then some. The rain throughout the night was relentless and even surpassed the predicted levels of precipitation. As a result, the river was flowing dangerously fast. Again this year, uprooted trees and logs were floating on the course. At the morning coaches' meeting, the head official announced that it was too dangerous to race, and that if the rain continued at this pace, they might have to cancel the entire regatta.

I couldn't believe it. The 2013 racing season had been a gong show because of severe weather, and now here we were on the first stop of our regatta circuit and Mother Nature was up to her old tricks. Part of the reason for racing the quad here was that Stotesbury was a qualifying regatta for Henley. If we won our event, it would likely mean we wouldn't have to race in the qualifying time trial in England. For obvious reasons, winning in Philadelphia was our preferred route. If we could then win at our own Schoolboy Championships, it would likely garner us "selected crew" status, which also had its benefits. Understandably, there was a lot riding on this race.

I sent Winston a text to let him know what was up. He was on the West Coast with his girlfriend. She was a rowing coach at the University of British Columbia in Vancouver. Winston, always willing to lend a hand, had agreed to fly out and help coach at their training camp. He was scheduled to join us on Saturday. I could tell from his response to the weather news that he was unnerved.

Thankfully, the rain let up later that morning. At an emergency coaches' meeting, the head official announced that they would send off as many time trials as possible for the remainder of the day, pending conditions and the safety of the crews. If they were unable to complete enough of the time trials, the regatta committee would be forced to scrap the semi-finals and go straight to a six-boat final based on times. Meaning, crews were now racing for lanes as well. With the current flowing like it was, we had to have an advantageous lane for the final.

I returned to the boathouse to meet with the boys and share the news. They were already anxious; now they were more so. "Look, it's going to be hairy out there no matter what," I said. "Get your boats down the course as clean as possible. Just control the controllables! You've heard us say that often enough."

We had opted to bring Jesus instead of Steve to this regatta so that our duo from the March camp could get a shot at racing the American crews. Both Josh and Jesus were well-seasoned scullers by now, but they were still in a tough position.

After the boats shoved off for the time trials, I went back upstairs and made myself comfortable. With my foot still giving me grief, there was no point in rushing off to watch the trial; I wouldn't be able get to the finish line before they were done. I chose to stay at the boathouse and patiently wait for the results to come in on my phone. Patience not being a virtue of mine, it was going to be a long afternoon.

Finally, times started to appear online. The double finished ninth, which in all likelihood meant they wouldn't race again. The women finished fifth, but twenty-two seconds back of the leaders, which on a day like this could mean any number of things. They might have hit something or caught a crab. There was no way of telling what may have caused such a gap. We'd have to wait to hear from them when they got back.

The boys came first—and by five seconds.

I texted Winston immediately, but he'd already seen the results and was as relieved as I was. Then I met the quad at the dock. They were quiet.

"How'd it go?" I asked.

"Shitty," answered Cosmo.

"Really? How so?"

"The conditions were terrible. There were logs all over the place. No lane markers. The wind came at us in every direction." While Cosmo continued with his take on the race, they all got out of the boat and gathered around me. "Once when we were passing St. Joe's, I hit this massive log. We must have turned sixty degrees in the water. I yelled to stop rowing because we were sideways. I was certain there was a hole in the boat. It was awful the entire way down."

They were clearly rattled. And by the sounds of it, for good reason: those were brutal conditions.

"Any times up yet?" asked Daniel.

"Yup. You guys were first. By five seconds," I said calmly.

"What? Get out of here!"

I smiled. "You guys were first. Have a look."

I gave them my phone and began carrying some blades up from the dock. That's when the yelling started. They couldn't believe it. True to my commitment to let them experience success more fully than I ever did, I let them cheer. There was no one around, and besides, why not? Five seconds over those fast US crews in these conditions was something worth cheering about. The main thing for me was that we would see another day.

On Saturday we awoke to clouds, but also sunshine, a stark contrast from twenty-four hours earlier. Mind you, with all of that rain, the Schuylkill was flowing at rocket speed. The race would be over before they knew it. It would be a real challenge for our boys. We had been training all year for the seven-minute race we would likely see at Henley. Today's finishing time would be closer to half that. Sure, we were fast off the line, but I wasn't certain that we could maintain that pace for 1500 metres.

Yesterday they'd been anxious; today they were eager. Even at breakfast, I could feel their quiet confidence. What they had achieved in their time trial was no small feat. The American schools prided themselves on winning this event every year. Having an unknown Canadian crew show up and post the fastest time went over like an unwanted guest. In fact, word got back to us that some of the Americans weren't just mad; they were gunning for retribution in the final. That was music to my ears! I knew damn well if those crews were focused on revenge, it meant for certain they would be focused on us and not on their own race. I understood all too well that that approach was a recipe for underperforming. The final would be a showdown between love and hate. Our boys were going to race for one another, with intrinsic motivation, whereas some of the Americans were going to race to get even with us—an extrinsic motivation. My money was on our crew.

Given the conditions of the previous day, our girls' quad, like every other crew out there, had been challenged to row at their best. Despite those horrendous conditions, they had managed to qualify. Knowing that each time they backed their boat into a starting gate they were only going to get better, Siobhan was pleased. In the final, they finished fifth again in their group, but they did manage to make up two seconds. It was an improvement, and they still had three weeks until our Schoolboy Championships.

Rob Silk, an old Ridley crewmate of mine, lived just north of Philly. The great thing about rowing was that the friends you made through this crazy sport often stuck around for life. Decades earlier, in our last race together at this regatta, Rob and I had defeated some imposing American schools to win the Stotesbury Cup. After four years of rowing at Temple, he had married his university sweetheart and then started a business and a family. Every year, Rob would take the time to come out to cheer on our crews. As always, it was great to see him. The funny thing was that the weather then was just like this weekend; there was heavy rain and a fast current. Shortly after four o'clock, when the boys gathered by our boat, Rob shook their hands and wished them good luck.

Now it was time for me to have one last talk with the boys. "I'm sure you can well imagine that given all of the rain, the course is fast. My guess is you'll come in just over four minutes. That's nothing. This race will be over very quickly. You'll barely have time to think. However, it's important that you do. Just try to slow the race down in your mind. Okay? Chances are the start will be crazy. They'll want to get you off as quickly as possible given how hard it will be for the boat holders in that current. Be ready for that. Otherwise, do what we've trained to do—race!"

When they were all ready and standing on the dock by their boat resting in the water, I grabbed Mathew's blade to assist them in shoving off. As they paddled away, I said what I always did: "Have fun out there, boys!"

Larry Laszlo, my freshman coach at Syracuse University, was the first coach ever to say that to me before a race. When he did, I thought it was stupidest thing I'd ever heard. I took his suggestion to be weak and somehow unmanly. *Have fun!* It was something you said to kindergartners before a game of dodge ball. It wasn't something you said to an elite athlete heading out to win a race.

Larry's approach challenged every promise I had about racing. I'd been taught a race was like a fight between you and your competition; the idea of fun had never figured into my equation for winning. It wasn't until years later that I recognized and appreciated the clever strategy behind Larry's parting words. Not to mention the obvious attempt at setting the right tone and giving his young athletes a holistic perspective on competition.

The expression Larry used creates an environment in which competitors don't just strive to win; they strive to get better, because it's fun. The bonus is, as a by-product, they improve their chances of winning more often—imagine that!

When I finally understood the competitive strategy of what Larry used to say to us, I borrowed it unabashedly. Given we are inherently driven to want to have fun in what we do, when coaches use that innate desire by creating a fun culture, they actually turn on the intrinsic motivation of their athletes. The results of that are often surprising.

There was no chance I was going to sit in the boathouse and wait for race results to come in over my phone. Instead, I borrowed a bike and immediately made my way up to the finish line.

The bike path was busy. It was a beautiful weekend day, and it appeared as though the entire city was out enjoying a reprieve from the heavy rain. By the time I arrived at the finish line, the grandstand was packed. I locked my bike to a lamp post and slowly made my way to a spot that provided me a clear view of the racecourse. Decked out in my Ridley stuff, I could feel the attention of those around me. I was surrounded by mainly US school supporters. Just as I was pulling out my camera, I felt a tap on my shoulder.

"Hey, good luck today." It was the coach of one the crews we'd be racing in a few moments.

"Thanks very much. And to you as well." We smiled politely, shook hands, and quietly returned to the agony of waiting.

Watching the crews come into sight, I could tell we were out front. *Come on, boys . . . push!*

Halfway through the race, it was still close, but they looked in control: a good sign. Coming into the last 500 metres, they still looked clean. But so did everyone. This was a class field. As Winston and I had predicted, the race had turned into a 1500-metre sprint. Our boys were still striking a stroke rate in the high thirties. The rates hadn't come down much at all.

Pictures, Jase, take some pictures!

I quickly raised my camera and began snapping shots, hoping that my shaking hands wouldn't ruin the photos.

With the crews fast approaching, the grandstand was deafening. I was surrounded by high-spirited cheering fans. Parents. Coaches. Friends. Other athletes. It reminded me of a time gone by when Ridley students would pack the grandstand in Port Dalhousie and cheer for us. Today there was no one here cheering for Ridley but me.

With twenty strokes to go the boys had open water, and it was clear they would win. My guard came down, and I smiled. A wave of tremendous satisfaction came over me. Our process was working; they had done it. I was thrilled for them.

The same coach approached me. "Congratulations. Your boys looked impressive. Will we see you at Mercer Lake next week?" He was assuming that we would race our same crew at their US High School Championships.

As crazy as it was, an old habit of mine was dying hard. The same dilemma about compliments that I experienced as a rower still lived on in me as a coach. I agreed, our boys did look impressive, but I wasn't about to acknowledge it. We had more work to do, and I wasn't letting up.

"Thanks," I answered. "Yes, we're going to be there, but we're actually going to race the coxed four event."

"With those same athletes?" he inquired.

"Ah, kinda. We'll be using our spare this time. It's a long story. But we'll see how it goes."

He was obviously taken aback. "Wow, that's crazy. Good for them!" Then, as we were walking out together, he added, "You know, for your boys to have that kind of lead in such a short race and in that lane," he shook his head.

"I thought we had a good lane," I said.

"Actually, when the current is moving like this, your lane would have been slower than some of the others. Tell your boys they did well. I've got to go. Congratulations, again, coach."

We shook hands one more time, and he was off.

Basking in my giddy sense of accomplishment, I had to tell someone. *Winston!*

I pulled out my phone and began to text him. "They did it!" Immediately, those little texting bubbles appeared; I knew he'd be waiting.

"Fuckin' A!" he replied. I laughed aloud.

I then shared with him what the other coach had told me about the lanes.

"England, here we come!" came back from Winston. Clearly, he was as thrilled as I was.

As the boys made their way to the grandstand for the medal presentation ceremony, I worked my way down the dock to join them. I congratulated them quickly before they got up on the podium to receive their medals. With my camera in hand, I began to snap photos. It had been over thirty years since I had stood on this dock and received my medal with my crewmates. Those memories came alive in that moment.

The boys gestured for me to join them on the podium for the official team photo with the cup. I declined. I appreciated their sentiment, but I saw this as their moment. I'd had mine. Sure, Winston and I had trained them, coached them, and, in some way, were a part of why they were standing here, but they had done all of the work. This celebration was about them.

CHAPTER FOURTEEN

OSMO AND JESUS had left directly after the race to get home and study for an IB chemistry exam. With the boats loaded on the trailer and everyone in their respective vans, we left for Princeton and the US Schoolboy. On our way out of Philly, we pulled over at the "*Rocky* steps" just outside of the Museum of Art.

We jumped out of the van, and I took some commemorative photos of the group bounding up the massive steps two at time in Rocky Balboa fashion, then posing beside the Rocky statue. Years ago, when I was sixteen, my own crewmates and I had run up those steps the same way. Today this crew jumped up and down at the top of the stairs, blaring out the theme from *Rocky* with arms stretched out above their heads. Not much had changed.

With the trailer secure at the Princeton boathouse, our next stop was the hotel. We had Lori to thank for this one. It was perfect. Modern and clean, it had a great workout room. It was also idyllically located near our training centre at the university, as well as the regatta sight. The other bonus was that we were just a few moments from a collection of good restaurants and grocery stores, especially Trader Joe's.

One of my favourite things about going to the States was Trader Joe's: great food at ridiculously cheap prices. As soon as we had got settled, I took off for a quick shop. Aside from the groceries, the store had two things I loved—dark beer and dark chocolate. I was set for the week.

Winston flew in late, and Siobhan joined us in the foyer briefly before calling it a night. I could tell she had something on her mind.

"The girls are getting faster," I started. "You should be pleased with their progress."

"I am. Believe me, they've come a long way since March. But I'm not sure what to do about Brigitte and Ashley."

"What do you mean?"

"Well, Ashley has worked incredibly hard. She's fit and rows well. But Brigitte has more power than any of them. She's getting faster in the single, and I think by the time we get home, she'll be ready to move into the quad."

"How's that a problem? I mean, surely those girls understand that the fastest four rowers will sit in the boat at Schoolboy?"

"No, they get that. It's just that Ashley so deserves to be there. It's going to be hard."

That was small consolation for what was coming. Crew selection is never easy, especially late in the season. But Brigitte was new to the School this year. She had won every ergatta so far. She was big and strong. Although she had struggled to transfer her erg score to the water, she was slowly but steadily improving. Ashley on the other hand was like Jesus. Pound for pound she was as tough as any rower, but she couldn't make up for what she didn't have, which was size. Siobhan had some tough moments ahead.

"What did I say to you at our camp in Shawnigan?"

Siobhan shook her head.

"That's why we pay you big bucks."

She smiled.

"It's never easy, Siobhan. But remember, they pick the crew them-selves by providing you with the information. Ashley knows there's a chance she may not sit in that boat for long. She'll be upset, but she'll also understand."

"Get some sleep," I added. "We've got a big week ahead." Siobhan nodded and left for her room.

"A good day for the boys," said Winston.

"It was so awesome to watch. They looked amazing. Strong. In control. It was beautiful. They've got more in them, though."

"They'll have to. Those Brits will be faster than these US crews. Guaranteed," he added.

"We'll get there. Now, we've got a four to figure out."

"See you in the morning," said Winston, as he went off to bed.

The big screen TV in the hotel's foyer was running the highlights from the news of the day. Thankfully the sound was low enough that I couldn't hear it. It looked like the usual stream of depressing trash that featured prominently on those twenty-four hour news networks. I wanted to feel good about the day a while longer, to savour what the boys had accomplished. I looked away, laid my head back, and closed my eyes. I was exhausted. Not so much from any physical work, but from being mentally and emotionally *on*. As a coach, part of the job was the thinking and worrying that went with being responsible for so much. Any number of things could have gone sideways in the race, but none had. The boys had done exactly as we planned; they had controlled their controllables.

With the weather looking clear for the week, I figured we were in for smooth sailing. Compared to what we had just been through, US Schoolboys would be a breeze in terms of logistics. And given the way Josh was sculling under Jack, four days was plenty of time for him to get used to the rest of the crew in the coxed four.

Knowing I'd be better prepared for the week well rested, I forced myself out of my comfy chair and limped down the hall to my room. Once there, I put my foot in a bucket of ice and took a quick moment to check my emails. Among the usual congratulations from family and friends, there were emails from two US coaches who had watched our crew race earlier that day.

They introduced themselves and spent a paragraph each reminiscing about the good old days of watching Neil's crews from the 1970s and 1980s. Both coaches were extremely generous in their heartfelt tributes to Neil and the boats that he used to bring down here to race, in some of which my brothers and I had rowed. Both of them also congratulated me on what our boys had done earlier that day, and said that it was fantastic to see Ridley back on the international stage racing the way the School once had.

I had been ready for the comparisons that had come from the Ridley Old Boys. I knew that was going to happen. These ones were different for some reason. I never expected it from my peers, especially ones of this calibre.

I shut my computer and flopped onto my bed. *It's no big deal, Jase. Don't make it mean any more than someone politely acknowledging what you've managed to do in short order. That's all it is. For once in your life, just take it in and feel what it's like to have somebody notice your efforts and compliment you for them. It won't make you weak. It won't diminish your desire to take these boys further. And it certainly won't make you cocky. Just let it soak in and enjoy.*

Sunday morning, we all slept in. It had been a challenging few days of racing, coupled with the emotional stress of the weather-related conditions on the crew's first real international test.

I checked in with the boys while they ate their breakfast. Everyone seemed playful, rested, and recovered. Winston, our resident insomniac, had been up for hours checking emails and working from his phone. We met briefly as a group to go over the plans for the day and the remaining week.

"Let's head to the course in thirty minutes. Winston and I will rig the boat. You guys get warmed up on the ergs. Then we'll head out for a paddle just to make sure the rig is right for Josh and to give you guys a chance to flush out any remaining lactate left over from the weekend. Sound good?"

I had always worked a two-kilometre erg test into the final weeks of preparation. Not because of selection, but more as a final team-building exercise and a chance for them to garner more confidence. In most cases, athletes would reach personal bests on the test, which provided them with more reasons to feel confident about our training and how much they had committed themselves to the process. Also, any time a crew engages in an activity as challenging and painful as a two-kilometre test, you give further reason for that crew to come together in support of one another. It was essential to setting the stage for the final push to our Schoolboy Championships.

In a word, the Princeton boathouse was stunning. Perfectly situated. Aesthetically unparalleled. Not to mention the world-class facilities that were housed within the main building. Weights, ergs, a tank, all of it contained in one beautifully designed boathouse. We were incredibly fortunate to call this our training site for the next four days.

Greg, the head men's coach, came down from his office to meet the boys and welcome us for the week. Having lived in New Jersey for a number of years, his Canadian accent was slowly disappearing. With NCAA rules being as stringent as they were, not only were we forbidden to train with the Princeton crews, we couldn't even be on the water when they were. In his generosity, Greg assigned us specific times when we could be out training and not run the risk of rowing alongside a Princeton crew. Those rules hadn't existed back in 1982 when Neil brought us down for our March camp. He could let us do pieces with the varsity athletes. I was disappointed we couldn't go up against some fast college crews with our boys, but I also completely understood why and made sure we stayed out of their way.

With the boat ready and the boys warmed up from their work on the erg, we set out for our first row as a new coxed four. Josh was noticeably apprehensive; I would have been worried if he wasn't. The others, however, were relaxed and joking around, and this helped to put Josh at ease. They all seemed up for the challenge. Instead of racing the crew with the line-up we had at the Early Bird Regatta, with Josh on port side and sitting in bow seat, we decided to try him back on his preferred side: starboard and sitting in two seat. Plus, Daniel was very adept at changing sides and rowed equally well on both. It was the way they did things in Germany. Athletes learned how to scull first before learning how to sweep. Once they did move into a sweep boat, rowers became proficient on both sides. It just made sense.

After the crew rowed away from the dock, Winston and I loaded up our wakeless coach boat and set out to get the four ready for racing. Knowing that it could take a number of rows before they got used to the changes, we chose to sit back and watch. Once again, they knew what would make the boat fast, and any yelling from the coach boat wouldn't amount to much more than a frustrating experience for everyone.

Eight kilometres into the row, the crew was still struggling to find their rhythm. At each turnaround, we would offer some suggestions based on the feedback the crew and Sandy were providing, but it was taking longer than we had hoped for them to find their stride. As they set out for another trip of drills and steady-state, we followed along, watching closely for any signs of improvement. Finally Winston concluded, "I think they rowed better three weeks ago with Josh on port. I say we switch 'em back."

"It sure seems that way. This is taking longer than we have. Let's see how tomorrow goes. We can always change the rig mid-row and go from there," I suggested. And he agreed.

Back at the hotel, Tim and Elaine had lunch ready. They had once owned a catering company and had volunteered to organize all of the meals for this trip. The athletes wasted little time in diving into the spread that had been laid out.

I was pleasantly surprised with what Tim had concocted. He had previously joked that he'd never had to cook for a *vegan* before. If this were any indication of the food that was coming for the week, I'd be in good hands.

After lunch, Tim informed me that one of the boys' mothers had arranged for a truckload of produce to be dropped off, and that he would need some help unloading. Thinking a van might drop off a few bags of groceries, we were shocked to see a full delivery truck pull up with enough produce to feed the entire hotel. This was another example of the generosity and support we had from the rowers' parents.

Later, back at the hotel, I joined Siobhan in the weight room for a workout before dinner. I asked her how the girls were doing.

"Good. They're excited to see how much faster they can get in one week's time."

"Nice. Good to hear. What about selection? Any talk of that?"

"I told them we'd revisit that when we got home," she answered. I said we would likely do two days of seat racing, plus some erg testing. "I need to make it crystal clear about why we're going to switch, if in fact we do."

"Sounds fair. And you seem better about it, so that's good."

"I am. If we make the changes, it'll be hard for Ashley. But that's how things go sometimes. She knows that." Then, as I climbed onto the bike, she asked, "How's your foot?"

"Ugh. It still hurts. Looks as though it's the bike and elliptical machines for me until this thing mends. No biggy—a change of pace never hurt anyone."

After another delicious meal, the rowers cleaned up while we coaches shot the breeze over a beer with Tim and Elaine. This was one of the many enjoyable parts of coaching, a chance to sit around and chat with fun, passionate people.

Between Tim's interesting hockey stories and Winston's hilarious rowing ones, we listened and laughed until bedtime. It was a great ending to our first day. If this was a sample of the week that was coming, 2014 would easily go down as my favourite Princeton trip by far.

Later, and once the boys were in their rooms, I went around and said goodnight like I always did. Part of it was because it was my job, but the other bigger reason was because I enjoyed their company. They were a fun group of boys. Plus the mess, the smell, the jokes, all of it—every time I walked into one of their rooms, I was sixteen years old again and back in high school. I loved that about coaching.

They were all well recovered from the racing. It had been a good day. The row hadn't been so great, but we knew that after the erg test in the morning, we'd get back at it and figure things out. I went off to bed more excited about the week than I had been before we arrived. The boys seemed as excited about racing as Winston and I were. It was going to be a terrific ending to four years of coming here.

At breakfast the next morning, given what was on the schedule, the boys were their usual quiet selves. On competitive days like this, I left them to their own routines to prepare as they saw fit. We'd gone over all of the strategies that they would need for this two-kilometre test multiple times. Sure, this one was their last chance to reach a personal best, but we had nothing new to add to their bag of tricks. They were trained, rested, and ready to get started.

It was shortly after 10:00 a.m. when they finished their warm-up. I gave them their starting commands and they were away. Winston, Sandy, and I stood behind them watching intently. With a little less than a 1000 metres to go, the girls and Siobhan came into the room. I had never been one for allowing cheering during erg tests. I believed it was up to the rowers to figure out each kilometre on their own.

Yes, I sometimes offered one-on-one encouragement if I thought it would help, but otherwise I just watched. The other part of it for me was there was no cheering section in a boat race. There was just you and that voice in your head.

So when the girls began to encourage our boys, I had a choice to make. Leave it alone and let them feel like they were contributing to the boys' best efforts, or shut it down and run the risk of killing a potentially positive team moment. I chose to let them cheer. In the end, it was no big deal, and the girls felt welcomed and appreciated. Winston and I agreed it was a positive start to the morning.

As usual we had some personal bests and other scores that were just shy, but still solid performances. For example, Josh pulled 6:27. That score secured his place in our group, putting to rest any concerns the others may have had about his power output in the boat. Luc took four more seconds off his personal best and came in with a 6:03 performance. For a guy who barely reached "five foot twelve with messy hair," as we use to say, he was an outlier. His ability to push beyond his pain threshold was exceptional, even if the aftermath was ugly. When I came out of the building ten minutes later, I found him face down in the grass. I knelt beside him.

"You okay, Luc-monster?"

He moaned, turned his head, and replied, "I don't feel well, Jason."

I couldn't help myself. I laughed out loud. Insensitive? Perhaps. He knew I loved him.

"Hate to break it to you, Luc. But if you're going to go that hard, your body's going to object. Do you need some water?"

"No, I'm good."

"Okay, well if you're goin' to puke, at the very least turn your head. And lying there isn't helping much, my friend. So, when you can, try to get up and walk around. Okay?"

He moaned again.

I smiled as I walked off to find Winston.

On my way over to the boat, Daniel, looking unusually stressed, came up to me.

"What's up? How was that test for you?" I asked.

"Not great. I was distracted," he answered.

"Oh yeah, distracted by what? What did I miss?"

"Well, I've been thinking. I've got something to ask you and I don't think you're going to be too happy about it."

Moments that began with that kind of introduction never ended well. "Daniel, what's going on? What's on your mind?"

Expressionless, Daniel answered, "I want to go back to Ridley early and spend a few day with my parents. I want to fly back on Thursday night."

"What do you mean, you want to fly back early? What are you talking about?"

"If I wait to go back after our race this Saturday, I'll only see my parents for a few days. They're flying all the way from Germany. They want to see me graduate and spend some time with me. And I want to spend time with them too. Besides, with my dad's health, this is important to me."

"You're just realizing this now? Holy shit, Daniel!"

"I know it's not great. But—"

"Not great?" I interrupted him. "*Not great?* It's incredibly not great. I can't believe you're asking me this four days before we're supposed to race. We've got this close, and you want to risk screwing it up for the other guys, go back to Ridley, and spend some time with your folks? This is nuts." We both stared at each other for a moment. "I'm trying to get my head around the fact that you think this is a reasonable request."

There was a long uncomfortable pause. I was reeling.

"I spoke with Cosmo," Daniel added. "He's willing to fly down here Thursday after his exam and jump in the boat so that they can race. We've checked flights, it can work."

"You've checked flights? How long have you been scheming this idea? Forget it, I don't want to know. I need a moment to think about this." I walked off to find Winston.

"Holy crap!" I said.

"What the hell happened?" he asked.

I shook my head. "Daniel wants to fly back to the School on Thursday to see his parents. He doesn't want to race on the weekend. He thinks Cosmo can come down and fill in for him."

If I was mad, Winston was off the chart. In fact, I hadn't even finished telling him and he was storming across the patio in search of Daniel.

By now the boys knew what was going on. How could they not? Everyone could hear the yelling between Winston and Daniel.

Tim had arrived at the boathouse to set up lunch for the crews. I walked over to see if I could help. I needed something to do. Tim was as shocked as I was, which, in an odd way, I took comfort from. For a moment, I thought that I had completely lost touch with what was a reasonable request and what wasn't. It didn't solve our problem, but it gave me a moment of feeling justified in my anger toward Daniel. Meanwhile, the exchange between Daniel and Winston continued. Thank goodness we were the only ones at the course at that time of day. It got ugly.

Winston had flown down on his nickel to be with us for the week. He had given up time with his girls at home and, furthermore, this was time away from his business. He didn't have to be here. But, as he made it clear, he had agreed to commit to the crew and he was following through on that commitment. Only to have Daniel decide that he wanted something different and was willing to compromise the performance of the crew at the upcoming championship. He felt, as I did, that Daniel was being incredibly selfish and thinking only of himself and not the other boys.

Winston reminded him that he was a volunteer coach. He didn't take a dime for his services. He coached whom he wanted. He went where he wanted. He didn't need the money, nor did he want it. He only got involved with teams that he thought would appreciate his years of expertise and who shared his passion for rowing and going fast.

During lunch and after, their exchange hung heavy in the air. I wondered how on earth we were going to get past this problem and manage a productive and positive week for everyone.

"I need some time," said Winston. "I'll go back to the hotel with Tim. You take the boys out. I need to cool down. Fuck me, that boy is something else!"

I agreed to take them out and also call Jay to let him know what was up. I told him I needed to call Cosmo to see how he felt about coming down to fill in.

"If we are going to race with Cosmo, we need to make a plan," I said to Winston.

"Yeah, I get that," he agreed. "I'll see you back at the hotel. Me and Johnny Walker are going to have a long chat."

I laughed. At least we were starting to find some humour in this. "You behave, Winston."

"Don't worry."

The phone calls went well. With Jay in the loop and Cosmo on board, we designed a plan. Back at the hotel after our second row, I met with each member of our crew except Daniel. I wanted to get a sense of how the others were feeling and, more importantly, how they wanted to proceed.

"So, given what you know now, what do you think we should do?" I asked the group.

Surprisingly, it was our two quiet ones that spoke up first. "I completely understand how Dan's feeling. I mean, it's his dad. I would want to spend time with my dad, too," said Mathew.

"Yeah. I kinda feel for Dan here," Luc added. "He's in a tough situation. True, it's going to make things a little more challenging for us, but I want Dan to see his dad. And we can do this. We can make this work."

I had been expecting the same sort of outrage that Winston and I had felt and displayed. Now I was stunned at the boys' take on the situation. Both Sandy and Josh shared similar sentiments. They saw it as a completely reasonable request given the circumstances. They had no problem with Dan heading back early. By the time I left the room, their biggest concern was deciding on which movie to watch. I was flabbergasted.

After a quiet dinner, I phoned Robyn and filled her in on the day's events.

"You sound really disappointed, Jase."

"Are you kidding me? Robyn, I could come home right now and just screw the whole thing. I can't understand how Daniel thinks this is okay."

"I know this is really important to you. And that your perception of Daniel's lack of commitment is genuinely what's got you so riled up. But we're talking about Daniel's father here. Not just a race. I think you need to step back and look at the bigger picture. You have a young boy who lives away from home. His dad is sick, and he wants to see him. I understand that."

I was shaking my head. I didn't want to hear Robyn's take on the situation. After twenty years of living with a frustratingly level-headed partner, I wasn't surprised that she didn't see my side of it. It drove me crazy when she did it. I just wanted to be pissed at Daniel. Instead, she was trying to open me up to being understanding and compassionate. I wasn't ready for that. On some level, I needed to be right. Now my anger was coming from the fact that maybe I wasn't. That just maybe, perhaps, it was the boys who were right.

After hanging up the phone, I thought more about what Robyn had said. With lots more to process, I pulled out my journal and got to writing. Three pages later, I was more understanding of how the boys had responded to Daniel's request. All year long I had been speaking unapologetically about love in front of the boys. That it was love that was going to see us through to our best race. I encouraged them each and every day before practice, before each piece, during pieces even. Any time things got challenging, I told them to dig in and build the love that existed in their crew.

Little did I appreciate that they had been doing just that. They truly loved one another. That's what enabled them so easily to understand and empathize with Daniel's situation. They understood right from the get-go that our race was important, but that Daniel's time with his dad was more important. I had completely misconstrued my principled stance on commitment to serve my needs, not the crew's. I had argued that Daniel was putting his needs before those of our boat. The boys didn't see it that way. Instead, for them the crew's needs were Daniel's needs, period. If Daniel needed to see his dad, then that's what should happen. Clearly, it was their love for one another that made their decision so easy. As I had years earlier with my Shawnigan crews, I was still learning from my rowers. Slowly, maybe. But still learning.

Hobbling out to breakfast, I found Winston reading the paper and managing his morning emails. He looked rough.

"Whooooweeeeee, Johnny and I had a good chat. Man, I haven't done that in a while."

"Holy crap, Winston, you look like shit."

"Yeah, well—you should be inside my head right now."

"No thanks."

He took a sip of his coffee while I peeled an orange. "So, how are you doing with what happened yesterday?"

Winston thought for a moment. "Yeah, well, I'm still really mad at Daniel, but we do need to move forward. It's not like we're going to say, 'No, you have to stay here.' That wouldn't serve anyone. So let's just make the best of what we've got. We can still do this."

"Agreed."

"I wrote down this quote," he added. "I was going to share it with the boys before we head out this morning." He pulled out a piece of paper and read: "We are all faced with a series of great opportunities brilliantly disguised as impossible situations."

"Listen to you, fancy boy. Where'd you get that one?" I asked.

"Can't remember. It might have been Johnny Walker," he answered, then grinned and told me it was a quote from Charles Swindoll.

"Ha, I love it. I think it sets the stage beautifully. Thanks for that, Winston."

Neither one of us was a quitter. We now had one hell of a challenge in front of us. And, more importantly, we were both determined to see this through. We had 10 two-minute pieces scheduled for the morning, all at or above race pace, and some with starts and finishes. It was supposed to be a confidence-building exercise, but two pieces into the workout, it was apparent the row was heading in the wrong direction.

"Just hold on a sec, Sandy!" I called out over my megaphone. "Okay, this is a waste of time," I said to Winston.

"Yup. I say we head in and change the rig. Put Daniel in bow seat and back on starboard. Move Josh into three seat and back on port. Having him right behind Mathew will help him with his rhythm. Otherwise, this is going to be a shit show."

"Okay, let's do it. I've never coached a bucket rigged four, so this'll be fun. I'll have to let Cosmo know he'll be rowing on starboard when he comes down—certainly not ideal. But this line-up just isn't working," I replied.

With the boat on stretchers, Winston got right to work re-rigging while I gave our new spare a phone call.

"Cosmo, have you ever rowed starboard?"

"Not really. Maybe a few times in the tank."

"Well, guess what, my friend. You're going to this weekend."

The phone was quiet. "Okay."

"I want you to get over to the tank every day this week and spend some time on starboard. I'll send you some workouts for the erg, but I want you to warm up and cool down in the tank. Got it?"

"I got it," said Cosmo. "But Jason, why am I rowing on starboard?"

"The boat's not going well with Josh in bow, so we're going to change things up. It's all good. How are your exams going?"

"Pretty well. They're actually not that hard. I think I'm doing okay."

"Good to hear. Okay, keep me posted through email. And let me know when you're arriving on Thursday. You're going to be just fine, Cosmo. You'll head out to race on Friday, and you guys'll come down as best you can. No problem. I'll talk with you soon."

"You bet, Jason. Oh, and my dad's going to fly down with me. So, we'll just meet you at the course. Okay?"

"Perfect. Say thanks to your dad."

As I walked back to the boat, I noticed that Daniel was helping Winston with the rig. Smart boy!

"How's our Cosmo?" asked Winston.

"A little surprised. But you know Cosmo. He'll manage this."

Back on the water and warmed up again, we began our second attempt at the morning's workout. Just as we'd hoped, it clicked beautifully. The boys ended up having a great row and came off the water reinvigorated and actually looking forward to the weekend.

With each day, Josh rowed more effectively and the boat got faster. By Wednesday, even Winston and I were impressed with how quickly our crew was coming together.

For three years, I had used this row to do some short sprints and starts. The plan was to put the rate up as high as they possibly could without blowing up. In previous years, every crew had reached into the fifties. Hitting fifty strokes a minute in any boat let alone a coxed four was no easy challenge, but by the end the boys were not just hitting that target, they were holding it remarkably well. After our last piece of over-rating, I had Sandy do one more twenty-stroker at race pace. This was the moment that we had been heading for as a crew—when you slow things down from fifty-plus strokes a minute to the mid-thirties. The idea was that, with that much more time, the boat would light up, as the rate was achieved that much easier. At the end of the piece, I asked how it went. Even Mathew smiled. They were ready.

Our Thursday morning row was another solid workout. The crew was developing some consistency and, with that, some much-needed confidence as well. Given the circumstances, we couldn't have asked for a better last few days of preparation. Despite how Monday had been, the remainder of the week was positive. With the boats washed and now loaded onto the trailer, Tim took off for Mercer Lake in search of a good location for our weekend of racing.

Earlier in the week, I had purchased some graduation cards from the Princeton bookstore. The handy thing about training at Princeton was that our school colours were the same as our mascot's—a tiger. I wanted to write a note to each of the boys congratulating him on his graduation from Ridley. Given that I wasn't going to be at their graduation ceremony, I figured it was a simple gesture to acknowledge their accomplishments.

Before Daniel left for the airport, I gave him his card. I also added a note explaining that I was done with what happened and ready to move forward with him in support of the team. When he left, we were on as good terms as we could have hoped. The healing had begun, and we were both excited to see what June and July would bring our crew.

The rest of us left for the racecourse to meet up with Cosmo and try out our new bowman. However, once more, Mother Nature had different plans for us. After a beautiful week of blue skies and plenty of sunshine, a new weather system was moving in. Thunderstorms were now expected for much of the afternoon and evening, and quite possibly for the weekend as well.

The park where all of the boat trailers had jockeyed for position was packed. Amazingly, Tim had managed to find us a great spot, but the long hike to the finish line meant it was going to be a painful few days for me. My foot was still no better, and walking was proving more frustrating with each day.

We had no sooner rigged the boat and told the boys to get stretched when an announcement came over the speakers informing everyone that the course was closed for the remainder of the day. We looked at each other knowing exactly what that meant. Cosmo's first row on starboard would be in their heat the next day. When they heard the news, the boys were a bit stressed, to say the least.

"Look," I said. "Just like in Philly, we can't control the weather. Cosmo's had some time in the tank all week. It's what we've got. There's no point getting upset about something we can't change."

"What about an early morning row before racing starts?" asked Cosmo.

"Good idea, but they've already said because of the weather, there'll be no training rows allowed. Winston just told me they've moved the schedule ahead and will start racing first thing tomorrow morning. We go at 12.25 p.m. We've spoken with the coaches from Malvern; they're going to let us use their ergs to warm up. We're all good."

"Wait, didn't we beat them at Stotes?" asked Mathew.

"Yup. Can't say as we would've asked to borrow those ergs if we were racing the quad here," answered Winston.

Everyone laughed. It was time to go for dinner, and a good night's sleep.

CHAPTER FIFTEEN

MANY COACHES AND athletes in Canada refer to the Stotesbury Cup Regatta, the US Schoolboy Championships, and our own Canadian Schoolboy Championships as the Triple Crown of high school rowing. Although a few Ridley crews had achieved the honour, it had been many decades since.

Winston and I certainly didn't talk about it in front of the crew. We knew they were thinking about it. As they should have. It was something within their reach, but achieving all three titles was going to be challenging, regardless of how we were choosing to do it. Changing events. Changing athletes. This was going be some test. Furthermore, there were thirty-six crews in our event, which meant six heats of six boats. The first two crews in each heat would advance to the semi-finals the next morning, while the next two crews would race again that afternoon in the repachage. *Repachage* is French for "second chance." If you were in the top three in the repachage, you would advance to the semi-final. From the semis, the first two crews in each would go to the final. The next two would go to the petite final. It was a great system. It was as fair as they could make, and one of the reasons why so many schools entered. In my opinion, it was the most athlete-centred regatta of all. Any time you have a regatta organizing committee that incorporates a full FISA (Fédération Internationale des Sociétés d'Aviron/International Rowing

Federation) race schedule, you know that they want to ensure that the fastest crews make it into the finals.

An hour before our heat, the boys began their warm-up. A storm had come through in the night, but so far that morning things were looking all clear. With the oars and the boat ready, we made our way to the launch dock.

A regatta official, dressed in khaki pants, blue dress shirt and tie, and a United States Rowing Association rowing blazer, met us on the path. This was a class event, one of the other reasons that I enjoyed coming here. He went through his safety check before wishing the boys, as well as Winston and me, good luck.

With the crew ready to shove, I grabbed Cosmo's blade and helped them get away from the dock. As they tied in, it was no surprise that Josh was looking a bit anxious.

"Josh, put your hand in the water," I instructed him.

He sunk his left hand into the lake. "How's it feel?" I asked.

He looked confused. "I don't know. Wet?"

"Perfect. Just like home?"

He smiled. "Yup. Just like home."

"Probably a little cleaner here, but it's no different than what we've been training on. Understand?"

"I got this, Jason."

"I know you do. We wouldn't have put you in there if we didn't believe that."

Sandy called out for Cosmo to take a stroke and straighten the boat.

"There!" he said. "See! Starboard's easy, Cosmo!"

He laughed. Then Sandy called his crew to attention before rowing away.

"Have fun out there!" I yelled after them.

As had been the case in Philly, the course at Mercer Lake was 1500 metres. Even without the current, these races would be fast. Walking down to the 1000-metre mark, the place we would watch from, Winston and I were quiet. We both knew this was a long shot.

Getting settled at our new perch for the weekend, we ran into Todd Jesdale. He was considered an iconic junior rowing coach in the United States. He'd been coaching since the early 1960s and had achieved tremendous success both nationally and internationally. He and I had connected in England at the Henley Royal Regatta in 2012. He was coaching Shrewsbury at the time, and his crew defeated our Ridley boys on the Thursday of racing. Speaking with him after the race at Henley, it was clear to me that he was from a different era of coaching. He was a true gentleman. He both accepted my congratulations and acknowledged our boys' efforts. He told me some stories about Neil from back in the day, and we shared some good laughs. We later reconnected through my book, *Chariots and Horses*, and at a US rowing conference where we had a wonderful conversation.

He had recently returned stateside where he was coaching at a high school in Virginia. Todd was here with that crew. It was great to see him. We had a brief catch-up and wished each other well for the weekend.

"I think they're away," said Winston as we both stared toward the starting gates.

"They look okay," I said a few moments later.

"They sure do. In fact, I think they're out front!" said a very surprised Winston.

They were indeed out front and hanging on to about a half-second lead when they went past us and stretched that out to a full second by the time they won the heat. Their winning heat time put them third overall. We had made it through the toughest part of the day. We also knew that the competition would only get stiffer with each race, but the boys were convinced they could race faster. So were Winston and I. Cosmo had caught a couple of little crabs in the early part of the race and knew that he would get more comfortable as racing progressed. The girl's quad had finished second in their heat, but once again were almost twenty seconds back from the leaders. They would have to find a significant amount of boat speed if they wanted to medal.

Saturday morning, the boys were different. I could sense it as we drove to the course. Friday, they had been thinking about surviving the race. Today, they intended to win. Our strategy was similar to that for the Mother's Day Regatta: get out front and try to drop as many crews as we could in the first 500 metres. Because we were an unknown crew with a fast start, if we could disappear from the line of sight of the other crews, my experience told me younger athletes were more likely to pack it in early.

Once more, Winston and I stood silently waiting for 10:55 a.m., the boys' starting time. Two minutes into the race, we had a déjà vu moment when our crew came into sight. They were holding onto a very narrow lead. The field was tight. There were five crews all within striking distance of one another. But, as they had done the day before, the boys managed to hold onto and win, posting the fastest qualifying time of the three semi-finals.

Their excitement was hard to contain. It wasn't just that they could possibly win this event; they'd never been in races this close before. They were obviously enjoying the thrill of intense competition.

"We can go faster," said a much more confident Cosmo. "We just have to break away as much as possible at the start and push for the line sooner."

"Agreed. This is where our fitness is going to shine," I added. "I'll guarantee no other crew here has done the work that we have. So, just like Cosmo said, let's extend the start phase of the race. Keep the rate up for ten more strokes, Mathew. Okay, Sandy?"

"If you can knock the wind out of these crews early, they'll fold," added Winston. "But, in order to do that, you have to focus on your own three feet. Everyone keep your heads in the boat. Understand?"

They were all listening intently.

We'd also just heard that they'd moved the start time up because of another storm system coming in, so that meant we would head off in less than two hours. Plenty of time for us, not so much for the other crews.

"They won't be nearly as recovered as you'll be," I added. "We can't emphasize enough how important it is for you to be really aggressive off that start."

I could feel my excitement build. It was times like this I wished *I* were racing in a few hours.

"Like Jason said, make it so that if they want to play with us, they'll have to be willing to hurt as much as you are. Got it?" Winston wasn't much for mincing words.

We had the boys rehydrate and refuel, then stretch and relax as much as possible. With thirty minutes until we launched, I went around and checked on each of them. "How are you doing, Josh?" I asked.

"Great. Jason, this is so much fun," he answered.

"Good. It's supposed to be," I said smiling.

"I understand that, but I didn't know what to expect. I didn't know we'd come together this quickly and that these other crews would be this fast. The racing has been so exciting."

"Nice. Good to hear. Well, you get one more shot. Make sure you enjoy it, okay?"

"Don't worry, I will."

We couldn't have asked for a better time for Josh. To come down here as our spare and have the experience that he was having. A personal best on the erg. A few days of solid training. And now this? What a week it had been. We were thrilled for him. Hell, for all of them.

I checked over the oars and the boat one more time, both to make sure that everything was secure and because I needed something to do.

Finally, it was time to go. We called the boys in and had one last word just to make sure that they were clear on the race plan. Then we were off again—going out this time as the favourites to win. Hardly the place we thought we'd be in a little more than twenty-four hours earlier.

Waiting in line to get on the dock, we heard something I would've never guessed we'd hear this far from home. "Good luck, Ridley!"

We turned to see who it was. The E.L. Crossley crew that we had leant some equipment to in Philadelphia was standing there with their boat. They'd just raced and won the junior boys quad event. Our crew acknowledged the gesture and congratulated them on their victory, then made their way to the dock.

This time, Winston and I were joking around as we waited for the race to start. We were almost giddy by this point. The exhaustion from the drama that we'd been through in the last few days had taken its toll. It was unprecedented for both of us. It's not like we doubted them at this point; it's just that given all that they'd been through, it was crazy to think they were possibly five minutes from winning.

Watching the race come down, there were five even boats, with one clearly out front. "Would you look at that," said Winston. "They're doing exactly what we talked about. This race is over."

Coming past us, they were just shy of open water on the field. And they weren't letting up. Within three races, they'd come far enough as a crew that any coach watching would've been hard-pressed to tell that this was only the third time they'd rowed together.

I turned to Winston; my gruff and tough coaching partner was teared up. I reached out to shake his hand. "Congratulations, Winston. Thanks for all of your help, my friend."

"You bet. That was fuckin' impressive."

Back at the trailer de-rigging the boat, we were inundated with dozens of young athletes from the other crews. That was the other thing I liked about this regatta: the majority of the coaches here understood that regardless of whether you won or you lost, you found the winning crew and congratulated them.

"Dude, you guys were crazy fast off the start. I was like, whoa, where'd they go?"

"Thanks. Thanks, very much," said a very satisfied but gracious Cosmo.

Then the Canucks became a bit of a novelty for the other crews. With all of the congratulations over, the young American boys began to ask our boys to pronounce all of the classic words that meant we were from north of the border.

"Okay, say *about*. Or, wait, no, no, say . . . say *boat*!"

Yes, these young teenagers who had been racing one another for a national rowing title less than sixty minutes earlier were now discussing the finer details of being Canadian. It was as it should be; they had competed fiercely against one another, but now were realizing that despite the subtle differences in how we pronounced certain words, we were all pretty much the same.

It had been quite a day for us, as well as for some of the other Canadian crews. E.L. Crossley had won, as did the girls' double from Holy Cross, and Dan de Groot from Governor Simcoe had easily won the senior boys' single as he had the week before at Stotes. During the medal presentation, I joined the Ridley parents who had made the trip down. Everyone was incredibly appreciative of the efforts made by our athletes. It was also nice to see Sandy launched into the water by his crewmates, a long-held tradition in rowing. Bill, his dad, was glowing.

Back at the trailer we had a brief chat before heading back to the hotel to shower and leave for the airport.

"I hope you were all paying attention when those American crews came up to you after our final and said what they did about the start of the race. At this age group, it can be such a huge advantage to break away early and discourage the other crews. We have to carry that lesson forward to our Schoolboy when we get home, and then again in England. Understood?" I didn't want that moment to go by unnoticed.

"Furthermore, Daniel sent me a text congratulating you guys for winning. I'm sure you've been in touch with him since. But his text raises the point: what we've been through in the last week has been like nothing Winston and I have ever experienced as athletes or coaches. I know I speak for both of us. What you guys pulled off these last two days was nothing short of miraculous. Your maturity. Your patience with one another. Your determination. Your care for one another. Your love. All of it came through in how you showed up as a crew and as individuals. You've heard me say this many times before, but let me say it again: You boys got the race you deserved."

They smiled and sheepishly looked at one another. They could sense that both of us were extremely proud of them.

CHAPTER SIXTEEN

————⊦ ⊦————

WHEN I MET with Ed and Jay back in the fall, we had discussed the date of the US Schoolboy Championships at Princeton and how to resolve the conflict with the boys' graduation ceremonies. Knowing how important this regatta was to the crew, Ed had agreed to postpone graduation by twenty-four hours. That was a huge concession from the School, but it meant that we had to fly the boys home Saturday night directly after the regatta. It made for a hectic departure but was worth it in the end. Cosmo won the Headmaster's Award, one of the School's most prestigious, and Luc went home with the Athlete of the Year Award. Not only did it recognize accomplishments, which for Luc there were many, it was also a reward for an athlete's attitude and commitment to his or her individual sport. It was great to see such a soft-spoken soul like Luc be recognized for his efforts.

With school now officially over, there was nothing more to focus on other than our preparation for the upcoming Canadian Schoolboys in two weeks' time. That was a huge advantage for us. I knew what life at those West Coast schools was like at this time of year, and it wasn't like what we were experiencing. They were thick into their exams, and their training was taking a back seat.

We met at the course Monday afternoon and, after a long hiatus from the quad, went out for a spin. Both Winston and I were encouraged to see how quickly the boys picked up from where they had left off back in Philly. They hadn't missed a beat.

After spending the majority of April and May in small boats, we would now focus solely on the two boats they would be racing. Every session from here on served a specific purpose. Some would be longer recovery rows. Others would cover precise racing strategies and would be tailored to how we wanted to come down the course. Included in that would be lots of speed work and over-rating. It was a great way to continue building confidence and allow the crew to get used to the higher racing rates.

We had maintained our weight training in Princeton and intended on carrying it through to England. We had only backed off one day of hard training for both Stotesbury and the US Schoolboy. The boys' aerobic base was so well established, we weren't too concerned about their ability to recover from those 1500-metre races. For our Schoolboy, we would have six 2000-metre races over three days and, therefore, we would execute a more calculated taper for the event.

Our first Tuesday back, the erg and tank session was intense. We continued to push the seven-minute pieces at sub-race pace. If the current was running and the wind was blowing as they had at Henley in 2012, we knew we'd have to be more prepared for those longer more difficult races. As we had done all year, we linked the ergs in pairs using the sliders. It kept the boys awake to their technique, created a competitive situation, and made them rely on one another for their best performances.

After nine months of encouraging the crew to build the trust and love among them through these hard sessions, I no longer had to. They had picked up that message and built on it. It was a common occurrence to hear one or more of them say, "Come on boys, build the love," moments before each piece began. They had become a very tight unit on and off the water.

As predicted, Tim's Shawnigan crew had been dominating the West Coast regattas. More specifically, his coxed four had won every race so far this season. Not surprisingly, we knew they'd be our biggest challenge from the west.

As was more often the case these days, US schools were coming up to race their crews at our national championships to see how they fared against the best Canada had to offer. One of those crews was the coxed four from Mathews School in Virginia. They had won that event at Stotesbury two weeks earlier but chose not to attend the US Schoolboy Championships the following weekend. Therefore, we hadn't raced against them, which made them an unknown entity.

My feeling was that any crew in the lane next to you is worth racing. If they've travelled a long way to get into the lane, they're worth racing harder. Winning Stotes in the coxed four was quite an accomplishment. We all knew they would be a contender and another crew that we would have to keep an eye on. As for the quad, we had the same local crews to contend with plus a number of unknown entries. We'd know more once Thursday's racing was done.

Josh and Steve were back at it in the double. Their coach, Jack, was thrilled about the experience that his bowman had in the US, but wasted little time in running the two of them through some hard workouts in preparation for their upcoming event. They knew they'd be in tough. Although getting into the final was doable, landing on that podium would require a bit of luck.

Jesus was facing an even more daunting challenge. His event was chock-full of twenty-four talented lightweight athletes who easily had twenty pounds on him. If he got through the heat, that would be outstanding. In typical Jesus fashion, if he was worried about the formidable hurdle that he faced, you wouldn't know it. He was his usual positive self and simply looking forward to having the best race that he could on the day.

As for the girls, they were embarking on the selection process that Siobhan had laid out for them in Princeton. In two or three days we'd know which four athletes would be racing in the quad and who would be backing into the gates in the single. The process would likely be stressful for the girls, but a great experience that would only make them faster.

Further to the challenge of selecting the crew, Siobhan and I had agreed with Jay that if the girls could close the gap on Shawnigan by Schoolboy, they could join us in England. There was a new club event for the girls' quads at Henley. It was the equivalent to ours. With Shawnigan already committed to going, and Siobhan's crew getting faster, it could prove the ideal opportunity to showcase our girls' rowing program overseas.

At first the news didn't go over too well with our boys.

"That's bullshit!" said Daniel. "I've been training three years to get a shot at going to Henley. And now they get to join us after a few months? That doesn't seem right." The others concurred.

Understandably, the boys saw England as something that had to be earned over a number of years, and capped off with a decisive victory at home. But these circumstances were different and they just had to move on. Having the girls attend Henley was an important part of the strategy for building the entire program in the future.

"Look, it doesn't affect us whatsoever. If they come over, they'll be staying on their own. Our plans are independent of theirs. I know you've heard me talk about 'trip and tracksuit' and earning the right to represent Ridley. I get that. But I've been trying to build the women's program since I got here. If these girls come with us, it'll create some much-needed attention and help support the program. So I would ask that you be encouraging to them. I understand your point. I do. But you just have to trust that this is what's best for Ridley rowing. Let it go, and focus on having our best races come Schoolboy. Okay?"

By now all of the events surrounding Daniel and what happened at Princeton had eased. Daniel and the boys, as well as Winston and I, were back to our old selves. The playful banter resumed. Our relationships grew even stronger as a result of the adversity we had faced.

When I first arrived at the School in 2010, I produced a wish list that would help kick-start Ridley's rowing program. But there was one problem—the School's coffers were empty. Undaunted, I went looking for a donor. John Walker had graduated from Ridley in 1958. During his time at the School, he was both a prefect and an athlete. Football was where he had made his mark. After two years at McGill University he had joined his brother working in the family business, a quarry as well as a road construction company. They took that venture and ran with it.

Now that John was retired, philanthropy was a big part of his life. He was responsible for funding many local community projects both anonymously and through the Walker name. His oldest son, Dave, and I had been on numerous sports teams together at Ridley; we had both rowed for Neil on the heavy eight. I had known Mr. Walker, as he was to us then, since I was a young boy. He attended our football games as a passionate voice of encouragement on the sidelines and even travelled with us to our regattas. He was a keen supporter of Neil. When John heard that I was coming back to coach, he was eager to get involved. At our initial lunch meeting, he hinted that my wish list was too short and suggested that I add a few items.

"If you don't ask, you don't get, Jase."

I obliged.

"Now that's more like it," he said, looking at the new list. "I'll have a cheque to you this week."

We went shopping. We purchased the van. Two coxed fours. Another coach boat engine. Numerous other big-ticket items that allowed us to get up and running more quickly. At the time, we had some big athletes rowing with us. As a crew, there were four of them that averaged around 195 to 200 pounds. For high school rowers that was big. To manage that size, I ordered a coxed four that would support those body types. John insisted on naming one of them the *Carl*

Dorland, after my dad. John saw this as his way of ensuring that my dad's legacy within the Ridley rowing program wouldn't soon be forgotten. Eight months after that, at our 2011 Schoolboy, Dad and John christened the boat. Dad was thrilled. In fact, when John passed him the glass of champagne, instead of pouring it over the bow of the boat as is customary, he drank it instead. Everyone laughed. It was a classic "Dad" moment.

When the 2010 team graduated in 2012, we were left with a boat that was better suited for university or national team rowers. Our current crop of boys were big, but not that big. I called our rep at Hudson Boat Works and asked if we could make a trade. With a little top-up to cover the two years of use, we had a deal. In the fall of 2013, a new coxed four arrived. Once again, I asked Dad to christen it. Trouble was, he didn't remember the first time. His dementia, which had begun earlier as an annoying forgetfulness, which we joked and teased him about, had become more serious.

It was tough to watch. As a younger man, he had been incredibly knowledgeable. He read voraciously. He was a dynamic and articulate conversationalist. He was interesting to listen to as well as interested in what others had to say. And he had a terrific sense of humour. I've never met anyone who could laugh at himself as easily as he could. I commented many times to Robyn and Mataya, "I wish you had met my *dad* then."

As too many of us know, watching a parent or any loved one fall victim to dementia or Alzheimer's is brutal to witness. Of all of the diseases to take hold in one's autumn years, they're among the worst. Tragic. Cruel. Sad. Unfair. There were lots of ways to describe it. It was just shitty. He was still here physically, but mentally he was slowly leaving us and, worst of all, he knew it.

Putting him in a care home when we did had been one of the toughest things we'd ever done. Dad's condition prevented him from understanding why he couldn't be at home with his wife of over sixty years. Once his circumstances were explained to him, he would settle and seem accepting of the situation, only to wake up the next morning asking the same question. It was a painful cycle for him to live through and for others to watch.

In those first few weeks, Dad was on suicide watch. Having your father look you straight in the eye and say, "I don't want to live anymore," is a moment you don't soon forget. We made the best of the situation and eventually arrived at a place where he could exist without too much distress.

He was staying at Henley House in the north end of St. Catharines. It was close to Mom, and with daily visits from her and Paul, weekend visits from Scott and his wife, Rose, Dad managed. I got there as often as I could. On days when I didn't have to drive the boys back to the School from the course, I would stop in to visit on my way home. Other times, once Mataya was in bed, I would visit with him late in the evening.

Dad was the consummate sports fan. He loved all of Toronto's teams: the Leafs, Jays, Argos, and Raptors. We would watch as many of the games as we could on TV. Of course, the quality of those visits varied according to how his day had gone and which nurse was on that evening. As at many care homes across the country, staff used drugs to sedate their patients. If Dad was "sun-downing," a term used to describe dementia patients who became unsettled and agitated when the sun began setting, then he would be drugged to control his outbursts.

On some level, I understood the predicament, but there were other times when I would think, *Christ, I wouldn't treat my dog like this*. It was hard. Sitting there with him, holding his hand while he continually nodded off, I would say softly, "Dad, why don't you just let go? You don't need this."

Other times, he was incredibly lucid. He would ask about the School, about the boys and how things were looking for England. It was shocking to have him so "with it" on those nights. When I shared the tribulations I was experiencing, he was always saddened to hear of it. He remembered his own challenges running the program in his day, but encouraged me to keep at it and not get too discouraged.

I chose the week after being in the US to christen the new boat. It was Wednesday afternoon when Mom and Dad pulled up in the car. Paul jumped out first to grab Dad's walker while Mom made her way over to meet with the crew. Winston and the boys were incredibly patient and understanding of the circumstances surrounding my dad's condition. They all took the time to shake his hand and politely introduce themselves. They knew how much this meant to me.

It was hilarious to hear Dad once again ask Daniel if he played basketball. As he had a dozen times before, Daniel politely answered, "No, Mr. Dorland, I row for your son—remember?"

Oh well, I figured. *Once a basketball coach, always a basketball coach.*

Paul brought along an old bottle of champagne. We popped it open, and with some gentle prodding had Dad say a few words as he poured its entire contents over the bow. It was awesome. To have him there and still involved at this stage of the game—priceless.

Like so many young boys of my generation, I had spent a lot of my time trying to earn my father's approval and make him proud. It was a bizarre pastime to be sure. But nonetheless, one that consumed so much of our time. That desire was likely fuelled by an even older generation that believed emotions were something kept under wraps, and that love was inherently served up with a healthy dose of toughness. In my case, I chose sport—rowing, obviously—as my vehicle for earning Dad's attention. There were certainly some moments when I knew he was excited about my accomplishments, none more than the day that I shared I was going to the Olympics. The look in his eyes and on his face was of genuine approval. He was proud. And I'll never forget it.

Watching him christen the new boat, I was the proud one. Proud of a gentle man who had brought such grace and dignity to a world that could, at times, be anything but those things. His impact on sport was profound. I often saw him as a paradox within it, consistently going against the ever-strengthening stream of macho rhetoric that perpetrated the idea of sport as manly and combative. Instead, he encouraged a softer, even feminine, tone through his coaching and mentoring. He insisted that competition be about all of the good things it could be, even though at times he was publicly referenced as a fuddy-duddy for his "old-fashioned" beliefs in manners and humility and all things proper. If Dad was ever guilty of anything, it was of trying to fan a nostalgic flame of how sport could be. Of how sport should be. He held onto that flame right through to his last years of coaching.

I must have frustrated and confused him to no end when he watched me compete. Despite his progressive teaching and mentoring in those early years, I was obsessed with winning for all of the wrong reasons. Now I was grateful to have finally come around to his philosophy. On some level, I was hopeful that he understood how fortunate and grateful I felt for having him as my dad. I couldn't have asked for better.

CHAPTER SEVENTEEN.

———| |———

ON THE MONDAY after graduation, I'd had the pleasure of meeting Daniel's parents, Anja and Josef, who came down to the boathouse while we were rigging the boats for our first row. The eighty-year-old Josef looked amazing, despite his health concerns. He still had a mischievous twinkle in his eyes, and he greeted us with a firm handshake and warm smile. His English was spotty and most of our conversation happened through either Daniel or his mom. Anja apologized for the circumstances that we faced at the US Schoolboy, and added that, regretfully, there should have been more communication, and sooner, about what they had planned.

In hindsight, as much as I appreciated her comments, truth be told I was grateful for how everything had played out. Honestly, if Daniel had come to us months before and said that he wanted to take a pass on US Schoolboys, given Cosmo's situation with his exams, we wouldn't have gone. We would've simply decided to come home after Stotesbury. Winston and I would've never agreed ahead of time to having an athlete come down the night before his first race. As had been the case all year long, everything had turned out perfectly. Furthermore, trusting that everything was happening exactly as it was supposed to produced yet another memorable experience for the group, one that resulted in some exciting wins and tremendous life lessons.

We also talked with Anja and Josef about the boys going to Germany two weeks before Henley and training at Daniel's rowing club in Dusseldorf. Daniel had run the idea by us months earlier, but I wasn't sold on the notion. He saw it as a way to get home sooner and spend time with his dad. I sympathized with that but saw it as adding to an already expensive trip. For Winston and me, it also meant more time away from our families. And it presented a logistical nightmare in terms of flights and transporting our oars and other equipment. Basically, I had been building a case to not go.

When I spoke with Anja, she put all of my concerns to rest. I began to see the possibilities. Yes, it got Daniel home sooner, but it also created a focused preparation camp for the crew. Two weeks before the very regatta that we'd been training for all year long, we'd have limited distractions. She had a friend with a hostel in the heart of the city that could accommodate us and make reasonably priced meals available. The rowing course was a short bike ride away. There would be no rental fee for our shells at Daniel's club. Within the space of fifteen minutes, she had me convinced Dusseldorf might just work.

With less than a week until the beginning of our Canadian Schoolboy regatta, there was nothing left to do but manage the days leading up to it. Not only did the boys know they were capable of winning both races, they knew they were favoured to do so. Therefore, it was important for me to make sure they were aware of what was expected of them if they did come across that line first. Given the time that we had, I took the opportunity to revisit some key components of our philosophy about preparation and competition. Although we hadn't had reason to say anything thus far, because of the hometown crowd and who would be in attendance, I wanted to make sure we were all on the same page about how to win.

Since the Seoul Olympics, a trend had developed on the national and international rowing scene whereby when crews won, one or more members of the team would stand up in the boat, with arms raised signifying their victory. Personally, I wasn't a big fan of that behaviour. I was always curious about how those individuals mustered the strength to even stand so soon after racing. But that aside, I believed it sent the wrong message. I was fine with quietly celebrating, but never at the expense of other crews in the race. It was unsportsmanlike conduct, plain and simple. I believed that if championship regattas were decided with best two out of three racing, rules would probably be put in place so that crews didn't celebrate inordinately having won the first race, much like when football players got penalized for celebrating touchdowns with too much enthusiasm.

The same went for the all too familiar "we're number one" index finger that some athletes raised on the podium, especially during photo ops. For a number of reasons, I saw that gesture as more of a fleeting falsehood than anything, and most definitely an inappropriately cocky response. Yes, if you were standing in the middle of the podium, it was because you had won. But if you did the race again the next day, there was a chance you might not. I wanted our boys to appreciate that fact and show more respect for other competitors and our sport.

The other conversation centred on losing. I wanted to make sure that our crew was okay with the fact that they might be beaten. I saw this conversation as one of the most important, not only from a holistic approach, but also from a strategic one. We wanted our crew to have their best races in a week's time. If that happened, there was a good chance they'd be the victors. If they were worried about losing, however, they'd be directing their energy toward something that wouldn't help them win. With every crew that I had coached since meeting Robyn, I had made a point of having this discussion. My aim was to demystify the notion of what losing might look like. Or, more specifically, what they would make it mean.

Invariably, our society sees losing as a punishment and winning as a reward. They are neither. Athletes can still lose and have a personal experience that resembles being rewarded. And, conversely, they can win and still experience a sense of loss. As a society, we've made those two outcomes mean something more than what they are, which is one of the many reasons why so many young athletes leave sport to begin with. If they're not winning, then their experience is that of being punished. Who signs up for that?

Once our boys understood that life would go on, and that eventually they'd have another race and another challenge, and that losing wouldn't define them as people, then there was nothing to worry about. In my mind it was a logical conversation. Tactical through and through. They had to accept that losing was something they could live with; it didn't make them weak or any less intent on winning.

It was a discussion that I entertained with other coaches quite frequently. They saw this part of my philosophy as a shortfall, that on some level I was less competitive because I made losing mean "you got beat by a better team and now have more work to do," instead of the status quo, which was, "you're a loser and I hope you feel like shit because of it." They obviously didn't know me. I liked winning as much as the next guy, in my day, probably more. And any time the boys went into a race, it was our obvious intention to try to win. Therefore, we made our goals about all of the things that would allow us to show up with the best chance of doing just that: winning. With those important elements understood, we began the best final ten days of race preparation that I had ever experienced as a coach.

Friday racing went off without a hitch. It was overcast. Conditions were fast and fair and expected to stay that way right through to Sunday. I was excited to get these races going. As much as the regattas in the US had been fun, we preferred the longer 2000-metre course. I always had. Knowing the fitness of our crew, I knew that it would take a special group of athletes to be able to match the pace we intended on setting, but it was going to be a process. The boys had to be patient.

With the formidable schedule of racing they faced over the next three days, managing their energy output was essential to having their best performances come Sunday. Our prescribed race plan for the heats and semi-finals was simple: get out front and stay there. Nothing fancy. No big sprints at the finish. Just get across the line first and in one piece. We had no choice; six races was ambitious. Also, with that sort of long-range racing strategy, there was a good chance we may not have the fastest times on each day. Given the personalities we had in our group, we knew that wasn't going to sit well. Regardless, we kept hammering it home to them: Sunday's races were the ones that counted.

The selection process that Siobhan had used with her girls produced a different line-up for the quad. After months of struggling to have her off-water power transfer into the boat, Brigitte was finally able to generate enough boat speed to surpass Ashley and join the crew. A challenging moment for both coach and athletes, but that's the nature of sport: it's a competitive arena.

Ashley would now be racing in the girl's lightweight single and travelling as the spare to England if the girls were to meet the challenge that had been laid out for them. Based on the results of their first heat, the likelihood of that happening was looking quite bleak. Although they finished second to Brentwood, they were still fourteen seconds back. Siobhan's new line-up was faster, but the question remained: were they capable of putting together a 2000-metre race that would land them on the podium? They still had two races to figure that out. And, given that the heat was their first official race as a crew, there was reason enough to believe they just might pull it off.

Our coxed four won their heat easily but, as we had predicted, did so with the third-fastest time. Mathews, from Virginia, was two seconds faster. The American crew rowed well and looked strong, but neither Winston nor I were convinced they could match our boys over the longer 2000-metre course. It may not seem like much at first glance, but tacking an extra 500 metres onto a race is a significant game changer. There is an expression in rowing: "The race begins at the 1000-metre mark." We would find out soon enough who could handle that extra distance and who couldn't.

Josh and Steve finished third in their heat, but four seconds back. Not a huge amount of time to make up, but sizable enough to know the toughest racing was still to come. Jesus's season came to an end in his heat. He placed fifth but was pleased with the race and accepted the fact that he had simply been beaten by bigger and stronger athletes; there was no shame in that. It was now time to cheer on his teammates.

A little more than two hours later, the boys' quad came down the course and won their heat. They looked comfortable and relaxed, once again following our instructions perfectly. Blessed Trinity, a local school we had previously beaten at the Mother's Day Regatta, posted a two-second-faster time. The boys were pleased to be advancing in both of their events, but it was clear to us they were struggling with our limiting race plan. They weren't used to holding back. And, with multiple crews having raced faster than they had, we could sense their displeasure.

Saturday, the sun came out. The conditions remained ideal. There was a slight breeze, but nothing that would affect the day's results. Despite a tougher semi-final, Josh and Steve closed to within three seconds of the winning crew, thereby claiming an outside lane as theirs for the Sunday finals. Two hours later, the quad seemed determined to post the fastest time for this event as well. Despite our best efforts in containing their competitive mindset, they won their race by twenty seconds, beating Blessed Trinity's time in the other semi by ten. It appeared that we had hit our taper nicely, and that our boys had come to race this weekend.

The girls continued to gather steam. Although they had lost to Brentwood by five seconds in their heat, they defeated them in the semi, posting the same time as the Shawnigan girls' quad. You could sense a dramatic shift in their confidence. They knew they were in the hunt for finals the next day. If they could manage an even better race within twenty-four hours, they'd be on their way to England.

Knowing the boys still had their noses out of joint regarding the times from Friday, we weren't surprised to see them dominate their coxed four semi-final. It appeared they were intent on sending a strong message to both Mathews and Shawnigan Lake Schools, which were in the other semi. As they came by the Island, they looked relaxed and in control, but they were pushing a lot harder than they had the previous day.

Winston and I were surprised to see the Mathews crew defeat Tim's Shawnigan boat so easily. We had heard that Tim was dealing with some sickness among his boys, but we didn't think it would affect them that much. The Mathews crew looked strong, but still finished four seconds back from our crew. It would be an exciting final.

It was Sunday, the day of the finals. "Where's our Luc-monster?" I asked as the others quietly rummaged through their backpacks, sorting out their racing gear, food, and water for the day.

"Right here, Pappa-Jay," Luc answered back.

I turned to see his smiling face entering our boat bay through the back door.

"You all set, Luc? It's going to be an exciting day."

"You know it. I can't wait."

"Atta boy!"

Winston and I went over the coxed four and quad multiple times to ensure everything that had to be tight was. It was one of my biggest stresses. Given all that these boys had sacrificed to get here, it was our job to make sure that the equipment was not going to fail them.

The weatherman had been right thus far. Fair racing conditions were the order for the day, with a small chance of thunderstorms later in the afternoon. The course was relatively calm when crews began heading out for their chance to proclaim themselves national champions. Anyone who had been here twelve months earlier would've noted the stark contrast from the previous year's weather.

Knowing a podium finish was a long shot, Josh and Steve went out in search of their best race to end the season. They managed to finish fifth. Given their circumstances, they had done well to finish that high in the ranking.

After months of patiently waiting for her crew to click, Siobhan's girls chose their final to do it. They had a spectacular race, finishing a close second to Shawnigan. Reflecting upon how far they had come since their first encounter with a notable Shawnigan crew back in March, the Ridley girls were well deserving of their accomplishment. They were now on their way to Henley.

With their washroom visits complete, the boys gathered at the back of the bay and began their visualization exercise, otherwise known as mental rehearsal. When I was an athlete, I thought it was a bunch of hooey. Now, as a coach, I was familiar with the research and had seen the impact of what proper mental rehearsal could do. A Shawnigan rower from my 2004 crew put it this way: "When I finish visualizing the race, there's nothing left for me to do but get out of the way and let it happen." I figured that if a teenage boy could articulate his experience of mental rehearsal this clearly, pursuing it as a strategic practice was worthwhile.

Sandy took the crew through a race simulation, during which they visualized their best race. Everything was about detail. The key was to involve all of the senses. Imagining the sounds. The smells. The sights you would see while sitting in the boat before and during the race. Even the salty sweat taste in your mouth. What did the oar handle feel like in your hand? Just create that moment, and make it as real as you possibly could. The best that you could. As I always told them, "It's your race; make it as perfect as possible."

The final part was about generating the emotion that you wanted to associate with the experience of racing. How did you want to feel sitting in the gates waiting for the race? Calm and confident? Or nervous and unsure? You pick! How about with 1000 metres gone? What did you want to link to that part of the race? And, finally, what feelings did you want to associate with crossing the finish line? Proud and fulfilled? Or regretful and ashamed? Again, pick the best ones. It's your race to control. It's not like someone else was going to say, "No, you can't choose that emotion; that's wrong."

Years earlier, I had used this exercise with an athlete who would monitor his heart rate. It was remarkable to see how his body reacted physiologically to circumstances that were created in his mind's eye. He even felt the need to stretch upon completion. It was science that had originally enticed me into using this tool but, having seen the benefits, I was convinced it was instrumental in leading athletes to high performance.

When I heard that Mathew's dad, Mirek, was a massage therapist, I asked him if he would lend his expertise in helping the boys recover between races. His hands had been working their magic the past two days. As the boys began their visualization, Mirek quietly set up his table at the back.

With their visualization and massages done, our crew jumped onto the ergs. Athletes were given only thirty minutes from the first call of the race to the starting horn. I believed in completing a good portion of the warm-up before heading out onto the water. Thirty minutes just wasn't enough time in my opinion.

Winston and I stood by the large bay doors looking out at the races going by as Sandy called out instructions to the boys behind us. The whirring of those ergs was a welcome sound. It meant we were moments from heading to the dock. Winston was his usual self: playful and chatty. But I could tell that even he had brought a little more business with him for the day.

"All good, Sandy?" I asked as we gathered as a group before our race was called.

A simple nod was his reply.

"Okay, this is it. Just like in practice. Do what you're capable of and the results will take care of themselves. Having said that, one length open is all we need. Do you understand? No sprint, Sandy. Just get them across the line. Everyone clear on that?"

I looked intently at each of them. "You have a quad race ninety minutes after this one. No screwing around!"

They heard me that time.

"Like Jason said, get out fast and sit there," Winston added. "Dictate the race early, and let the others chase you down the course. If they move, you move. Understood?"

With that we walked to the dock. I stood back as they got into the boat. I loved seeing their one-foot push-off. A small detail, perhaps, but they looked so disciplined, so ready. I stood quietly and took a little longer to watch them row away. This was it. Our last race in the four.

Amidst my nerves and usual concern, I made a conscious decision to savour the moment. I would miss this. I would miss them. As much as the boys had become a tight group, so, too, had all of us. Winston included. They had successfully gotten under our skin. Not surprisingly, I suppose. When you spend that much time with a group of teenage boys the likes of ours, you develop a bond.

I had always made a strategic point of keeping just enough emotional distance between my athletes and myself. I believed being free to make unbiased and sometimes unpopular decisions was paramount to being an effective coach. I never wanted to be in a situation where I was concerned about whether or not the members of my crew liked me. Being popular with the athletes wasn't my job. Coaching them was. As in my work with other crews, sometimes that was easier said than done. These guys were a boatload of characters: fun, mischievous, passionate, caring, and, most of all, lovable.

Watching the crews go by and counting down the races until ours, I found it hard not to think about how many times I had either raced this course as an athlete or stood here watching a crew as a coach. I shared my nostalgic moment with Winston.

"You know, more than thirty years ago, you and I raced each other down this course."

Winston smiled and looked at me. Then he shared his favourite line. "Yup, and we were right with you."

"Until the race started," I answered. We both laughed.

True to form, our crew went by with exactly one length of open water between them and their competition. Shawnigan, Mathews, and Brockville were exchanging second, third, and fourth places with each stroke.

When the gun went off to signify that our boys had won, Winston turned to me and said, "Well, can't ask for much more than that! They did exactly as we asked."

"True enough. One down, one to go," I said, shaking his hand.

With the boat put away, I pulled out my phone to check the radar. I wanted to see how those thunderstorms were doing. If they were to develop, racing would be on hold. No sooner had I opened my weather app than a clap of thunder signified we'd be having a delay. By then, Cosmo was on the table having his legs worked on by Mirek. The others were on the ergs flushing out as much lactate as they could. Given the tight turnaround we'd originally faced, we had scheduled for ten minutes of massage time for each of them. With the change in weather, we could now double that.

As the thunder continued periodically, each lightning strike meant racing was delayed another thirty minutes. Winston and I were thrilled with the added recovery time. When our race was eventually called an hour later, the boys were fully recuperated and eager to get going.

"Okay, this time you can do things a little different. Let's see how quickly you can open up on the other crews off the start. Then, just hold onto that. Okay, Cosmo? With three hundred metres to go, you can let loose." They all smiled. "Empty your tanks and have fun with this one. Got it?"

"Okay boys, last one. Here we go!" called out Daniel as they walked to their boat.

I don't think I had ever felt so relaxed watching one of my crews come down a racecourse. They were such a disciplined group. They had worked incredibly hard for this day, and now, after all of the challenges that they had faced in the last ten months, they were finally seeing the fruits of their labours. They rowed past Winston and me with a number of boat lengths of open water on the following crews. As per our instructions, with three hundred metres to go, the crew took off. The shift was so visible; it looked as if they had stepped onto one of those moving walkways you find in airports. I had never seen anything like it.

"Wow!" said Winston quietly. "Look at them! Henley's going to be fun. They are going to have the time of their lives racing the best in the world. I can't wait."

Given the short turnaround between our two races, we had informed the officials that if our coxed four won, they wouldn't be able to come into the presentation dock to receive their medals. Instead, we asked and were given permission to let Sandy join them on the podium and receive both of their medals.

It was an incredibly satisfying moment for Winston and me to know that the five young men we had spent the last ten months with were standing together on the podium receiving gold medals as national champions. They had taken our challenge of being the first crew to win both events back to back and not only achieve it, but surpass it.

"Nice job, Winston! Next stop, England."

"Yeah, well, the crews they run into over there'll be a hell of a lot faster than these ones. Guaranteed!"

Back at our boat bay, alumni were gathering to congratulate all of the Ridley athletes and reconnect with their old crewmates. It was fun to listen in on their stories and see some familiar faces.

With no new boats to be christened this year, we didn't have an official reception like we'd had in the past. Regardless, I took the opportunity to acknowledge all of the people on our "bus" who had contributed to the day. There were some terrific Ridley coaches who had spent an inordinate amount of time away from their own families so that our rowers would have a good experience. There were school officials and administrators that needed acknowledging, as well as parents and other support staff.

I was doing just fine until I got to Winston. We had a strange ritual around talking to the boys before and after races. We never looked at one another. My take was that we were too concerned that one of us would set off the other's emotions.

Winston had found an inconspicuous place to stand while I was speaking. When it came time to thank him, I went looking for him and, as soon as my eyes caught his, my throat locked and my eyes welled up. Damn. After a brief pause, I managed to get through my words of acknowledgement and thanks for his generosity, knowledge, and selfless giving of his time to our program and, in particular, the senior boys.

Then came my family and, of course, Robyn and Mataya. Agreeing to come back to St. Catharines was one thing. Agreeing to me coaching rowing at Ridley was something beyond. Robyn knew my obsessive tendencies because of her experience with me while at Shawnigan. She also knew this wasn't just a job for me. I acknowledged her tireless support in backing me up through some trying times. Mataya, too, had missed having her daddy around, given the time it took to do this job properly. I explained that after I got home from Henley, she would be sick of me.

To have the boys ready for racing at Henley in four weeks' time, we had to allow for their bodies to come down after such an intense weekend of racing and a partial taper. After two days off, we hit the water again, reintroducing longer recovery rows as well as some sessions in the weight room. During the four days before we left for Germany we focused mainly on re-establishing good rhythm at low rates. Upon settling in Dusseldorf, we'd return to some more race-specific workouts, once more, steadily building to a peak volume of work followed by our last and final full taper.

Taking a group of teenagers overseas was no more challenging than anything we'd seen so far that year. Flights were booked. Blazers ordered. Accommodations were arranged, and our travel money allocated. Thanks in good part to Lori, we were set to go.

The one thing that wasn't ready to travel was my foot. It was still bothering me. Like so many times I'd been injured before, I hadn't sought out any help but, instead, tried to push through it. Not surprisingly, that strategy had never worked for me as an athlete, and still wasn't working. I finally conceded that I had to see someone.

Dr. Conrad Cowherd, a local chiropractor, had been our team's back cracker since I had returned to Ridley. He had the best hands I had ever come across. He manipulated bodies like butter and, in 2012, he had travelled to England on his nickel to keep that year's crew in one piece. He had worked with several of our athletes this year and had kept me in tune from time to time as well. Given his history with rowing and the community, he had proven a good sounding board during my visits.

With his clinic conveniently located right downtown, I opted to see him the day before we left.

"What's up? You all ready to go?" asked Conrad as I hopped up onto his table.

"We're all good. Boys are healthy. Everything's booked. Nothing left to do but get over there and race."

"Nice. Good to know. Now, why are you here?"

"I hurt my right foot a few months ago and it's still ... whoa! Jesus, what the hell did you touch?"

"That would be plantar fasciitis," Conrad answered, as he ran his thumb along the tendons near my heel. "And you, my friend, have got a good dose of it."

With searing pain, I hobbled out of Conrad's office with a list of exercises and stretches.

"Don't expect it to be gone overnight. These things tend to have a mind of their own," were his parting words. There was no point getting too upset. I would have to make do.

The next afternoon, the boys and their families, Winston, and I all met at the School before heading off to the airport. It was great to have Sandy there as well. Not one for small talk, Sandy simply wanted to be there in person to wish all of his crewmates good racing overseas. It was a classy gesture that didn't go unnoticed. With the van packed up, we were off. In twenty-four hours we'd be rigging our boat in Germany and beginning our final preparation for the most important races of the year.

The simple act of arriving in Germany two weeks prior to Henley captured perfectly one of the main reasons this crew had been so successful. I thought Daniel's ask was a big one. Forget about the logistics: the finances alone were an added burden to the parents. If any of them were hesitant, we didn't hear about it. If being in Dusseldorf was going to allow Daniel to spend time with his dad and still train with the team, they were all in. No questions asked.

After the fifth day, as per the one-day per time zone norm of acclimatizing when jetlagged, the crew was hitting their stride and logging some solid training sessions. The rowing facilities in Dusseldorf were more than adequate. We trained on two kilometres of protected water every day and had unlimited access to a training centre with ergs and weights. Unfortunately, some of the boats that were ours to use were poorly maintained and missing a number of parts. Having Winston along proved extremely valuable in those first few days. Winston worked his magic several times with our borrowed Empacher boat.

As per Anja's word, the hostel in Dusseldorf was ideal. The rooms were perfectly European: efficient in design, clean and comfortable, a great place in which to spend our down time. Plus, we were in a quiet part of the building, which meant we slept undisturbed.

Our day began with a typical German breakfast in the hostel's cafeteria: cold meats, yoghurt, muesli, fruit, cheese, and coffee or tea. The boys lasted one day before a trip to the local grocer resulted in boxes of cereal beginning to appear in the mornings. While waiting for our breakfast to digest, we gathered out front each morning on our bikes, our chosen mode of transportation, and left en masse for the rowing course. A bike-friendly sidewalk system throughout the city allowed us to manoeuver relatively free of any traffic challenges. With the hostel and rowing club located smack dab in the middle of town, we simply crossed one of many enormous bridges that linked the city districts separated by the Rhine River. Ten minutes later we'd be carrying the oars to the dock.

With the first week done there was a noticeable shift in the boys. Despite all of the unprecedented success that year, they were not content with the results from their season. They were determined to get faster and discover what we had committed to all year—finding our best race on the day.

The weight sessions took on a new intensity, as did the brutally demanding erg workouts we had scheduled. Winston and I never questioned the boys' fitness, but it was clear to all of us that they had more to give and even more to gain.

Before each ride to and from the hostel, I would repeat to all of them that the bikes were for transportation only. As I shared my nagging reminder, they all avoided my stare as if to say, *Yeah, yeah, old man. We're fine. Let's get going.* Truth be told, I understood their frustration with my instructions to not race or "dick around," as I clearly put it. Who was I kidding? They were competitive teenagers. Asking them not to race was like asking the wind not to blow. During the ride home each afternoon, I played the role of caboose. I enjoyed reflecting on the day's work. We had come with a clear mission, and the boys had bought into achieving it. Two years of exceedingly hard work was coming to the perfect storybook ending.

It was Thursday. With the training approaching its peak, we were three days from wrapping up in Dusseldorf. The scores from our scheduled erg work were indicating a fitness we hadn't seen all year. I had tapered many crews before, but none with this sort of conditioning. We'd surpassed our intention of being a sub-6:20 combined erg crew by five seconds—a respectable outcome for any club or university team, much less a high school team. As far as I knew, that score was unheard of. If our boys were anything, they were fit and strong. All we had to do was hit this taper properly, and they'd be ready to face the best the world had to offer.

On this afternoon, Daniel hung back with me. Even with his dad's condition, he wanted to talk about his options for the following year regarding schools in the US. Despite his challenges on the erg, when you'd won as many races as these guys had, US college coaches took notice. So far, every member of the boat was spoken for, except Daniel. As we rolled up the incline of our final bridge, I was sharing some things to consider. As I watched the car traffic whiz toward me on the other side of the guardrail, I was interrupted by Daniel's panicked voice.

"Shit! Someone's down."

I looked up to see that the rest of the boys had stopped. My heart stopped with them. As we got closer, I could see it was a serious accident. Josh and Luc were quietly trying to untangle the bikes when we arrived. Cosmo and Mathew, the two who had fallen, were up and limping in circles trying to displace the obvious pain. There was road rash everywhere: elbows, knees, forearms, hands, shoulders, shins. Not a word was spoken. They all knew this wasn't good.

"Can either of you walk?" I asked Cosmo and Mathew in as calm a voice as I could manage. They both nodded. "Good. Grab your bikes and walk back to the hostel. I'll meet you there."

With that, I was back on mine and pedalling home. And I was mad. Really mad. In fact, the satisfaction of repeating over and over again the one and only word that could even come close to processing the anger I was experiencing came spewing from my mouth quite generously. As I passed resident Germans on my decline toward the hostel, I'm sure they needed no translation to know something was up with the Canadian on his fast-moving bike. By the time I got there Winston was already back from the gym. One look at me and he knew something was up.

"Cosmo and Mathew are hurt. They collided bikes on the bridge."

He slowly shook his head. "Is it serious?"

"Serious enough."

We both stood in silence waiting for our crew to arrive. Eventually, two sore-looking bodies, with blood caking on their braised limbs, came toward us. Their bikes were in the care of their teammates. No one was speaking.

"What hurts, Mathew?"

He shrugged as he tried to downplay the reddish coloured Picasso-like masterpiece the sidewalk had left on him from head to toe. I gathered immediately we had found our culprit. Despite his quiet demeanour, Mathew was intensely competitive and a good part of the reason this crew had been so effective. It was hard to be mad at him; it was who he was—a racer!

"Here's the deal, Mathew. It's going to be painful but you need to go shower and scrub each of these wounds with a facecloth and soap.

If there's any gravelly bits in there, you need to get them out. Understand? If this road rash gets infected you're screwed. Which means we're screwed. Got that?" He nodded and disappeared into the hostel.

"How are you doing? What hurts on you?" I asked Cosmo, who seemed more outraged than anything.

"Okay. Aside from the cuts, my elbow hurts a lot," he replied.

Knowing Cosmo's pain threshold wasn't what most would consider normal, I knew that just mentioning his elbow meant it needed further checking.

Sitting in the waiting room of the Dusseldorf Hospital, it was clear that we weren't in Canada; there was no one else waiting. Within moments, a nurse appeared and Daniel explained our circumstances. No sooner were they finished speaking than Cosmo was on his way to the radiology wing. Thirty euros later, and we were driving home with a confirmed bad contusion but, according to the x-rays, thankfully no break. We stopped at a local pharmacist and stocked up on gauze, disinfectant sprays and ointments, tape, and painkillers. We were six days away from our first race. There was nothing to do but the obvious: take care of Cosmo and Mathew the best we knew how.

That night, after a quiet dinner, and using the hostel's painfully slow wi-fi, I connected with Robyn back home in Canada. When you travelled as much as we did, FaceTime was essential. Through a sketchy connection, Robyn could hear immediately that something wasn't right. I shared the details of the accident. Then, we both went silent. There was nothing to say. We both knew how long this trip had been in the making, and how hard the boys had worked. We were so close to reaching our goal. After some consoling words from Robyn, it was time for bed. It had been a rough day, and I was beat.

"I had this crazy dream last night," mumbled Winston as we both lay awake in our beds the next morning. "It was so real. Cosmo and Mathew got into this nasty bike accident. They were covered in road rash. And we had to stop training. Oh, but no. That's not a dream. That's really what happened. *Are you kidding me?*"

It did seem like a dream, a bad dream. The questions remained, however: Could we move forward from this? What sort of plan would keep the boys engaged and finish off this long journey in a positive way?

After breakfast we gathered in the boys' room. They were quiet and seemingly lost amidst some brutal life lessons. We're all on a path, predetermined or not, and the choices we make will invariably affect us for the rest of our lives. They were finding that out the hard way.

"So. How's everyone doing with this?" I began. Some shrugs and nods were their answers; I wasn't expecting much more. They were hurting as much as I was.

"The way I see it, we have one way out of this mess. And it's the same way we've used all year. 'How can this be the best thing that ever happened to us?' There's no other way, boys. We have to embrace this as an opportunity. If we don't, there's going to be resentment among us, which will breed bitterness and eventually will divide the crew. If that happens, we're pooched. Therefore, moving forward, we have to do what Winston and I have said from the get-go: take care of everything we can control and not let the other stuff bother us. That's it. That's our only way out. We've got less than a week until we race. We have to stay positive and do everything we can to put our fastest crew on the water. Period."

Their looks were accepting. It certainly wasn't the first time they'd heard that from me. And goodness knows, it wasn't the first time they'd faced adversity, but certainly nothing like this.

"How about you, Luc-monster? What are you thinking?" I chose Luc for a reason. I knew that his dogged determination and unwavering optimism would shine through even in these circumstances. He set the perfect tone with which to take our next steps.

No word of lie, Luc rubbed his chin. "Well, Jason, I think we can overcome this. We just have to remain positive and work extra, extra hard."

"Nice! I agree, Luc."

Biking to the training centre later that day, we chose an alternative route. It was cool and overcast as we travelled along the Rhine. Taking in the unfamiliar sights, we came upon some ruins from an old bridge. I quickly glanced over at the structure as we sped by. Not certain of what I'd seen, I hit my brakes and walked my bike back for a closer look. I called for the boys to join me.

The remaining stone frame, which had at one point supported a bridge that crossed the river behind us, was littered with holes where bullets and explosives had struck the stonework during the Second World War. Standing there, I imagined young German boys the same age as the boys beside me desperately defending their side of the Rhine from advancing Allied forces.

Suddenly, it was easy to find some perspective within our circumstances. Yes, our team had suffered a devastating blow. Yes, we had trained hard and made enormous sacrifices for this upcoming regatta. And, yes, to be so close and so well prepared and have the accident happen was, somehow, incredibly unfair. But the truth of it was that these young boys weren't going to war. They weren't running the risk of being killed. Instead, they were attending a regatta, one that many considered for the privileged elite. Sure, the accident sucked, but no one had died. Cosmo and Mathew would recover, and life would go on. Shitty situation? You bet. But, like everything that had happened to our group, we would manage. We got back on our bikes and slowly proceeded along the path. I was thinking that, maybe—just maybe—there was something bigger in store for this crew.

During our time left in Germany, Mathew and Cosmo spent their training sessions on stationary bikes, and the rest of the boys on the ergs. We tried one outing in the boat with Mathew's hand taped, but it was too painful even for him. His left hand had suffered a nasty gash when he'd tumbled off his bike. We probably should have had it stitched, but it was too late now. There was no way it was going to heal before the end of the Regatta, not without him tearing it again every time he pulled.

As for Cosmo, he was improving, but he was a long way from being able to straighten his arm, an obvious requirement if he was going to be able to race.

CHAPTER EIGHTEEN

REWS TRAVEL FROM every continent to race at the Henley Royal Regatta despite it being an odd course, as regatta courses go. Competitors race 2112 metres on the River Thames—against the current. While the course travels a straight line up the winding river, there are times during the race when you are at an advantage or disadvantage depending on which lane you're rowing. If the current is flowing, everyone knows the course can be unfair. Honestly? The Brits love it that way. Having underdogs win races only adds to the drama of the event. And, with tens of thousands of people lining the course, enjoying Pimm's and dressed in their finest, anything you can do to create added excitement is a bonus.

We arrived on the Sunday before the race with just enough time to drop off our gear at the athletes' enclosure moments before it was shutting down for the day. With our oars secured in the tent, we made our way back to our hotel in Marlow.

In 2012, my Dutch and Scottish heritage got the best of me, causing me to save money by billeting the team at a local home. It was a beautiful spot located in Henley-on-Thames, but we were five athletes sleeping in one room and four in another. We saved our parents money, but by the time racing started I noticed that nerves were becoming frayed and tempers heated. By the end of the regatta, I believed my decision had proved more costly: it had compromised our performance. As a result I decided that this time around,

I wouldn't travel minding our nickels and dimes. I enlisted the help of Josh's mom, who was originally from England, and she found us a hotel that was ideal. The boys were two to a room, and the restaurant food was outstanding. We were set.

At dinner, we outlined the plans for Monday, our first day onsite. We could tell the boys were excited, but there was some obvious tension in the air over who would be racing, Cosmo or our spare, Josh. As far as the rowing went, Josh's trip hadn't been a great one so far. He had received minimal coaching from Winston and me, and his boat in Dusseldorf was inadequate. That was the gig. He knew it coming in as a spare. The focus was the quad—period.

Nevertheless, I considered him a vital member of the team. And at no time had he ever complained or even implied that he was getting a bum deal. He adored his teammates. As the youngest in the group, he looked up to every one of them. In fact, he called his mom in tears after the bike accident because he was so worried for Cosmo. How Josh originally anticipated this week playing out had changed drastically. He had stepped into a pressure cooker of a situation—a lot to ask of a sixteen-year-old boy. If he was apprehensive or unsure about whether or not he was up for the challenge, we didn't sense it.

That first morning, while Winston rigged the quad, I went to find someone from the medical staff and inform them of our situation. I found the regatta's physiotherapist who would assess Cosmo each morning and give his recommendation on whether or not he could race. With Josh listed as our spare, we would simply wait each day to make the call and inform the regatta chair about which athlete would be racing. After speaking with the physio, I found one of the officials. We sat down, and I explained what had happened. He shook his head and smiled.

"I know. Teenage boys, right?" I said.

"Not exactly," he countered. "If you were familiar with our British men's team in the latter part of the 1990s and what happened to one member, Tim Foster, you'll understand me when I say, it's not teenage boys, it's just boys."

Foster punched his hand through a glass window at a party in May of 1998 and was unable to race in the early part of the season. He was a member of the legendary British straight four along with Stephen Redgrave, Matthew Pinsent, and James Cracknell.

We both acknowledged the physio's addendum. Then he continued, "You know, I remember your Neil Campbell and his crews of the late 1960s, 70s, and 80s. They were so impressively big and fast. Ridley was such an institution here during those years. I have some fond memories of Neil. He was absolutely brilliant."

"Those were magical times, for sure," I replied.

By the time I got back to the crew for the practice session, Winston had the oars laid out and adjusted. The boat was suspended in the stretchers ready to go. I walked up to it, put my hand on the bow. "Before we head out, I want to name our new chariot," I told Winston.

I found my backpack and went digging for the name decal that we had made before we left home. When you rent boats abroad, you get to name them whatever you want. What would have made most sense, perhaps, was to use the name we had used back home on our own boat—my name. I had christened the boat in 2005 when I was at Schoolboy coaching for Shawnigan. I won't lie. Having my name on that boat would've been a thrill, given I'd never had the chance to race at Henley, but I'd wanted to use this as an opportunity to acknowledge the fellow rower we'd have aboard—Peter Yates.

I carefully peeled the backing from the sticker and adhered Peter's name to the bow section of our boat. I stepped back and asked the boys to come in for a moment. I began with reminding everyone why using his name was so meaningful and important. Yes, Peter had been a tremendous friend and mentor when I was a younger man. But, that aside, he represented the spirit that had gotten us this far.

When we were in Victoria to say goodbye to Peter, I overheard someone say that seeing him was like visiting with the Buddha. Although Peter then had no hair and limited ability to speak, his communication was incredibly clear and present. The essence of Peter in that moment was love. Even in the face of his own death, he was all love.

It was hard to contain my emotion. I didn't care if the boys saw; they knew me well enough and, more importantly, they knew what Peter meant to me. They were quiet and respectful while I struggled to get my words out. In the end, we agreed that our new name was indicative of what our whole journey had been about.

With Cosmo still unable to straighten his arm, Josh was having his first row in the quad three days before the race. We decided to leave the line-up as it was, put Josh in bow seat and have Daniel call the races from three seat. Josh would have enough to think about with just following the powerful group in front of him while making sure they didn't run into anything.

During practice, there were lots of crews out on the course, but no coach boats were allowed. Winston and I were relegated to being spectators just like the rest of the coaches. Even though there was a bike path that allowed us to speed along beside our crew and shout out the odd command, given what had just happened the week earlier, I was reluctant to cycle and opted to walk on my gimpy foot.

Henley was a funny place. Coaches watched and even filmed other crews as they rowed by, seemingly trying to garner that little bit of information that might help their crew win. Me, I never bought into it. As Neil had taught me years earlier, if the work wasn't done by now, no amount of clever reconnaissance was going to help.

We had gone web silent since the day of the accident. I had been posting information online about the events and goings on of the crew up until that day. Another website, however, considered us favourites and had even posted some pictures of us from Germany. That told me everyone was watching. And I didn't want anyone to know what we had been struggling with.

After what appeared to have been a good first row, the boys came off the water less stressed, even a bit excited that things had gone as well as they had. With that, we called it a day and went back to our hotel.

Through our partnership as coaches, I had learned that Winston's approach to life was simple: if you want something badly enough, make it happen. This can-do philosophy defined his coaching. The night after Cosmo's accident, Winston found a person online who lived near Henley-on-Thames and owned some crazy healing gizmo called a Scenar machine; I referred to it as "that *Star Trek* thingy." Having been treated with a Scenar device himself after a painful back injury and finding it incredibly helpful, Winston felt it just might be our ticket.

When we arrived in Henley, he acquired the machine for a week. After a hefty down payment and quick tutorial, Winston took on the role of rehabilitating Cosmo. Essentially, the premise was that this machine, which used sensitive electronic vibrations, not only indicated visually where there was trauma, but also then went about helping to heal the injured tissue.

By Wednesday, the improvements that Cosmo had made were nothing short of miraculous. Each day his mobility was markedly improved. By Thursday, after a trial row on the erg, Cosmo felt he was ready to jump in the boat. Being a seeded, or favoured, crew, we had been granted a bye in the first round, which meant we had another day to treat and rest Cosmo while Josh continued acclimatizing in the quad. Although we were making strides with Josh in the quad as well as with Cosmo's physical health, there was still an ever-increasing tension in the group. As each day passed the boys became quieter.

At Henley, the lanes aren't numbered. They're named. Each name relates to the part of the town it's closest to. One lane is called Buckinghamshire or Bucks Station, and the other Berkshire or Berks Station. When the current is flowing—and this year it was—Berks Station is the favoured lane. We were told that drawing Berks Station this year was worth three or four seconds. With that sort of advantage, it was important to know when and where to make a push during the race in order to optimize, or minimize, that difference. Either way, we were under no illusion that the race was going to be easy. Even without the accident, racing the best junior sculling crews in the world is a tall order. We knew we would have to be sharp and focused to advance each day.

During the Thursday morning practice row, we did the first loop of the course with Cosmo and then the second with Josh. At the end of this second trip, the guys pulled over to the bank.

"What's up? How's it going out there?"

Daniel spoke quietly. "It's going well. We had a decent row with Cosmo, but no offence to Cosmo..."

Oh boy—be careful, Daniel, I thought, and quickly looked around to make sure Cosmo was out of earshot.

"It seems more stable with Josh. I think it's just because Cosmo is still testing his arm. It feels like he's a little worried to really lay on it."

"Okay. That's fair. Take it in and we'll see you back at the tent."

When Winston and I arrived at the tent, the boys were wiping down the boat and putting it back on the rack. With the blades put away, we all gathered.

"How was the row, Cosmo?" I figured there was no point skirting the issue.

"Pretty good. I could feel my arm by the end of the row. But overall not bad," he replied optimistically.

"You ready to race with it?" I continued.

"I think it's ready," he added.

I looked at Winston; his look said, *No way!*

We both knew that Cosmo's elbow wasn't ready. His heart was, but not his body. There was only one decision.

"I think we're going to wait one more day, Cosmo," I said. "Josh, you'll race this aft. Okay? Remember guys; come back to what's got us here, and trust that it's all happening as it should. Be patient, we're going at this one day at a time."

As I passed Patrick, Cosmo's dad, I patted him on the back and told him we'd catch up with him later. Once more, I was appreciative of the parents I had inherited with this package deal. They were incredibly supportive and never meddled in our coaching. Although Patrick, his wife, and her parents had travelled all this way to watch their son and grandson race, Patrick knew that Winston and I had a responsibility to the rest of the boys to put the fastest line-up on the water even if that didn't include his son. Knowing that support was there, however, didn't make the decision any easier.

After a light lunch and some quiet time back at the hotel, we returned to the regatta site intent on having the best race we could manage given the circumstances. As the boys went through their pre-race routine, Winston and I checked over the boat and the oars thoroughly to make sure everything was tight and measured up correctly.

With a little over an hour until we would head out, Joanne Yates, Peter's wife, and their daughters, Aly and Lizzie, showed up with our fifth rower, Peter. Five boxes that had been hand carved by a good friend with the intent of transporting Peter's ashes to the coinciding five places in the world he wanted to rest, Henley-on-Thames being one of them and the first on his list. I asked Joanne and the girls to christen the boat in Peter's name. After a few photos, I took the box containing Peter's ashes from Joanne and secured it in the middle of the boat. When one of the officials showed up to inspect our racing shell, I thought he might question the box, but all he did was check the usual things: shoes, slides, riggers, and registration, but not one word about the "ringer" that we had tied into the boat.

The crew was surprisingly composed as they shoved off. Even Cosmo, doing what he could to support his crewmates, was calm and upbeat.

Winston and I chose to head to different parts of the course rather than watch the race together. He chose a spot close to the finish line, while I limped farther down the river to about the 1500-metre mark. It was only two days into the regatta and already there were thousands of people lining the banks to watch the early qualifying races. As I walked among them, I reviewed our race plan in my mind. We were in the Berks Station, which meant we'd have the faster starting lane as well as some help from the current at the finish. That would support our usual fast start and hopefully provide Josh an opportunity to ease into the racing. That was the hope, anyhow.

Undeniably, the Henley Royal Regatta Committee set the gold standard for combining a sporting event and a celebration; there was none like it in the world. People were dressed to the nines and picnicking beside their Bentleys and Jaguars; it truly was quite a sight to behold.

Rowing races could be as exciting as watching the grass you were standing upon grow, so the current trend was to use technology to engage spectators right from the start. For a few British pounds, you could purchase an earpiece that provided a live, stroke-by-stroke call of the race. Regatta Radio struck just the right balance between reporting ongoing results and giving little bits of interesting side notes to keep the spectators entertained in between races or when the crews were too far up the course to be seen.

Waiting to see the crew racing or hear word of their progress wasn't enjoyable—it was agony—but eventually the commentator announced that our boys were out front and leading comfortably. As we came through the halfway mark, the time announced was the fastest of the day for the event. A good indicator. Rowing by me, Josh looked like one of the crew. He had done an outstanding job assimilating in such a short time period. The boys were all business back at the tent. They had won but they took the race in stride.

"How was that?" I asked.

"Good," Daniel offered up. "Josh did a great job. It felt easy. But I know we can get faster." They all enthusiastically agreed.

"Good to hear," said Winston. "Cuz you're going to have to."

I turned to Cosmo and smiled. When you're the guy sitting out, it's tough to hear that the boat went well. Full credit to him; he was genuinely excited for his crew and did what he could to show his enthusiasm. When I was his age, and given my attitude at the time, I'm not so sure I could've mustered the same graciousness.

That night, Winston treated Cosmo's arm once more in the hopes that he could still get a shot at racing. The next morning, Cosmo and I met in the workout room located in the hotel. We had to know how much his arm could withstand and if there was any chance of him getting through an entire race. We agreed to some starts and full pressure pieces. After a normal warm-up, he began a series of ten-strokers at full pressure. With each piece, his scores got better and his confidence seemed to grow. Then I suggested he try some starts. Again, no apparent discomfort, and the numbers registering on the monitor were where they should have been.

"Well, what do you think? Do we give it a try?"

Without any hesitation, Cosmo nodded and answered, "Let's do this."

As for Josh, if there was a guidebook on how to conduct yourself as a substitute in the most mature, supportive, and composed manner, he was now writing it. He had been neither excited when he was in the boat, for fear of emphasizing the disappointment that Cosmo was experiencing, nor disappointed when we pulled him that morning. He was expressionless and completely understanding of his place. He knew that his role was to fill in, not replace. That's the brutal truth of being a spare.

Before they shoved off for their morning paddle, just to empha-size the importance of this trial run I crouched down beside Daniel. "I know we all want Cosmo to have a race, but you still need to be hyper-critical of this row. If it doesn't go well, you have to promise me you'll tell me. Fair?" He nodded.

Winston and I made our way to the course to watch them row by. Everything appeared to be okay; however, they didn't stop to say anything this time. Did that mean it was bad? Should we switch back to Josh?

We returned to the tent to meet with them in very much the same way we had left—quietly. The stress that Winston and I were feeling was overwhelming. There was so much resting on this one decision.

As the boys waited for us on the dock, they were smiling. "Well, what's the verdict?" I asked.

"Felt great. We're good to go," said Daniel.

Daniel had changed a lot. He clearly understood what his crew and coaches had agreed to and the lengths to which we were all will-ing to support his spending time with his dad. Throughout the year, he had proven a bit of a loose cannon; now at Henley, he had stepped up his game and become far more accountable. Since Cosmo's acci-dent, Daniel had reached another level. He had assumed a leadership role in the group that was encouraging to witness.

While Winston made some last-minute adjustments on the oars, Cosmo and I went to find the regatta's physiotherapist again. Then we informed the regatta chairman of the switch.

We had barely seen the girls since their arrival at Henley. I had spoken briefly with Siobhan on the occasions when we had both been at the course for training rows, but given the situation with Cosmo, that hadn't been very often. She was well aware of what we had been facing and accordingly had been sensitive and supportive. The girls, too, had tried their best to remain positive in front of the boys.

Their first race was against a British club crew called Marlow. By all accounts, our girls were in for a tough first heat. They'd known that before coming over and understood that there was a chance they could travel all the way to England and get knocked out on the first day of racing. Sure enough, later that afternoon, our Ridley girls would go down to that Marlow crew, who would eventually lose in the final to Gloucester Rowing Club. The Shawnigan girls faced the same fate in their heat: defeat by a British club.

Later that afternoon, moments before it was time to launch, Jonathan Leigh, the headmaster who had hired me, came by our tent to see the boys and wish them well. It had been his vision to see Ridley rowing return to what it had once been, so it was great to have him watch the Ridley crew he helped start. It had been two years since we had spoken. Jonathan told me that the move back to England had been a smooth one and that he was enjoying his new headship. He was incredibly excited to see Ridley College back at Henley one more time. Needless to say, he was struck by how much the boys had grown since he had last seen them. Likewise, the boys were thrilled to see him. After one of his brief, rousing pep talks, he was off to find his seat and cheer them on.

Sitting on the bank of the Thames minutes before our race, listening to the commentators through my earpiece, I was nervous. Each new day brought a tougher race as the better crews advanced. The day before we had drawn the Berks Station, but today we had the Bucks. Leading from the first stroke in the slower starting lane was going to be a challenge. Our boys were used to getting out front quickly, but if that didn't happen this evening, I was concerned they might get rattled.

As 6:30 drew closer, I recognized the voice on the radio to be that of Freddie, a young man who had come by our tent earlier that day to speak with the crew. He had asked some good questions and conducted a respectful interview. As he shared that conversation live, I was impressed with how encouraging he was. He even gave a shout-out to all of the families and friends listening back home in Canada. He was a class act.

Then, the commentator at the start took over and began to go through our competitor's line-up, one rower at a time. The Nottingham crew had some impressive experience and accomplishments. We knew entering this event that we might very well go up against some exceptional club crews, meaning composite crews made up of boys who didn't necessarily row at the same school. As the commentator shared the bios of each rower, I began to doubt our decision.

Soon, the race was on. They called both crews striking forty-three strokes per minute off the line and sitting even. "Come on, Cosmo, you can do this, buddy," I said aloud.

At the first marker we were out front by only just a bit. But, given our slower lane, I'd take it. Our strategy for today was to hold Nottingham as best we could from the start and then make a push around the midway mark when the current crossed over to favour us. At the quarter-mile we had increased our lead, but it was still tight. At the next marker they called us up by three-quarters of a boat. At this point I was feeling good about our situation. At the halfway marker, I knew these boys would stretch out the lead and then hold it to the line. They were so big and strong, so fit that no one had been able to row through them all year. When they established a lead, they were quite adept at maintaining it.

The next commentator reminded everyone that with the current being active today, Nottingham would only have to keep in contact with us before having the full advantage coming into the final sprint, where they could make their move and win.

"Okay, I don't need to be reminded of that right now, thank you very much," I said quietly to myself as the crews remained out of sight.

At the halfway marker we were down to a half a boat-length lead. Then with a little more than 600 metres to go, our lead had been cut to one-third of a boat. Normally, at this stage in the race we should be stretching out to a boat-length lead of open water. Things weren't playing out as they should have; something had happened. When they came into sight, I could clearly see that Nottingham was slowly but steadily, one stroke at a time, rowing through us. I began to limp my way back to the tent and heard the commentators say the lead was down to a canvas. I was preparing myself for this being our last race when I heard the commentator again.

"*The rates are going up in both boats. They are neck and neck, as both crews sprint for the line. Can Nottingham catch the Canadians, or will Ridley hold them off? It's going to be too close to call.*"

"Come on boys, *push!*" I yelled. I was surrounded by strangers but didn't care who heard me.

"*Nottingham is starting to steer toward the centre of the course. I hope they don't clash blades. No, they're getting back on terms and Nottingham have taken the lead!*"

It was over. There was no way we could come back now.

"*Wait, Nottingham has crabbed. Oh, what a disaster for Nottingham. Ridley has gone on to win the race.*"

"*What?*" My limp became a run. With my foot burning, I made it back to the tent as fast as I could.

I found the boys gathered around our boat. Their heads were low.

As Winston joined us, I asked the crew, "What's wrong?"

"If those guys hadn't have crabbed, they would be advancing, not us."

I took a deep breath. "Really? Last time I checked, *not crabbing* was a requirement for having your best race, and possibly winning. They crabbed. Not you. You won. Fair and square." I paused to make sure they had all heard that. "That's the last time I want to hear anything about it. We're advancing to the semis tomorrow. Top four crews out of sixty-five entered. Think about what we've been through in the last week. You guys have no reason to hang your heads. Understand that?" I looked at each one of them. "Okay. Usual warm-down. Get showered and we'll head back for dinner. That was a gutsy race out there today. You didn't quit. You got what you deserved, I hope you can hear that, boys." They were now smiling.

I turned to Winston. "Winston?"

"Yeah, I'd be excited if I were you," he added. "You get to race tomorrow." He then pointed to the crew they had just beaten in the boat bay beside us. "They don't."

The point was made. They gathered their things and headed off.

"Holy shit, I couldn't believe it," said a relieved Winston. "Right there in front of me. Just a few feet from the finish line, the Nottingham crew had a boat-stopper. Their stroke man lost control of his oar, and they were done. Boom! Never seen anything like it."

"Well, shitty way to lose. Shitty way to win, too, as we saw from the boys. But I'll take it. The race is 2112 metres. Not 2110."

"Amen," said Winston.

Joanne came into the tent all smiles. "I don't know, Jase. That was pretty close," she said as she gave me a big hug.

"My guess is Peter's having so much fun, he wanted another race," I said. *"Thank you, Peter!"* We both laughed, then walked to the shell and unstrapped Peter from the boat. She smiled as she stuffed the box into her purse and made her way out.

"Great race, boys!" Joanne yelled to the crew. "We'll see you tomorrow, Jason."

Dinner was unusually quiet. Something was up. Winston and I had been doing this long enough to know that one of us needed to chat with the crew. Later that evening, I asked Cosmo to come by my room.

"How are you feeling?" I began.

"Good, I feel pretty good; nice to finally race today."

"How's your elbow?"

"A little sore, but not bad," he answered as he rubbed his arm and straightened it.

"How do you think the race went today? Are you tired? It's been a while since you've rowed that hard."

As we continued to talk, it became apparent to me that Cosmo was convinced the race had gone well and that he was as good as ever with no concerns going forward. I, on the other hand, wasn't so sure.

When Daniel, Luc, and Mathew came to see me, I asked them the same questions. Their answers were pretty much what I expected—vague. When I asked how the race had gone, there was a long pause. They looked at one another.

"Well? How did it go?" I repeated.

"The first half was great! We got away clean and kept moving," answered Daniel.

"Then..." He hesitated. "It got heavy. At the halfway mark when we were supposed to move and really open things up, the boat got really heavy."

"Heavy?" I enquired. "What do you mean heavy? Heavy as in something went wrong with the boat, or heavy as in someone stopped pulling?"

Silence.

"Look, we have to find out what happened today. We're not doing anyone any favours if we don't sort this out."

"I just don't think Cosmo was able to pull like he normally does; his arm was too sore."

"Hmmm. Well that's not good is it?" I looked at each of them. They were squirming as if they'd just ratted out a friend. "If Cosmo's not ready to race, he's not ready to race. It doesn't make him a bad person. We just need to figure out what we're going to do tomorrow."

"Will you put Josh back in the boat?" Daniel asked.

"I'll speak with Winston, and we'll let you know. In the meantime, you need to get some sleep. Either way you've got another big race tomorrow."

I knocked on Winston's door.

"What's up? How's Cosmo?" he asked.

"Not bad. His arm is sore, but he seems to think he'll be fine tomorrow."

"What do you think?"

"Remember when I asked Cosmo about the warm-down after the race and he got so defensive? The boys said he never even got on the erg, which would explain a lot. Clearly, he's in more pain than he's letting on. And, just before they went out to race today, he asked for another painkiller. I said no, but now that I think about it ... it all makes sense. Besides, his family's here, and he doesn't want to let them down. They didn't come all this way to watch him stand on the bank. He wants to race!"

"Well, that's Cosmo; he's a tough nut."

"I get that, but there's no choice here, Winston. I'll call Patrick in the morning and let him know we're going to make the switch. He'll understand."

With Patrick in the loop, it was time to tell Cosmo. I knocked on his door and asked if he had a moment. He followed me back to my room.

"Have a seat," I said pointing at the chair beside my desk. There was no other way to do this than just come out with it. I figured he knew what was coming, but it didn't make it any easier.

"I know you told me that your arm is holding up, but it's clear to Winston and me that you're not 100 per cent, Cosmo. Something went wrong yesterday. No one has ever rowed through you guys. Regardless of the advantage from the current, that just shouldn't have happened. Period. I'm sure you can appreciate that it's my job to put the fastest four guys on the water each race. We think it's better to have Josh in there today instead of you."

Cosmo looked away nodding his head as he let what I had just said sink in, that he wouldn't be racing today. I sat quietly and let him process the situation. Moments later, his hands came to his face and he began to sob.

"I know this sucks. Believe me, I'd do anything to keep you in that boat, but I just can't. It's not fair to the other boys."

"I know. I know," he said with tears now streaming down his cheeks.

"I spoke with your dad earlier. He's expecting your call. You take as much time as you need. Okay, Cosmo?"

"Okay, thanks, Jason." With that, he left.

That was the first time I'd seen Cosmo cry. Our strong, quiet, unshakable leader had finally released the emotion he had been carrying around for over a week. In many ways, I think it was as much about not wanting to admit to himself, and the boys, that he couldn't withstand the pain. Cosmo was as stubborn as they come, and we'd relied on that stubbornness all year to get us through races and hard training sessions. Having me tell him he couldn't race was a relief more than anything. At least it was me who was preventing him from racing. It wasn't him having to bow out.

The stress of that predicament on Cosmo, and on the others in the crew, became clear to me later that morning. I arrived at lunch to find the boys rolling out of their chairs in a fit of laughter, each one of them.

"What the hell's so funny?"

"No, no way, don't say anything!" objected Mathew. They laughed even harder at the thought of me knowing what had happened.

Standing there waiting to hear what had caused their roaring laughter, I could feel my tension release as well.

They were back. The crew that we had known all year was finally back. The politically incorrect comments, the toilet humour, the stuff teenage boys do that only teenage boys and their coaches find funny. All if it was back and spilling out of them. It was beautiful.

An hour before we left for the course, we gathered in my room to go over the race plan and then practise it with our visualization exercise. The boys were light, playful, and ready. But before they left my room to get dressed, I wanted to share some of the emails I had received throughout the week from grown men who had done exactly what they were doing today, only decades earlier when they were rowing at Ridley. It was a privilege for me to read the banter that went back and forth all week long on group emails between men who had gone on to lead remarkable lives, but still remembered where those lives had begun and who they had to thank for them.

The comments directed to one another and to their coaches, Neil Campbell and John "Munch" McIntyre, were as moving as they were revealing. All these years later, they still got nervous thinking about the starting gates at Henley. They still remembered the pain of "seventy-strokers" and, perhaps most importantly, they still held closely the friendships formed and the lessons learned pulling on an oar, all those years ago.

After reading the emails aloud to the crew, I looked up; the boys were captivated. They had truly heard and even felt what their large group of admirers had shared with them from across the Atlantic. Apparently, there was nothing more to say.

We were ready. The chair of the regatta was informed of our switch, the boat and the oars set, the boys warmed up, and Peter tucked securely back in the boat. We all stood around our chariot one more time.

Despite Winston's sometimes tough exterior, he was extremely sympathetic to the price of racing as hard as these boys did, and what that sort of commitment required. As I shared my final thoughts with the crew, I made certain to avoid his gaze for fear of choking. As usual, his eyes watered up; it was touching, and the boys respected his emotional buy-in.

We had drawn the Bucks Station again, so the plan was similar to the one for their previous race: hang onto the Windsor crew as best they could off the start and then go to work through the middle of the race. It was the best we could hope for.

Winston and I knew the boys were tired from yesterday's race. We had seen the photos from the finish. I had never seen them look so exhausted. Mathew and Luc, normally expressionless when they rowed, had looked as though they could barely hang on. That was undoubtedly the hardest they had ever been pushed. Today would be more of the same. The Windsor Boys were a composite crew that had already beaten two seeded crews. They were going to be our toughest challenge to date.

Windsor took the lead off the start, just like we knew they would. As they raced toward the halfway mark, the commentators were calling us even, neck and neck. Everyone close to the course turned to have a look at the crews as they rowed by. Once more, the comments were supportive and respectful of our crew, the last remaining international boat at the junior level.

The Windsor Boys held our boys off until the centre of the course, then they began to stretch out a lead. The current would kick in shortly. This would be our last race. There would be no final sprint, no Hollywood ending where we caught them at the line and advanced to the final. Our journey was over.

Walking back to the tent, my foot still objecting, I was sad for the boys, sad for how it had all ended. At the same time, I was incredibly grateful for the experience they would take away. A journey they wouldn't soon forget. As they stood at the back of the tent, our chariot still dripping Henley water, they were quiet and looked completely beat. They had given everything and lost.

"How was your warm-up?" I asked. Daniel smiled at first and then caught himself before he laughed as if realizing, *Why wouldn't he ask that? It's what he's done at the end of every race so far this year.*

"It was good. We felt ready."

"How about your start? How did that go?" I continued.

"It was clean, but they got us by a few seats," said Daniel.

"We were expecting that. And, the race? Did you execute our plan as we had discussed?" I asked all of them.

They nodded.

"What about the finish? How did that feel?"

"The rate came up, but we just couldn't come back on them."

"Was there anything that you think we could've done differently? I mean, aside from the obvious, anything you would've changed?"

Everyone shrugged their shoulders while shaking their heads.

"Perfect, there's nothing to be ashamed of then is there? We did exactly what we came here to do: find our best race on the day. Despite the challenges that we've had, you've shown up here and raced the best you possibly could. There's nothing more that Winston and I could have asked. We are both incredibly proud of all of you. Do you understand that?"

They all smiled.

"Beautiful. Thanks, boys. I'll never forget this year. Ever."

With that the hugs began, the tears flowed, and these young men shared a final moment as the crew they had become. Tenacious. Passionate. Strong. Loving.

Both Winston and I hugged and congratulated each of the boys. I could feel their gratitude. They were sad, but they truly believed what I'd said. They had given everything. Today, they'd given their best race.

Holding Josh, I could feel the stress that had built up inside of him during his incredible week. I could feel it release as he began to shake and sob in my arms. He had been through so much. Perhaps more than any of us knew. To have come here as a spare and fill in at the last moment was not what any of us had expected. And yet, what he'd done and how he'd done it was exactly what we expected. I hoped he was proud.

Soon after, the boys made their way out to the front of the tent where their parents were waiting. Winston and I stayed behind to de-rig the boat. There wasn't much to say. We were exhausted and simply needed some quiet time to think. I flashed back to Seoul where I'd helped de-rig our boat after racing in our Olympic final. Yes, Seoul was my last race as an athlete, and this was my last race as a coach, but the contrast between my experience in each was glaring.

In Seoul, my combative mindset had enabled our loss to mean more than it ever should have. It was a race—granted, the biggest of my life—but still just a race. The by-product of that race and the mindset that I embraced, however, was shame like I had never experienced it. Shame that took more than a decade to shake. Here at Henley, our holistic mindset had enabled our loss to be simply a moment in our journey. Aside from meaning that we got beat on the day by a crew that produced a faster race, it really held no other meaning for us.

This year would simply register as an experience from which these boys learned a tremendous amount about life, about one another, and about themselves. They would be defined more by how they chose to participate this past year as opposed to the results that this year produced. They would have more races. More challenges. More wins and losses. Much more of what life is about—a journey. Obviously, I was pleased with that.

Eventually, Joanne came in to grab Peter. We hugged in silence.

"That would've meant so much to Peter. I can't thank you enough, Gooseman."

There was nothing to say. There was nothing I could say.

Then, along with Aly and Lizzie, we walked Peter's ashes to the end of one the docks and released him into the Thames. The sun was setting. The clouds were glowing, scattered with brilliant reds and pinks. The parents and athletes behind us were quiet, knowing what was happening. With my arm around Joanne, we watched as Peter danced in the current beneath us. This man who had done so much for the young rowers he had brought to Henley over the years was now back to rest forever in her waters. After a few quiet moments of reflection, we moved off the dock to join the rest of our group. We gathered for a final team photo. Everyone smiling. Everyone joking. Everyone pleased. Everything good. I loved it.

P.S. UPON RETURNING to Canada, I received an email from Cosmo. He'd had his arm x-rayed again. It was broken.

EPILOGUE

——┤ ├——

A LOT HAS CHANGED since my presentation at that fateful 2011 CAC Conference in Ottawa, most of it good. In 2016, the year of the Rio Olympics, a nationwide initiative called "Game Plan" was formed to help Canada's national athletes more easily transition out of their lives as elite competitors.

Game Plan's mission is to support our athletes' health, education, and skill development, and it's a program long overdue. It's also one that has had to convince many a coach and administrator that it is time—and money—well spent. In fact, funding for Game Plan was uncertain until research from other countries with similar programs started to report findings that proved that athletes who took care of their post-Olympic plans performed better in their final Olympic Games, and actually won more medals. When athletes aren't distracted by concerns about life after the Olympics, they're more able to focus on preparation and performance. Sadly, it wasn't enough simply to want to take care of an athlete's entire needs just because that was the right thing to do; it took research supporting an increased medal count to garner the final approval.

Interestingly enough, the word "holistic" is used in Game Plan's mission statement. That simply means that sport governing bodies are now focusing on the whole athlete, including their mental well-being. You may ask, "Why is that a big deal?" When I, and others, have used the word "holistic" at coaching conferences, people saw it as "New Age jargon" and not applicable to high-performance athletes. It's an example of a simple change in language creating a shift in perspective. For me, it is an indication that athlete-centric coaching will soon become the new normal.

What I find even more inspiring is the evolution that I've been seeing in the athletes themselves. In this case, the students—our athletes—have become the teachers. Watching Rio was a reminder that our young up and comers have not necessarily bought into the same combative mindset that many of us did. Countless times during pre- and post-competition interviews I heard our athletes express excitement with their performances, regardless of the results. Even those placing fourth, despite leading questions that implied, "you must be disappointed," explained that taking part had been great personal experiences for them at this stage of their careers—and that they couldn't wait for the next Olympic Games. Their language was about reaching for personal bests and having great performances on the day.

Many of them also talked about how much fun they were having competing on the world stage and how focusing on fun was translating to podium performances. Despite some members of the mainstream media using the old "revenge" and "retribution" rhetoric in pre-competition interviews, I didn't hear one athlete take the bait and go down that old-school path. To me, that says we are at a crossroad in our society.

Recently, we have seen the influence of fear and hatred in shaping the opinions of millions on a national scale. Sport has the opportunity—some might say the duty—to counter that influence with examples of hope and love. Sport can choose to maintain the status quo that says competition is a battlefield where combatants use any means to destroy one another in the pursuit of winning. Or, it can choose something more meaningful. Therein lies the truest opportunity for sport. If more coaches and athletes were to adopt a holistic mindset, we could see an enormous shift in the future direction of sport. And not just in the ability and performance of our athletes, but also in their roles as global citizens.

We must all raise our game—as athletes, coaches, and spectators—and make sport more relevant in the evolution of humankind. Only then will sport begin to serve the greater good on a level it's always been capable of reaching.

And finally, I would be remiss if I didn't provide an update on the current state of rowing at Ridley. As was my hope, Dereck and Siobhan have continued to build the program that we were fortunate enough to kick-start in 2010. After three years, they have the largest number of committed athletes vying for positions in their top boats that they've seen since 2014. In 2016, the team won medals at the CSSRA and Stotesbury Cup regattas. All great news as for the future of rowing at Ridley!

WHERE ARE THEY NOW?

WINSTON COOK

Winston still spends the majority of his time running his business, Henley Financial & Wealth Management. Although he and Jason declared that Ridley would be their last coaching adventure, Winston continues to guest coach on his terms. Calgary Rowing Club, University of British Columbia, and Brock University have since been the lucky recipients of his vast experience and knowledge. When not working or coaching, Winston can be found chasing little white balls around the golf courses of the Niagara region and travelling with his daughters as they pursue their interests in basketball, lacrosse, soccer, volleyball, and rowing—yes, rowing!

WINSTON'S TAKEAWAY

If you have passion and camaraderie, and you choose to be the best you can be within your discipline, the sky is the only limiting factor. If you choose to work together as a team, you can develop a natural persistence, determination, dedication, resiliency, work ethic, and respect for one another that determines your outcome long before the race even begins. Win or lose, you will understand if you continue on this path; your hopes and dreams will be realized.

JOSH GATCKE

After his grade eleven year at Ridley, Josh transferred to Shawnigan Lake School. This allowed him to study at another top academic school and take part and win in two national championships, as well as another trip to English Henley. Josh is currently enrolled at Georgetown University where he is studying international relations in the School of Foreign Service. He is also a member of the Georgetown rowing team.

JOSH'S TAKEAWAY

My time spent as a member of the Ridley rowing program was undoubtedly the highlight of my four years in high school. Before this program, I was like every other athlete: driven by the incentive to win. In the ninth grade, I revered the Ridley heavy eight as gods. They were strong, tall, and exceptional oarsmen. I never thought that I would be able to achieve the kind of success they did because I believed I was inferior. Jason's process-centred philosophy allowed me to let go of those beliefs and focus on living in the moment and taking each practice and race stroke by stroke.

SANDY MORRISON

Sandy also transferred to Shawnigan Lake School after grade eleven. The playful banter that he had grown used to at Ridley was alive and well within his new Shawnigan crew, but the philosophy was a little different than what he had grown used to at Ridley. Hearing the word "win" from his new teammates was strange and took some getting used to. Sandy knew what had worked at Ridley and, therefore, always tried to phrase his suggestions convincingly while trying to remain modest about the results he and his Ridley crew achieved the previous year.

At the 2015 Canadian Schoolboy Championships, Sandy coxed the Shawnigan eight and four to gold medal performances. He then travelled with Shawnigan to England to race in the Princess Elizabeth Challenge cup at English Henley. They were knocked out in their second race. Sandy has just finished his third of four years in the Bachelor of Science program at Queen's University and is no longer coxing.

SANDY'S TAKEAWAY

The paramount thing for me is the ability to be completely okay with whatever the outcome is, not only in sports, but also in everyday life. I quite frequently ask myself, "How is this the best thing that could have happened to me?" I came into rowing as a shy and reserved kid and left as a much more self-confident young man.

COSMO STEIER

Cosmo just finished his third year at the University of Pennsylvania where he's enjoying studying both economics and chemistry. In March of his first year, Cosmo tore a ligament in his left wrist and, at the moment, no longer rows. The transition from healthy athlete to injured athlete was much more difficult than he anticipated. Given how much he misses rowing, Cosmo hopes to return to the sport at some point in the future.

COSMO'S TAKEAWAY

It took me a while to digest everything that happened at school, and more importantly the last week of our rowing season. Understandably I was disappointed, but whenever I look back at that time I remind myself how lucky I was to have had that experience. One of the reasons we were so successful that season was because of our passion and the commitment we had to one another, as well as to our goal. If you put that much effort and concentration into a task or a goal, you will be satisfied with yourself regardless of your initial target. Doing the best that you can possibly do is such a rewarding experience, and it is something that I strive for in my studies and in all parts of my life. It is the journey that truly matters. It's the most important thing.

MATHEW SZYMANOWSKI

After Ridley, Mathew enrolled at the University of Victoria where he is pursuing a degree in software engineering and competing on the UVic Vikes rowing team. Since joining his new UVic varsity crewmates, he and Luc have won the Brown Cup, an annual race between UVic and the University of British Columbia, and recently became national champions, again, this time at the university level.

MATHEW'S TAKEAWAY

The philosophy that I learned at Ridley continues to influence my passion in rowing. The idea of having your best race on the day and controlling the controllables has allowed me to truly discover my potential while competing for the UVIC Vikes. Because of this approach, I feel like I can continue to compete at a high level for a long time, not really having a destination in mind, but just loving competition. My goal is to make the national team someday and compete against the best in the world.

DANIEL TKACZICK

Daniel returned home to Germany to pursue a lifelong dream of representing his country at the Olympics. He is currently training under the tutelage of the German national team, with the intention of rowing for his homeland at the 2020 Olympics in Tokyo. He is also studying business engineering in Dortmund, where the Olympic Rowing Training Centre is located.

DANIEL'S TAKEAWAY

The mindset of using love as the foundation for your goals isn't easy, but so far that strategy has worked for me. Not only did it provide our Ridley crew with the best possible outcome that we could have had on the day, it also helped to bond us as a group. Cosmo, Josh, Sandy, Luc, Mathew, and I will remain best friends for life. In hindsight, this is far more important than any wins or losses could have ever been.

I still live by the approach that we learned at Ridley and encourage the people around me to do the same.

JASON DORLAND

After a death-defying trip home in a dilapidated U-Haul truck, Jason, Robyn, Mataya, and Katie began the arduous task of reclaiming their home. Jason's options were to return to teaching and coaching at a school on Vancouver Island, continue freelancing as a graphic designer, or get back to the food business that he had started twenty years earlier. Although any of those choices would have proven fulfilling on some level, he decided to take what he had learned as an athlete and coach and share it on a broader scale.

JASON'S TAKEAWAY

When I reflect on our journey, what resonates as my most profound, and ultimately my proudest moment, was how these remarkable young men handled themselves in defeat. Sure—winning those national titles was fun. Each was a tremendous accomplishment. I won't argue about that. And, yes, there's no question in my mind that our crew was more than capable of winning at Henley. But that's not the point. If we had gone on to win in the final, it simply would have re-affirmed what Winston and I already knew: they were an exceptionally fast crew. On so many levels, however, the challenges they faced and endured in the days leading up to and including Henley truly defined them beyond their racing abilities, much more than winning ever would have.

Cosmo nailed it: the journey is truly what matters most.

ABOUT THE AUTHOR

JASON DORLAND IS an Olympian, coach, entrepreneur, and the author of the memoir *Chariots and Horses*. He has dedicated his life to the pursuit of excellence for himself and those he supports. Dorland is a graduate of Emily Carr Institute of Art and Design, taught high school for fifteen years, and is  the co-founder of Left Coast Naturals, an organic and natural food manufacturer and distributor in Vancouver. During his ten years of coaching high-school rowing, Jason's crews won twelve international championship events, set a Canadian course record time, and won back-to-back events with the same four athletes—a feat never before achieved at a national championship. Jason now shares his experiences and life lessons through his keynotes and workshops, and he consults as a high-performance coach for athletes, teams, artists, and executives. Jason lives in Victoria, BC, with his wife, Robyn Meagher (two-time Olympic runner), his daughter, Mataya, and their family dog, Katie. Learn more at jasondorland.com.